Praise for *All the Knowledge in the World*

“Garfield’s witty history captures the obsessive, quixotic and sometimes error-filled quests of those—from Pliny the Elder in the first century AD to Wikipedians in this one—who have attempted to corral all the world’s information into a single source.”

—*New York Times Book Review* (Editors’ Choice)

“The life and death of the encyclopedia is recounted in Simon Garfield’s excellent new book. . . . Garfield is lucid, witty, learned and clearly a bibliomaniac. . . . In *All the Knowledge in the World*, he has produced a lively threnody to the encyclopedic impulse. . . . Impressively comprehensive.”

—*Wall Street Journal*

“A fascinating history. . . . Lively and informative. . . . The story of the encyclopedia, in Garfield’s telling, is a continual push for more and bigger: knowledge’s widening gyre.”

—*Washington Post*

“Witty and geekily eclectic. . . . Celebrates encyclopedias in all their quirky, leatherbound glory.”

—*The Times*

“A wealth of research wrapped into an eccentric, charming package. . . . Fits easily into [Garfield’s] unpredictable canon, combining information, entertainment and insight. . . . Garfield’s great affection for his subject shines through, making this book a pleasing, intriguing read.”

—*Kirkus Reviews*

“Recounts the history of the encyclopedia—a tale of ambitious effort, numerous errors and lots of paper. . . . A delightful curated sampling of what seekers before and after [Denis] Diderot have tried to actualize. . . . A playful history. . . . Having grown up with a hunter-green leatherbound set of *Britannicas* in the house, I relate to Garfield’s nostalgia and delight. . . . Garfield’s deep dive into encyclopedia-making would merely involve summarizing scholars’ studies on the subject, which he acknowledges often and with reverence, if it did not also spotlight some of the wonderful, eccentric personalities that animate this history. However bookish knowledge can be, Garfield counters this tendency with a light and personable touch.”

"Simon Garfield is the only author who could ever keep me up at night reading about encyclopedias. A brilliant book about knowledge itself."

—Deirdre Mask, author of *The Address Book*

"Anyone fascinated by the origins, evolution and the ultimate mortality of print encyclopedias will love this book. Wikipedia enthusiasts, from casual consumers to dedicated contributors, will also gain much from reading the book. . . . *All the Knowledge in the World* is excellent at telling the long historical story of all encyclopedias, including those that predated *Britannica*. The book does a great job of detailing the twentieth-century history of *Britannica* and the full story of Wikipedia's creation, challenges and impact."

—Inside Higher Ed

"An erudite and amusing exploration of the human quest for knowledge."

—*Financial Times*

"An enjoyable tour."

—*Science*

"A pleasure. Garfield writes fluidly, cheerily and charmingly, even while the breeziness does not detract from the scale of his ambition: to understand nothing less than humans' need for knowledge and how to convey and preserve it."

—*The Spectator*

"This entertaining compendium is a worthy tribute to the pursuit of knowledge."

—*Publishers Weekly*

"Illuminating. . . . An infectiously enthusiastic history, inspired by genuine affection."

—*Times Literary Supplement*

"Illustrates Garfield's capacity to synthesize wide-ranging research and present it in a lucid, vibrant style. . . . A valentine to the monumental significance of encyclopedias."

—*Irish Examiner*

"[A] suitably encyclopedic book—written with all [Garfield's] usual wit and sharp eye for memorable facts."

—*Reader's Digest*

ALL THE KNOWLEDGE IN THE WORLD

The Extraordinary History of the Encyclopedia

SIMON GARFIELD

wm
WILLIAM MORROW
An Imprint of HarperCollins*Publishers*

ALL THE KNOWLEDGE IN THE WORLD. Copyright © 2022 by Simon Garfield. All rights reserved. Printed in the United States of America. No part of this book may be used or reproduced in any manner whatsoever without written permission except in the case of brief quotations embodied in critical articles and reviews. For information, address HarperCollins Publishers, 195 Broadway, New York, NY 10007.

HarperCollins books may be purchased for educational, business, or sales promotional use. For information, please email the Special Markets Department at SPsales@harpercollins.com.

Originally published in Great Britain in 2022 by Weidenfeld & Nicolson, an imprint of the Orion Publishing Group Ltd.

A hardcover edition of this book was published in 2023 by William Morrow, an imprint of HarperCollins Publishers.

FIRST WILLIAM MORROW PAPERBACK EDITION PUBLISHED 2024.

Library of Congress Cataloging-in-Publication Data has been applied for.

ISBN 978-0-06-329230-7

23 24 25 26 27 LBC 5 4 3 2 1

For Justine

"A large work is difficult because it is large."

Samuel Johnson, Preface to *A Dictionary of the English Language*, 1755

"Books can be useful from so many points of view. In my early days, for example, I used to use the *Encyclopaedia Britannica* as a trouser-press, and certainly the house that was without it was to be pitied."

Ford Madox Ford, letter to the *Philadelphia Inquirer*, September 1929

"This great mass of human knowledge—so vast in its range that not even its editors can hope to read all through the complete work."

BBC News report on the fourteenth edition of *Encyclopaedia Britannica*, 1951

Contents

Introduction

On Friday, 4 June 2021, I made peterhodgson1959 an offer for his encyclopedias. He was selling what he described on eBay as "Encyclopedia britannica pre-assembly suppliment set 4th, 5th & 6th editions." Seven tall volumes, condition "acceptable." They dated from 1815 to 1824, with articles on acoustics, aeronautics and Spain. I was intrigued by the prospect of a twenty-nine-page entry on Chivalry, and frightened by the forty-page treatise on Equations. I hoped to learn what 1819 knew about Egypt, and what 1824 understood about James Watt.

peterhodgson1959 had set the opening bid at £44, which I liked for its randomness. I offered him £50 to end the auction a few days early and was delighted when he agreed. Peter told me he had owned the books for about twelve years. "For some reason" he had decided to obtain a set of each of *Britannica*'s fifteen monumental editions spanning 1768–2010, several hundreds of volumes and hundreds of millions of words. But now he was downsizing his home, and evaluating his reasoning, and things had to go.

My seven supplementary volumes arrived via UPS four days later. "Acceptable" may have been better described as "flaky" or even "deplorable," because they were foxed, water-stained, falling apart and they smelt of armpit, but they were still wholly legible and fascinating, and more than acceptable to me.

They were additionally acceptable because all but one of the opening pages carried the elegant signature of P.M. Roget. Peter Mark Roget, a well-regarded physician and active Fellow of the Royal Society, had not only found time between teaching and surgery to purchase the greatest encyclopedia of his age, but also, in his late thirties, to contribute regular articles. At the front of Volume 1 he had written a list of his entries: Ant, Apiary, Bee, Cranioscopy, Deaf & Dumb, Kaleidoscope and Physiology.

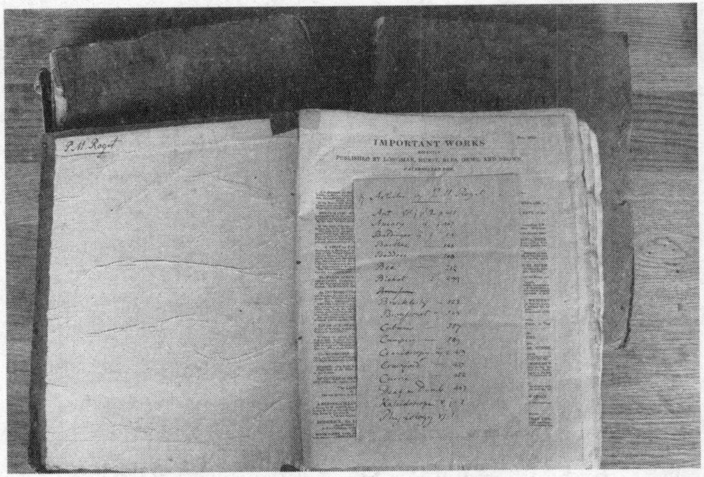

From Ant to Physiology: Roget's *Britannica* and a list of his contributions

And of course he had found time for something else, for while he was writing his *Britannica* entries he was also writing/composing/compiling/producing/penning his *Thesaurus*. I was enchanted by the conflation of these two great reference works, both of which I'd consulted all my life. But perhaps I shouldn't have been: Roget's fellow contributors to my Supplements included Walter Scott, William Hazlitt and Robert Stevenson.*

* There was also an entry by David Ricardo on Money. Ricardo was one of the few contributors to *Britannica* to have refused payment on the grounds that his article wasn't good enough to merit it.

A few weeks later I came across another set of *Britannica*, in the basement of Henry Pordes Books in Charing Cross Road. They were just there, in a row on the floor, kickable. It took a bit of effort to crouch down, ease one volume from the pile of other reference books above it (the *Australian Encyclopaedia*, the *Encyclopaedia of Restoration Comedy*), and bring it up to a level where it could be identified as Volume 11 of the 1951 London printing of the fourteenth edition (twenty-five volumes, 38 million words, 17,000 illustrations, slippery black faux-leather binding, gold embossed lettering, nine-hole side-stitching, whiff of tobacco and fish). Once I was upright the volume was tricky to hold—large, heavy and unwieldy, all the things one hopes an encyclopedia will be, always suggestive of a proper bounty.

Volume 11 (Gunn to Hydrox) contained, in very small print, important information about the herring, the herringbone pattern and homosexuality. This edition, launched in 1929 and updated every few years, had four founding aims: to promote international understanding; to strengthen the bonds between English-speaking peoples; to encourage interest in and support for science; and to sum up the ideas of the age for future generations. It contained original articles by Alfred Hitchcock (Motion Pictures), Linus Pauling (Ice; the Theory of Resonance), Edward Weston (Photographic Art), Margaret Mead (Child Psychology), J.B. Priestley (English Literature), Jonas Salk (Infantile Paralysis), J. Edgar Hoover (FBI), Harold Laski (Bolshevism), Konstantin Stanislavsky (Theatre Directing and Acting), Helen Wills (Lawn Tennis) and Orville Wright (Wilbur Wright). What a line-up! The articles on flying and homosexuality would now be considered off-beam, to say the least.

The week after I bought Peter Hodgson's nineteenth-century supplements, I went on eBay again. I was becoming hooked on old knowledge—and how cheap it was. A seller called 20111230kay from Haywards Heath was willing to part with a complete nineteen-volume *Children's Britannica* from 1993 for 99p. Davidf7327 from Buckfastleigh was selling a twenty-six-volume 1968 *Britannica* (with yearbook and atlas) for £1. And cosmicmanallan from the Rhymney Valley offered a twenty-four-volume set of the fourteenth edition, condition good, for £3. There was a lot of talk in the papers at the time of how we were all searching for certainty in our lives: amid Covid-19 and disruptive social change, we yearned for an element of stability and control—something trustworthy and authentic, the reliable pre-pandemic world in reliable physical form. Not the case with encyclopedias, it seemed; not if the items on eBay were anything to go by.

Someone calling themselves thelittleradish was selling the complete fifteenth edition, the last in the line, originally published in 1974, thirty-four volumes including yearbooks. This particular set was last updated in 1988, and they were in near-perfect condition. The starting price of the auction was £15. I thought they might reach £30 or £40. But no one else wanted them, so the set was mine for £15, which was obviously incredible considering that it contained the work of around 4000 authors from more than 100 countries. And these authors weren't just random people. They were experts, PhD people, men and women who had not only attained excellence in their specialisms, but were able to share their knowledge with others, with me. According to *Britannica*'s own account, the editorial creation of this work cost $32 million, exclusive of printing costs, which made it the largest single private investment in publishing history. And the price now—44p a volume, less than the cost of a Mars bar—made it the best value education one could possibly buy, and the fastest depreciating assemblage of information ever known. If the market assigned true worth, then the stock in encyclopedias had tumbled into the basement, if not back into the soil.

Of course, I had to add petrol to that. I drove down to Cambridge—Cambridge!—to collect the set in my seething Toyota (Cambridge University Press had published *Britannica* in its heyday at the beginning of the twentieth century). thelittleradish turned out to be a thirty-two-year-old named Emily, who was not particularly little and lived in Sawston, about seven miles from the city center, and she joked that the extra weight I was about to load into my car was nothing, for she'd just had to carry all the books down the stairs. They were waiting for me in the front room, six piles spread across one wall, and as I shifted four books at a time into my boot, and then my back seats, and then my front seat, Emily apologized for the possible scatter of cat hair.

Emily told me she had never actually consulted any of the volumes herself. During my drive to her home I assumed she'd inherited the set from a recently departed parent or grandparent, and their value to her wasn't justifying the space they were taking up, and her loss would be my gain. But no: she had a side hustle buying and selling on eBay, usually selling for more than she bought. Not this time. She had bought the set three months ago from someone who said his children had used them all through school, and now that they were young adults he had no use for them anymore. She didn't want me to reveal how much she'd paid for them, but it's safe to say she wouldn't be buying any more sets for profit. As we'd both just experienced, an old encyclopedia was about as popular as a burst balloon. Emily's young daughter toddled through from the kitchen. "You don't want to keep these for her?" I asked her mother, but I had already guessed her reply.

The great set from thelittleradish in Cambridge joined three other sets in my study. Two were from my childhood: the first, shared with my brother, who received it as a bar mitzvah gift, was the *Everyman*. Launched by J.M. Dent & Sons in 1913, my fifth edition from 1967 contained 4000 illustrations and 8 million words. The jacket flap promised nearly 50,000 articles "easily and lucidly written . . . the care given to the whole production is meticulous . . . the *ideal* encyclopaedia . . . handsome but not too bulky . . . detailed and comprehensive but not too voluminous . . . the lowest priced major encyclopaedia in the English language is incomparable value for discerning purchasers." It had cost someone only £28 for twelve volumes, and for that I got everything I needed to understand everything around me. There was a huge confusing universe out there, and a child of eight who wasn't even allowed to go to school alone on a bus could easily feel overwhelmed by it. But now that universe had come to me in twelve alphabetical volumes. I would never need another book again; the concept of school was suddenly outmoded, except for sports. And if I did still have to go to school, the encyclopedias would be useful for an additional reason: teachers and examiners could always tell how much of one's schoolwork had been lifted from *Britannica*, but I was confident that a more obscure publication would be harder to detect. Alas, as its title implied, the *Everyman* was more popular than I suspected.

In my younger days, what I really liked were the spine codes. Or at least I thought of them as codes, those alphabetical guides to each volume, the Bang to Breed, Chaffinch to Colour, Dachshund to Dropsy, Xerxes to Zyfflich. The encyclopedist's official name for these codes was "catch titles," which didn't at all rule out a secret resonance. They were a cipher, surely, ushering in something big, something final. Aliens? Critical answers in exams? Perhaps in the far future women with huge foreheads from *Amazing Worlds* would explain them all, although by then we would be their captives. If encyclopedias were the ultimate gathering of knowledge, then the spine codes had to be the ultimate refinement of this, the filtered pure essence of deep learning. In other words, the Enlightenment. Transcendence. The Truth. Dachshund to Dropsy.*

Over the years, I occasionally thought of the set I had consulted at school. ("Consulted" is probably too polite a word; between the ages of seven and thirteen, the collection in the school library was mostly used for tracing and tittering. Inevitably, we scoured it for rude biology and pictures of Amazonian tribes.) *The Children's Encyclopaedia* was ten volumes, quite a formidable carry, lithographic color, seemingly endless amounts of texts on the subject of knights. It was edited by a man called Arthur Mee, and the trinity of beliefs deeply embedded within his writing—God, England, Empire—must have left quite a dent in our minds.

In the early 1970s my parents had invested in the *Encyclopaedia Judaica*, which occupied a large part of my father's study for thirty years, and has since taken up residence in the Hampshire home of my parents-in-law, where even if it is rarely consulted, it certainly looks proud in its blue and gold binding.

Then there was a 1973 printing of *Britannica*, an updated version of the fourteenth edition, which pulled up in my septuagenarian father-in-law's car about ten years ago. He couldn't see the use for them anymore, now that all the information appeared to be inside his computer. He had a point, of course: any factual

* Sometimes the codes revealed more obvious and natural connections, particularly for younger readers. Volume 2 of the 1976 edition of *Britannica Junior*, for example, had the catch title "Animal to Bacon."

disputes could be settled far more quickly online, exposing the printed volumes as outdated at best, and inadvertently offensive at worst. And they were woefully insubstantial on the Munich Olympics and Pink Floyd. But I certainly couldn't bear to part with them: scholarship of any era is still scholarship. So for a while they sat beneath a table supporting my iMac, and they never once groaned at the irony. For someone whose entire working life has been based on the accumulation and elucidation of information, a good encyclopedia will always be the historical backbone of broad knowledge—familiar, unshowy, faithful, exact. Yes, they're unwoke, and yes my attraction to them is rooted in musty nostalgia, and even though I may not consult them as much as I did, just knowing they *may* be consulted I find as comforting as an uncut cake.

Many encyclopedias had passed through my hands over the course of my life. The only thing my current burgeoning collection couldn't teach me was how to know when enough domestic encyclopedias was enough domestic encyclopedias.

And then the inevitable happened. Cambridgebaglady listed a complete set of the 1997 *Britannica* for 1p. I looked at my screen again: it really was £0.01. The seller described the books as "pristine." There was even a bonus book, *Science and the Future*, predicting everything but the demise of the encyclopedia. The item was "collection in person only," and all thirty-five volumes were in southeast Cornwall. (Quite beautifully, for something on which I could spend a penny, they were in Looe.) Would the 500-mile round trip be worthwhile? Could I pick up the books during a Cornish holiday? Did I really need these volumes, cheap and pristine as they were? Yes, yes, and no/yes.

What had happened to this brilliant world? How had something so rich in content and inestimable in value become so redundant? Why were so many people giving these wonderful things away for almost nothing? I knew the answers, of course: digitization, the search engine, social media, Wikipedia. The world was moving on, and access to knowledge was becoming faster and cheaper. But I also knew that information was not the same as wisdom, any more than the semiconductor was the same as the turbine. And I was fairly certain that relinquishing so much accumulated knowledge so dismissively was unlikely to signal good things. At a time when researchers at MIT had found that fake news spread six times faster on social media than factual news (whatever that is), and when false information made tech companies much more money than the truth (whatever *that* is), we should necessarily ask whom we can trust. Despite its numerous and inevitable errors, I have always trusted the intentions of the printed encyclopedia and its editors. That we don't have the space in our homes (and increasingly our libraries) for a big set of books suggests a new set of priorities; depth yielding to the shallows. The process of making an encyclopedia informs the worth we place on its contents, and to neglect this worth is to welcome a form of cultural amnesia.

This book is as much about the value of considered learning as it is about encyclopedias themselves. It is about the vast commitment required to make those volumes—an astonishing energy force—and the belief that such a thing will be worthwhile. Those who bought them did so in the hope of purchasing perennial value. An encyclopedia is a publishing achievement like no other, and something worth celebrating in almost every manifestation.

As I spent more time with the old volumes at the London Library, and bought more from eBay, I wondered about the collective noun. An academy of encyclopedias? A wisdom or diligence? Alas, increasingly an *overload* and a *burden*. It is the task of this book to correct this perception.

Like an old atlas, old encyclopedias tell us what we knew then. Not so long ago—just before we all got computers in fact—they did more than any other single thing to shape our understanding of the world. It is no surprise that many of the greatest minds contributed to their success, from Newton and Babbage to Swinburne and Shaw, from Alexander Fleming and Ernest Rutherford to Niels Bohr and Marie Curie. Leon Trotsky wrote about Lenin. Lillian Gish considered motion pictures. Nancy Mitford courted Madame de Pompadour. W.E.B. Du Bois summarized "Negro Literature." Tenzing Norgay tackled Mount Everest.

And it should be no less surprising that our encyclopedic story has a role for Chaucer, Shakespeare, Francis Bacon, Coleridge, Voltaire, Rousseau, Flaubert and the founding fathers of the United States. The role of women in this saga went underappreciated until the eleventh edition of *Britannica* in 1910; only with the leadership of Wikipedia has this markedly improved.

After I had decided to write about encyclopedias I fell under their spell once more. And I found them everywhere. I read Thomas Savage's magnificent *The Power of the Dog* when the film came out, and discovered that the malevolent Phil Burbank had learned chess from a *C* volume a century ago; I read the celebratory tributes to Alice Munro on her ninetieth birthday, all of which mentioned *Lives of Girls and Women,* her book with that rare thing, a mother flogging encyclopedias to local farmers; I read Colson Whitehead's *The Nickel Boys,* with young Elwood Curtis winning what he thought was a complete set of *Fisher's Universal Encyclopedia* in a competition, only to find that all but the first volume were blank (he still wowed them at school when the Aegean and Archimedes came up).

And then I turned on the television. Streaming on Apple TV+ was a series based on Isaac Asimov's futuristic *Foundation* trilogy, in which almost 150,000 "scientists" had been toiling in a distant galaxy for more than half a century to write *Encyclopedia Galactica,* containing all the knowledge in the world and the worlds beyond. (Only later do we find the project to be a fraud, an invention to keep the cleverest minds occupied while their fellow citizens are forced to surrender their free will by a new fascist regime. But you probably saw that coming.) There is, possibly, a moral here, or maybe three: too long in ivory towers will blind you to the real terrors of the world; fifty-five years spent on producing the first volume of anything is probably excessive; the attempt to capture the definitive sum of all human knowledge in one place—ever looking back, seldom looking forward—may, after all is said and done, be a wholly fruitless enterprise. As someone explains early on, working on an encyclopedia "Is all very interesting . . . but it seems a strange occupation for grown men."*

Of course there was a reason for this ubiquity: encyclopedias were once as common as cars. Attracting both esteem and derision, they occupied the literature because they occupied the life—the weighty backdrop to an intelligent discourse, the

* It made me think of Douglas Adams, who once observed that *The Hitchhiker's Guide to the Galaxy* had already supplanted Asimov's *Encyclopedia Galactica* as the standard repository of all wisdom, for although it had many omissions and contained much that is apocryphal, or at least wildly inaccurate, it scored over the older, more pedestrian work in two important respects. First, it is slightly cheaper; and secondly, it had the words "DON'T PANIC" inscribed in large, friendly letters on its cover.

stern status symbol on the shelf, a reliable target of satire. I've come to rob your house, a man tells a woman on her doorstep in the first series of *Monty Python*. Well OK, she replies, just as long as you're not selling encyclopedias.

The printed *Britannica* is printed no more, but it exists as myth, as plagiarized schoolboy homework, as parental guilt-ridden purchase, as a salesman's silver-tongued wile, as evidence of a ridiculously bold publishing endeavor, and as a mirror to the extraordinary growth of cultured civilizations.

This is not an encyclopedia of encyclopedias; it is not a catalogue or analysis of every set in the world, just those I judge the most significant or interesting, or indicative of a turning point in how we view the world. The only mention of the *American Educator Encyclopaedia* and *Dunlop's Illustrated Encyclopaedia of Facts*, for example, has just occurred. If your favorite is Johann Heinrich Alsted's *Encyclopaedia Septem Tomis Distincta* of 1630, I can only apologize for its absence. Specialist guides are also missing—the *Encyclopaedia of Adoption*, say, and the *Christopher Columbus Encyclopaedia*, brilliant as they both might be. No room either for the *Encyclopaedia of World Crime* (six volumes, Marshall Cavendish, 1990), or even the *Concise Encyclopaedia of Traffic and Transport Systems* (Pergamon Press, 1991, $410). If you live in the Netherlands, I hope you already know all about the *Grote Winkler Prins Encyclopedie* (twenty-six volumes, Elsevier, 1985–93). Almanacs and catalogues of miscellany—astrological charts, lists of capital cities, seasonal gardening tips—are also excluded. I was tempted to include the *Pragmatics Encyclopedia* (Routledge, 2010, £125), but I took the pragmatic approach myself, reasoning that the fact it was possible to compile entries on "implicative, deixis, presupposition, morphopragmatics, the semantics-pragmatics, syntax-pragmatics and prosody-pragmatics interfaces" was probably knowledge enough.

But I am happy, in passing, to include a few outliers in this book, including the three-volume *Encyclopedia of the Arctic* (Routledge, 2005), the nineteen-volume *New Catholic Encyclopedia* (Catholic University of America, 1995) and the thirty-two-volume *Great Soviet Encyclopedia* (Moscow, 1970; New York, 1975), the latter of particular interest for its subject choices, many of which have both lost and gained something in translation from the Cyrillic.*

My history focuses on the West, on the great European and American tradition. Chinese and South American volumes get a look-in along the way, but they are exceptions in my attempt to record not just the monumental achievements of encyclopedias as objects, and the admirable if sometimes maniacal ambitions of their compilers, but to set these objects within the framework of Western knowledge-building. They were as much a part of the Enlightenment as they were the Digital Revolution. I'd be missing a trick if my book wasn't in alphabetical order, and with the exception of the letter *A*, it will follow a vaguely chronological pattern. I count myself fortunate that *Britannica* was first published near the beginning, and Wikipedia was launched near the end.

---

* Who would want to miss Additional Penal Measures, Apartment House, Auxiliary Gearbox, Batman, Children's Excursion Tour Station, Cleavage, Daily Milking Block, Decontamination (nuclear agents), Danube Cossack Host, and Declaration of the Rights of the Toiling Masses and Exploited People? Astonishingly, these are all in the first third of Volume 8. For those wondering whether Cleavage and Daily Milking Block are connected, I am happy to report they are not, and that Cleavage is defined as "a series of successive divisions of an egg into increasingly smaller cells," while Discoidal Cleavage is the same, but refers specifically to those animals—scorpions, certain types of molluscs—producing eggs with a much more dominant yolk.

I didn't buy the books in Looe. Not merely because Looe was a step too far, but because spending 1p on thirty-five volumes would have been obscene, and unforgivably insulting to the notion of intelligence.

I began to wonder what a set of unwanted encyclopedias cheaper than firewood says about the value we place on information and its history, particularly at a time increasingly decried as rootless and unstable. Perhaps the story will help us understand ourselves a little better, not least our estimation of what's worth knowing in our lives, and what's worth keeping.

A

AAH, HERE COMES ANDREW BELL

That's what they said when he approached.

Andrew Bell was a novelty to himself and a wonder to others. He was born in Edinburgh in 1726, and achieved many things in his life, but nothing was as great as his great and extraordinary nose.

His wasn't an averagely large nose, or even a very large nose. His was a nose that won rosettes, and you could pin the rosette on his nose and he'd hardly notice, such was its pocked and fleshy expanse. It was the size of an avocado. It made the proboscis monkey look like Audrey Hepburn. When people met him they found it impossible to look away, such was its implausibility.

When historians wrote of Andrew Bell long after his death they recalled "a spry fellow of unusual appearance." The American writer Herman Kogan noted in 1958 how "He stood four and a half feet tall and had an enormous nose and crooked legs." His nose was so large that its owner made fun of it himself. According to Kogan, when guests stared or pointed to his nose at parties, Bell would disappear, only to reappear with an even larger nose made of papier-mâché. His nose became the subject of academic interest. The scholars Frank A. Kafker and Jeff Loveland, writing in a publication of the Voltaire Foundation at the University of Oxford, observed in 2009 that Bell's nose rendered him "grotesque." An appreciation of Bell's career as an engraver by Ann Gunn in the *Journal of the Scottish Society for Art History* (vol. 22, 2017–18) mentions not only his nose, but also his appearance in etchings by the caricaturist John Kay. One of these shows him side-on, talking to a colleague, his knock-kneed legs forming a triangle from his knees, his face with a baking potato where his nose should be.

A spry fellow of unusual appearance: Andrew Bell and colleague compare profiles

But Andrew Bell's entry in the *Encyclopaedia Britannica* makes no mention of it. Presumably this is out of politeness, for Bell's other claim to posterity beyond his outstanding appearance was his key role in *Britannica*'s formation. He contributed more than 500 engravings to the first four editions, and for the last sixteen years of his life he was sole owner of one of the greatest publishing achievements of his age. Bell and his co-founder conceived a work of accumulated learning so wide in its scope and so lasting in its significance that *Britannica*—"the great EB"—is the first name most people associate with the word "encyclopedia." Launched in 1768, it was far from the first, and obviously far from the last. It emerged in what was certainly the golden age of encyclopedias: the eighteenth century produced at least fifty sets in Great Britain, France, Germany, the Low Countries and Italy. Fifty!

In English the *Britannica* was the figurehead, the watershed and the gold standard. It proved itself and improved itself over many editions, hundreds of printings and hundreds of thousands of articles. Its contributors were revered and its words were trusted, so much so that when Wikipedia launched in 2001, it plundered huge amounts of *Britannica*'s (out-of-copyright) eleventh edition as its core knowledge base. Wikipedia currently mentions not only Bell's achievement as an encyclopedist and possessor of a not-small nose, but also carries a sketch of a tiny man riding around Edinburgh on a huge horse, with a ladder brought for his mount and dismount, forever cheered on by a crowd delighting in his fearless ambition.

ACCUMULATION

Andrew Bell's involvement was artistic and inspirational; by contrast, the role of his colleague Colin Macfarquhar, a printer in Nicolson Street near the University of Edinburgh, was businesslike and practical. Both men appreciated the money that a groundbreaking new publishing enterprise might accrue. We shall see how the principles of the ancient Chinese or Greek encyclopedias did not share these considerations: theirs was a philosophical concern, usually founded on privilege and social class. But by the 1750s, knowledge, or at least the accumulation of information, was seen as a marketable commodity, as saleable as cotton and tin. This principle wouldn't be reversed for more than 200 years, and not until the emergence of the Internet would it be seriously challenged. For Bell and Macfarquhar, the collation and summation of the world's practical thinking into a few manageable volumes presented nothing so much as an opportunity of trade. One could view it more radically still, as a bourgeois accumulation of goods—intellectual property—to be obtained, ordained and refigured, and then sent on its way again at a profit.

Bell was not a wealthy man; when he wasn't carving copperplate illustrations for books he was engraving dog collars. Macfarquhar was the son of a wig maker, and his printing works faced such strong competition that he had developed a reputation for the piratical. He had been fined for the unauthorized printing of a Bible and Lord Chesterfield's *Letters to His Son*. One may assume his financial affairs received advantageous guidance after he married the daughter of a Glaswegian accountant in 1767, the same year he was honored as a master printer.

Together Bell and Macfarquhar announced their intentions: a weekly part-work in 100 installments, sold initially from Macfarquhar's printworks, each twenty-four-page installment (or "number," or "fascicle") costing 6d on ordinary paper and 8d on more refined stock. Every week would see an advancing accretion of letters until the installments were compiled into three volumes, and the volumes were compiled into a set. The first volume ran from Aa to Bzo, "a town of Africa, in the kingdom of Morocco." The second covered Caaba to Lythrum, while the third stretched from Macao to Zyglophyllum.* The second and third volumes contained significantly shorter entries, or at least distinctly fewer long ones. The page size was quarto and the typeface was small. The enterprise, in double-columned text we might now regard as 8-point, and sometimes 6-point, benefited from the application of a magnifying glass (not supplied), especially if a reader hoped to tackle all of its 2391 pages. The first complete leather-bound set was published in August 1771 at a cost of £2 and 10 shillings on plain paper and £3 and 7 shillings on finer. The number of its pre-publication subscribers is not known, but after moving its sales efforts to the bookshops of London it sold its entire 3000 print run within a few months.

Who had written and compiled this magnificent thing? Almost certainly the same people who bought it. Collectively they were known as "A Society of Gentlemen in Scotland" and their names appear at the beginning of the first edition. It's a list of more than 100 experts and authors, a small handful of whom were direct contributors. Most of the names were simply sources, the authors of books filleted and condensed for a fresh purpose. The titles were arcane, at least to us today: *Bielfield's Universal Erudition, Calmet's Dictionary of the Bible, Cotes's Hydrostatical Lectures* and *Sloane's Natural History of Jamaica*. Then there was *Priestley's History of Electricity* and *Macquer's Chemistry*. The use

* Caaba "properly signifies a square building; but is particularly applied by the Mahometans to the temple of Mecca . . . It is toward this temple they always turn their faces when they pray, in whatever part of the world they happen to be." Lythrum was a purple flowering plant, "a genus of the dodecandria monogynia class." Macao was "an island on China, in the province of Canton, fifty miles south of Canton." Zyglophyllum was another flowering plant, of which "There are eight species, none of them natives of Britain."

of the authors' surnames suggests a long-standing familiarity with the standard text, in the vein of *Gray's Anatomy*; the full and correct title of Pierre-Joseph Macquer's textbook (translated into English from the French and published in Edinburgh five years earlier) was *Elements of the Theory and Practice of Chymistry* (the author was a Parisian chemist). These works underlined one of the *Britannica*'s prime objectives: the accumulation in one publication of the key titles one might expect to find in a university library.

But the precise content of the first *Encyclopaedia Britannica* was ultimately the responsibility of one man, its principal editor William Smellie. Perhaps it was inevitable that a man with an enormous nose would engage a man with such a surname, but Smellie also possessed other attributes. He appears to have been rescued from a possible life of debauchery and alcoholism by the twin redemptive forces of education and remuneration. He was a Presbyterian with much experience of proofreading, editing and printing, while his regular attendance at a wide variety of classes at Edinburgh University had rendered him a polymath, and he became an expert in bees and plant sexuality, the telescope and the microscope, and botany. Bell and Macfarquhar paid him £200 for four years' work, his contract demanding Smellie oversee the entire publication and compose fifteen articles on "capital sciences," which included, in the first volume alone, lengthy entries on anatomy and astronomy.

In his preface to the first edition, William Smellie claimed his "professed design" was to "diffuse the knowledge of science." To this end he and his compilers had "extracted the useful parts" of many books, "and rejected whatever appeared trifling or less interesting." In other words: astute editing.

The historian Herman Kogan found Smellie a "roisterer," "as devoted to whiskey as to scholarship." He was fond of reciting his father's "tedious" poems in Latin. At the age of twenty-eight he already had many literary friends and connections, rendering him something of an intellectual show-off. There may have been no individual in the whole of the British Isles better suited to marshaling such an august and high-reaching publication.

Despite his own modest status (his father was a builder), Smellie held a generally elitist view of his fellow beings. In his entry on Mythology, he suggested "common people were prone to superstition" and "born to be deceived in everything." Ignoring for a moment his Scottish environs, he believed that "people of distinction" tended to live in London. His employment was intended initially as a part-time occupation, but it entirely consumed him.

It is not certain precisely how much of the first edition was written by Smellie himself, nor how much was created anew by his band of gentlemen scholars. All the articles went uncredited. "I wrote most of it, my lad," Smellie announced facetiously in his later years, "and snipped out from books enough material for the printer. With pastepot and scissors I composed it!"

Agriculture spanned thirty pages ("Agriculture is an art of such consequence to mankind, that their very existence, especially in a state of society, depends upon it"). Algebra occupied thirty-eight pages ("A general method of computation by certain signs and symbols, which have been contrived for this purpose, and found convenient"). Medicine ran to 110 pages, with much on gout, quinsy and other agues, but it did not cover Midwifery, which merited its own forty-six-page entry, providing a step-by-step guide that assumed to eliminate the need for training and experience. The accompanying three pages of highly detailed anatomical engravings outraged many, not least churchmen, who urged readers to tear them out and burn them.

The birth of *Britannica*: an anatomical guide to midwifery upsets the church in 1771

Among his personal contributions, Smellie almost certainly composed the entry entitled Abridgement, for within it he laid out his intentions for his entire enterprise. "The art of conveying much sentiment in few words is the happiest talent an author can be possessed of," he declared, in an entry much longer than those surrounding it (Abrax, an antique stone; Abrobania, a town and district in Transylvania). "This talent is particularly necessary in the present state of literature," the entry maintained, "for many writers have acquired the dexterity of spreading a few critical thoughts over several hundred pages . . . When an author hits upon a thought that pleases him, he is apt to dwell upon it . . . Though this may be pleasant to the writer, it tires and vexes the reader."

Smellie's conclusion may be judged abusively anti-academic. "Abridging is particularly useful in taking the substance of what is delivered by Professors," he writes. "Every public speaker has circumlocutions, redundancies, lumber, which deserve not to be copied." He recommended concision, elision and omission. This "would be more for the honour of Professors; as it would prevent at least such immense loads of disjointed and unintelligible rubbish from being handed about by the name of such a man's lectures."

Smellie's suggestion was unmistakable: *Encyclopaedia Britannica* was an alternative university, the modern way with knowledge. Buy these volumes, he seemed to be saying, and you need buy nothing more; this set will set you up for life. Those whose task it was to sell *Britannica* and other encyclopedias to cynical households in the years to come would seldom waver from this pitch.

ACCURATE DEFINITIONS AND EXPLANATIONS

But how, in the late eighteenth century, in the age before door-to-door salespeople, in the age indeed before the train, was such a hefty, new and ambitious publication to be explained and sold? Principally by newspaper advertisement. Announcing the publication of the first volume in December 1768, a notice in the *Caledonian Mercury* claimed it would contain "ACCURATE DEFINITIONS and EXPLANATIONS of all the Terms as they occur in the Order of the Alphabet."

This did rather make it sound like a dictionary, and with good reason. The encyclopedia as we understand it today—a work of reference on a great variety of topics, a gathering of information and instructional articles intended as a summation of contemporary human knowledge—began life primarily as a definition of words.

Between the exhaustive entries on Agriculture and Algebra, for example, there were a great many briefer ones, many of them banal. These included (in their entirety):

Aid: In a general sense, denotes any kind of assistance given by one person to another.

Aighendale: The name of a liquid measure used in Lancashire, containing seven quarts.

Alarm-bell: That rung upon any sudden emergency, as a fire, mutiny, or the like.

Other entries read like the erratic index of an atlas:

Aberyswith: A market-town in Wales, lying 199 miles W.S.W. of London, in 52.30 N. lat. and 40.15 W. long.

ANGERMANNIA: A maritime province of Sweden, lying on the western shore of the Bothnic gulph.

Many other entries were anecdotal, whimsical, circumlocutory, contradictory and pointedly subjective. Some were blind alleys. Others, rather than self-evident and brief, may now appear to us excessively detailed, given their subject matter.*

ABESTON: A blundering way of writing Abestus. See Abestus. [There is no entry for Abestus.]

ACRIDOPHAGI: Locust-eaters. A famine frequently rages at Mecca when there is a scarcity of corn in Egypt, which obliges the inhabitants to live upon coarser food than ordinary. The Arabians grind the locusts in hand-mills, or stone mortars, and bake them into cakes, and use these cakes in place of bread. Even when there was no scarcity of corn . . . they boil them, stew them with butter, and make them into a kind of fricassee, which . . . is not disagreeably tasted.

ANNUITIES: A sum of money, payable yearly, half-yearly, or quarterly, to continue a certain number of years, for ever, or for life.†

* For reasons of space and comprehension I have not included samples of the lengthier and more detailed treatises, relying for favor instead on these shorter definitions. But there was a conscious difference between the definitions in *Britannica* and those in the basic dictionaries that preceded it. The aim in the encyclopedia was connectivity: definitions were often cross-referenced, and when two or more were considered together, greater knowledge would be attained. For a closer examination, visit: https://digital.nls.uk/encyclopaedia-britannica/archive.

† This entry lasted five pages, and often read like something from the Marx Brothers: "The probability that a person of a given age shall live a certain number of years is measured by the proportion which the number of persons living at the proposed age has to the difference between the said number and the number of persons living at the given age."

Armadillo: In zoology, a synonime of the dasypus. See Dasypus.

Dasypus: A genus of quadrupeds belonging to the order of Bruta. The dasypus has neither fore-teeth nor dog-teeth; it is covered with a hard bony shell, intersected with distinct moveable zones or belts. This shell covers the head, the neck, the back, the flanks, and extends even to the extremity of the tail; the only parts to which it does not extend are the throat, the breast and the belly, which are covered with a whitish skin of a coarse grain, resembling that of a hen after the feathers are pulled off.

Linnaeus enumerates six species of dasypus, principally distinguished by the number of their movable belts.

1. The novemcinctus, or dasypus, with nine moveable belts.
2. The unicinctus, or dasypus, with eighteen (*sic*) moveable belts.
3. The trichinous, or dasypus, with three moveable belts.
4. The quadricinctus, or dasypus, with four moveable belts. Linnaeus is mistaken with regard to the trivial name and specific character of this animal; it ought to be called the sexcinctus, or dasypus, with six moveable belts; for, according to Briffonius, Bouffon, and most other natural historians, none of the species of this genus have four moveable belts.
5. The septemcinctus, or dasypus, with seven moveable belts.
6. The dasypus with twelve moveable belts. This is the largest species, being about two feet in length, of dasypus.

Questioning precisely how useful this might be to the general reader—or indeed to the dasypus—would be to miss the point: the information was conceived with expertise, and believed accurate, and so it went into the encyclopedia. The broader question is: what exactly is an encyclopedia?

The word entered common usage in the seventeenth century, originating from the Greek notion of *enkyklios paideia*: "learning within the circle" or "all-round education." This circle would in turn make a well-rounded man, someone versed in all the liberal sciences and practical arts. Previously, such an accretion of knowledge would be experiential, or at least personally taught. Only now, with the enlightened *Britannica* and some of its European predecessors, was the word "encyclopedia" employed to define a book or a set of books that made universal learning possible from one extended text. A complete library was hereby filleted and compressed, and the wisdom of experts was attainable to anyone with a solid grounding in comprehension (or what William Smellie called "any man of ordinary parts") and the financial wherewithal to expand it. (It was no small irony that the principal purchasers of this condensed library were libraries: now even those with limited means could attain information in a concise and direct manner.)

Although the first edition of the *Encyclopaedia Britannica* had as many strange inclusions as it did odd omissions, it carried two clear messages for its purchasers: buy these volumes and become one of us; read these volumes and take your place in modern society. The cross-referencing of its entries applied equally to its subscribers: the connections, both textual and personal, united its readers in a shared purpose, a desire to contain what was known and could be agreed upon.

Edinburgh was the perfect place for such a project. Its progressive university attracted students and teachers who were leaders in their fields; the university's self-esteem fomented only greater expertise. The Scottish Enlightenment was born of a large number of humanist individuals (among them the economist Adam Smith, the architect Robert Adam, lawyer and author James Boswell, surgeon John Hunter, philosopher David Hume, botanist Erasmus Darwin and engineer James Watt) who proposed a rationalist, forward-thinking attitude to matters of the intellect; at the dawn of the steam age the educational dominance of the Church was neither an attractive nor workable proposition for these men, all of whom were overtaken by the demands of practical advancement and the rigors of empirical reasoning.

Intellectually, even viscerally, 1768 was a hugely exciting time to be alive. Every possibility was expanding. The great early breakthroughs of the Industrial Revolution had already been made, not least Watt's early advances with the steam engine and James Hargreaves's revolution of the cloth trade. In other fields, the philosophies of Jean-Jacques Rousseau, David Hume and John Locke were transforming the way we approached scientific argument and moral judgment. But no one was expanding the realms of the possible that year more than Captain James Cook, who embarked on the first of his voyages across the Pacific to New Zealand and Australia a few weeks before the first part of *Britannica* went to press, and arrived just as the final volume was being completed three years later.

By the time the news of Cook's discoveries reached Edinburgh, it was clear to *Britannica*'s founders that their city was home to one other valuable asset: an abundance of avaricious readers, not least at its academic institutions. *Britannica* was born of market demand, and the market demanded a continually updated version of the world. In 1771, when its publishers claimed every set had been either sold or reserved, and would therefore require a second edition, their creation had become a living, lasting organism.

ALPHABETICAL ORDER

Before a page of *Britannica* was compiled, William Smellie and his publishers faced a dilemma that wouldn't trouble us now—the question of how to organize such a vast tower of information in a way that would make its compilation rigorous and its reading seamless.

The method chosen, alphabetical order, was far from universally accepted; this easy collation of characters might indeed be anti-intelligent. To take the *A*'s, on the first page of the first edition: could a reader gain a rounded knowledge of the world from a discordant appreciation that Aabam is "a term, among alchemists, for lead," or that Aarseo is "a town in Africa, situated near the mouth of the river Mina," or that Abactores is "a term for such as carry off or drive away a whole herd of cattle by stealth" and that Abactus is "an obsolete term, among physicians, for a miscarriage procured by art?"*

Wouldn't this be just a speculative, subjective and irregular collection of what today we may dismissively call factoids? Would such a random process not be considered absurd in any other constructive situation in life, such as the placement of skilled workers on a production line ordered to work next to the person closest alphabetically in surname, irrespective of their role? Or would this method inadvertently reflect the true nature of *Britannica* and most encyclopedias before and since—that is, a scattershot accretion of geographic, philosophic and scientific miscellany, a grand admission that the organic amassment of human knowledge is an unattainable and maybe even fruitless endeavor?

---

* A "miscarriage procured by art" is achieved by interventionist means; a deliberate abortion.

The alphabet is a concept, an abstraction. Its letters began as representative symbols, in much the same way as a coin became representative of money: the worth is not in the item itself but in the promise of indicative value, in this case the wealth of communication. Language symbols appear in the West first as Egyptian hieroglyphics, and around 1800–1700 BCE appear as a twenty-two-letter abjad, a system consisting entirely of consonants. This North Semitic script was similar to Old Hebrew, and we know its order was firmly established by the time nine acrostic Old Testament psalms were composed between the sixth and second centuries BCE.

The primitive alphabet was swiftly adopted by Middle Eastern craftsmen and merchants, who found the symbols far easier to remember and record than the thousands of previous cuneiform or hieroglyphic symbols (it was perhaps the earliest example of a communication technology promoted by commerce). And from Egypt and Israel this alphabet passed to Greece around 1000–900 BCE. The Latin rendering removed the "zeta" and added *G*, before incorporating both *Y* and *Z*. The Roman alphabet used in the West derived largely from Etruscan characters, and extended to twenty-six letters in medieval times when *I* was differentiated into *I* and *J*, and *V* was split into *U*, *V* and *W*.*

The appeal of alphabetical order was recognized by Aristotle in the fourth century BCE, and there is some suggestion that the

* This is necessarily a highly truncated account: I have made no mention, for example, of the parallel Arabic script that emerged in Petra, nor the role played by Phoenician traders in the second millennium BCE. For a full and illuminating history of this development see *A Place for Everything* by Judith Flanders (Picador, 2020). Flanders observes that the word "alphabet" was not itself employed until surprisingly late. The Romans preferred either letter (leterae) or element (elementae), and it wasn't until Hippolytus of Rome wrote "ex Graecorum alphabeto" to mean "from the Greek alphabet" (and derived from the first two letters in that language, alpha, beta), around 200 CE, that the word probably entered regular usage.

Library of Alexandria employed it in its classification of scrolls (by author). But it was only in the fifteenth century, with the advent of the printing press and the subsequent use of paper as a popular system of storage and trading records, that the alphabet came to be used regularly as a method of ordering and reference. The development of movable type necessitated a distinct and fixed physical placement of letters that had never been required before. The liability and speed of making text depended on knowing a set order, much as we know the QWERTY layout of the keyboard; if this was to change every time we sat down, we would probably not sit down. In the age of Gutenberg, strict placement was doubly necessary, as the carved metal letters were visible only at the tip of their metal strip; the best way to mind or find your *P*'s and *Q*'s was by careful advance assignment.

The alphabet's printed roots lie in glosses or glossaries: the definition, usually at the end of a text or book, of words considered unfamiliar to the general reader (or as the first edition of *Britannica* has it: "Glossary, a sort of dictionary, explaining the obscure and antiquated terms"). Often, as in the case of the Roman physician Galen from the second century CE, glossaries would appear in medical textbooks, and it seemed natural that these terms would appear in alphabetical order. But it wasn't until the demand for bilingual dictionaries in the sixteenth century that the logical tradition for an instructional reference book running from *A* to *Z* was established.

But all this seemed to run counter to *Encyclopaedia Britannica*'s stated aim of creating a circle of human knowledge (after all, an alphabet was linear not circular, a progressive string of characters). To *Britannica*'s founders and editors, there was no doubt that the alphabet eased accessibility. It created order where none existed, particularly in a work of almost a thousand pages. And it helped with retrieval, enabling a fact, definition or explanation to be more easily found. What it didn't do was assist in the interpretation of a more detailed concept, or in the presentation of one of *Britannica*'s proud treatises on the practical arts or sciences.

To see how William Smellie and his publishers wrestled with this dilemma, one need only consult the title page.

Encyclopaedia Britannica;
or, A
DICTIONARY
OF
ARTS and SCIENCE
COMPILED UPON A NEW PLAN
IN WHICH
The different SCIENCES and ARTS are digested into
distinct Treatises or Systems
AND
The various TECHNICAL TERMS, &c. are explained as they occur
in the order of the Alphabet

It was a compromise, an attempt to produce something both generally useful and academically detailed, in which thousands of brief definitions arranged alphabetically combined with extended expert sections on such things as Horsemanship (eight pages), Hydrostatics (nineteen pages) and Law (seventy-five pages). These longer entries—each of which could have been published as an instructive pamphlet on their own—were split into sections or chapters, these subdivisions only occasionally adopting alphabetical order.

While William Smellie's listing of his major sources and contributors also appeared in alphabetical order (from *"Albini tabulae anatomicae"* to "Young on Composition"), the editor made it clear in his preface that the system could not be extended to the more complex entries. There was a "folly of attempting to communicate science under the various technical terms arranged in an alphabetical order." He found this concept "repugnant to the very idea of science, which is a connected series of conclusions deduced from self-evident or previously discovered principles." The key to a reader understanding these principles depended on them being "laid before him in one uninterrupted chain."

His dual approach suggested perhaps that the publishers saw two distinct sets of prospective readers. It was entirely feasible that the "Society of Gentlemen in Scotland" who had both written and subscribed to the first edition, and were most likely to have rallied for the in-depth articles, were regarded as a quite separate reader to the intelligent lay figure who may have been encouraged (by newspaper advertisement or fanciful bookshop whim) to purchase the set to improve their prospects.

But it may also be that *Britannica*'s publishers had seized upon a brilliant system of marketing. Few people would buy just one part of an encyclopedia arranged alphabetically; once persuaded to buy the letters *A* and *B* for a shilling each, a reader would either have to be disappointed with the text on offer, or be straitened financially, not to proceed to the end of the set.

There is a compelling word for this concept: abecedarianism. While in its most neutral form it means something arranged in alphabetical order, or the process of learning an alphabet, or indeed buying something in alphabetical order, it has also taken on a slightly condescending tone, not least in tech circles, where it may be applied to something rather simplistic, perhaps a piece of programming progressing in an uninterrupted or obvious fashion. As such it may also suggest a lack of imagination, a strict pedagoguery. And then there is another apt definition: an Abecedarianist is one who rejects all formal learning. Applied most commonly (and with some disputation) to the sixteenth-century German sect of Anabaptists, it suggests a person wholly reliant on spiritual, instinctual and religious guidance on how to live one's life. An encyclopedia, therefore, of any description and in any order, would not have been part of an Abecedarianist's armory.

ANCIENT MARINER

Samuel Taylor Coleridge took a dim view of Smellie and his schemes. Today, his reputation as a fantastical poet tends to overshadow his work as a vociferous literary critic, but in late-eighteenth-century London his influence was considerable. And his criticism of *Encyclopaedia Britannica* was the literary equivalent of gunboat diplomacy.

For a start, he regarded the concept of alphabetical order as absurdly random and completely nonsensical. In its place he offered a superior intellectual approach to the organization of knowledge (and thus, almost by definition, a less marketable one). He advocated a "rational arrangement" and a strict "scientific method," a circular philosophical relationship between all subjects in an encyclopedia, organized into "one harmonious body of knowledge," an organic connection of past and present. The historian Richard Yeo has suggested that Coleridge wished for all branches of sciences and fine arts to be arranged in terms of class, order, genus or species, each of which derived its "scientific worth, from being an ascending step towards the universal."* By contrast, any encyclopedia organized around the alphabet was "mechanically arranged," a caged animal compared to Coleridge's promotion of the safari park.

Despite its alphabetical strictures, Coleridge argued that *Britannica* was characterized by "more or less complete disorganization" of its subject matter. In 1803, Coleridge wrote to the poet Robert Southey of the "strange abuse" that "has been made of the word encyclopaedia!" He found the "huge unconnected miscellany" of the *Britannica* too frequently determined "by the caprice or convenience of the compiler"; knowledge was splintered and fractured, he complained, and thus rendered almost useless.

The complaint was a simple one, and William Smellie had heard it before. The reader might be obliged to search back and forth through several entries in several volumes to acquire a thorough understanding, say, of industrial growth or meteorology; the experience was comparable to printing chapters of a novel in an order that made comprehension purposely difficult. Also, there was a tendency for entries appearing in *Britannica* late in the alphabet to be condensed in order to meet printing deadlines and financial constraints (in the first edition, the letters *A* and *B* occupied 697 pages, with the remainder squeezed into 2000). What was Coleridge's solution to these dilemmas? It was called *Encyclopaedia Metropolitana*, a publication as big, burdensome and doomed as the albatross. We shall mark its rise and fall a little later in this chronological alphabet.

* *Encyclopaedic Visions: Scientific Dictionaries and Enlightenment Culture* by Richard Yeo (Cambridge University Press, 2001).

ANOMALIES AND APOLOGIES

By today's standards *Encyclopaedia Britannica* was not wholly enlightened. The fact that it was compiled by men for men may be borne out by consulting the entry Woman, which read, in its entirety: "The female of man. See Homo."*

Women do fare slightly better when it comes to religious affairs. Here, the entry for God runs in its entirety: "One of the many names of the Supreme Being," while Goddess receives the greater coverage, in length at least:

> A heathen deity of the female sex. The ancients had almost as many goddesses as gods; such were Juno, the goddess of air; Diana, the goddess of woods etc. And under this character were represented the virtues, graces, and principal advantages of life; Truth, Justice, Piety, Liberty, Fortune, Victory etc. It was the peculiar privilege of the goddesses to be represented naked on medals.

* Thirty years later, with the publication of *Britannica*'s fourth edition (1801–09), the consideration of women in relation to men had entered a new phase. "The man, more robust, is fitted for severe labour, and for field exercise; the woman, more delicate, is fitted for sedentary occupations, and particularly for nursing children. The man, bold and vigorous, is qualified for being a protector; the woman, delicate, and timid, requires protection . . . The man, as a protector, is destined by nature to govern; the woman, conscious of inferiority, is disposed to obey." One may, at this point, believe this to be parody, but it is not. And it goes on: "Men have penetration and solid judgement to fit them for governing, women have sufficient understanding to make a good figure under a good government; a greater portion would excite dangerous rivalry between the sexes, which nature has avoided by giving them different talents. Women have more imagination and sensibility than men, which make all their enjoyments more exquisite; at the same time they are better qualified to communicate enjoyment . . . With respect to the ultimate end of love, it is the privilege of the male, as superior and protector, to make a choice; the female preferred has no privilege but barely to consent or to refuse."

There were similar anomalies elsewhere, and many idiosyncratic editorial choices. The entry on Mahometans, the outdated term for those who followed Muhammad and would be now regarded as Muslim, runs to seventeen pages, covering all forms of cultural history and religious observance. The entry on Jews and Judaism, by contrast, extends to one paragraph ("Those who profess obedience to the laws and religion of Moses . . . they lay great stress upon frequent washings . . . every Jew is obliged to marry, and a man who lives to 20 unmarried is accounted as actually living in sin").

Elsewhere, bloodletting from the penis is a bit of a cure-all, squinting is a contagious disease (and may be caused by nurses placing a child's cradle in a wrong position with regard to the light). And you didn't necessarily want to buy the first edition if you were hard of hearing. "Some say, the eggs of ants bruised and put into the ear, with the juice of an onion, cure the most inveterate deafness."

In his preface, William Smellie excused himself early. For all the fanfare, and for all the work employed in its creation, he explained that in his opinion *Encyclopaedia Britannica* was still a little rushed. The editors, he said, "were not aware of the length of time necessary for the execution, but engaged to begin the publication too early." Even though the publication was delayed by a year, "still time was wanted."

And then there was a plea for forgiveness. A work of this kind, Smellie argued, was bound by its very size to contain errors, "whether falling under the denomination of mental, typographical or accidental." He reasoned that those familiar with a work of such an extensive nature "will make proper allowances."

Any reader—indeed any writer—would surely have

sympathized. Of course there would be mistakes in a work of this complexity. And most of them were straightforward: St. Andrew's Day—for the thirteenth, read the thirtieth; Interlocutor—for extacted read extracted; Law—read 1672, not 1972. And then there were entries that would only prove suspect with time.

Asbestos: A sort of fossil stone, which may be split into threads and filaments, from one inch to ten inches in length, very fine, brittle, yet somewhat tractable, silky, and of a greyish colour, not unlike talc of Venice. It is almost insipid to the taste, indissoluble in water, and endued with the wonderful property of remaining unconsumed in the fire, which only whitens it . . . Pliny says he has seen napkins of it, which, being taken foul from the table, were thrown into the fire, and better scoured than if they had been washed in water. This stone is found in many places of Asia and Europe; particularly in the island of Anglesey in Wales, and in Aberdeenshire in Scotland.

By the time the first edition of *Encyclopaedia Britannica* sold the last of its 3000 sets in the 1770s, the notion of this grandly ambitious multi-volume publication attempting to encompass the sum of human knowledge had became a sport, a pastime and an enduring sensation. *Britannica* was one of the eighteenth century's most enduring brands. Although at first there was no indication that the first edition wouldn't also be the only edition, it was decreed that like the dasypus it should in future come in different sizes, with updates and printings and additions.

But the second edition would require a new editor. William Smellie declined to continue in the role, for he had other plans, with alcohol once more a prominent part of them. Twenty years from his initial engagement, and after years as an influential founding member of various philosophical and natural history societies, including the Royal Society of Edinburgh, Smellie found himself the celebrity owner of a drinking club on Edinburgh's Royal Mile called the Crochallan Fencibles. His biographer Robert Kerr found him increasingly disheveled during this period, and in financial disarray, while one fellow club member, the poet Robert Burns, reveled in Smellie's inebriated joshery, and found him a "veteran in genius, wit and b[aw]dry." Smellie, according to a source quoted by Kerr, used to "thrash the poet most abominably."

Nonetheless, Burns honored him with a verse:

His uncomb'd, hoary locks, wild-staring,
thatch'd
A head for thought profound and clear
unmatch'd;
Yet, tho his caustic wit was biting rude,
His heart was warm, benevolent, and good.

Colin Macfarquhar died in 1793, William Smellie in 1795 and Andrew Bell in 1809. Their extraordinary publication lived on, surviving controversy, calumny, mutiny, bankruptcy, parody, ignominy and perfidy until it announced in 2012 that it would print no more.

B

BACKSTORY

In 1964, the historian Robert Collison compiled a chronology of more than forty encyclopedias that predated *Britannica*. Not all of these exist to be perused today, and not all are what we might recognize as encyclopedias. A great many Latin works contained a varied display of intellectual artistry without holding to a recognized or ordered system, while others seemed unnecessarily ambitious. In 1245, for example, the French priest Gautier de Metz composed *L'Image du Monde*, laying claim to be the first encyclopedia written in verse (it was part fact, part religious fantasy, with references to angels and dragons and a belief that the sky was made out of some sort of very early concrete).*

Collison's list highlighted a diverse attempt at uniqueness—the first German encyclopedia, the first encyclopedia for

* *Encyclopaedias: Their History Throughout the Ages* by Robert Collison (Hafner, New York, 1964).

women, the first encyclopedia with a specifically Catholic view of the world—but they shared with *Britannica* a familiar intention: "The chief mirage that hovered tantalisingly before so many generations was that it was possible to compile a work that would supersede all other books and render them unnecessary."

Collison claims that the first encyclopedic work was written by the Greek philosopher Speusippus, Plato's nephew, around 370 BCE, although later scholars question this.* It may be that the philosopher's writings should be considered encyclopedic in their scope, given that they covered such topics as mathematics, legislation and the gods, and that Speusippus believed that knowledge stemmed from the ability to understand not one thing alone, but one subject's relationship to others. Perhaps Aristotle may stake the greatest claim to have studied matters so wide in variety that his knowledge may be justly classified encyclopedic, no matter how unsystematic in form was the result. An encyclopedia by Aristotle would surely be a thing to behold, his knowledge arranged perhaps into the strict taxonomic disciplines of metaphysics, ethics and poetics; alas, what we know of his mind was principally written down by students at his Lyceum, a university by all but name.

The first Roman encyclopedia is sometimes named as Cato the Elder's *Praecepta ad Filium* (*Precepts to His Son*), *c.*185 BCE, a collection of teachings derived from his speeches, although nothing of this survives in the original. But as great a case may be made for his encyclopedic if particular *De Agri Cultura* (*On the Cultivation of the Field*), a ramshackle and exhaustive guide

---

* See for example Jason König and Greg Woolf (eds.), *Encyclopaedism from Antiquity to the Renaissance* (Cambridge University Press, 2013).

to agriculture and husbandry, combining the latest scientific practices with superstition, including much reverential consideration of asparagus and cabbage.*

Today, the oldest writing we may recognize as encyclopedic is from Pliny the Elder. Begun not long before the eruption of Vesuvius in 77, and completed by his son after its author perished in its aftermath, Pliny's *Naturalis Historia* runs to thirty-seven books, from astronomy to zoology, purposely monumental. Its author claimed that such a thing had never been attempted before, although he makes reference to those who had attempted less ambitious efforts, notably the medical reference work of Aulus Cornelius Celsus and the nine-volume illustrated guide to the liberal arts, *Disciplinarum* by Marcus Terentius Varro (116–27 BCE), which included meditations on grammar, rhetoric, geometry, astrology and music. Most significantly, and unlike Varro's compilation, Pliny's writing survived: it is known to us now as one of the most influential and earliest printed multi-volume works, first appearing in Venice in 1469.

Naturalis Historia was neither alphabetical nor cross-referenced, but it did have the sort of clearly defined contents page (the *summarium*) we may expect to see in efficient modern textbooks. It was consistently enthusiastic in tone: Pliny seemed to be in love with the entire world. The books encompassed geography and anthropology, botany and mineralogy, the cosmos and "Mother Earth," olive and wine growing, mammals and insects, gemstones and dyes, sculpture and portraiture—"the world of nature," Pliny wrote, "or in other words life." In

---

* We do have an account of Cato's teachings from Pliny, a report of a lecture to his son on the untrustworthiness of his rival Greeks. "They are a worthless and unruly tribe. Take this as a prophecy: when those people give us their writings they will corrupt everything . . . They call us barbarians too, of course . . ."

one sense it was the Great Library of Alexandria arrayed along a single shelf.

Pliny defined his intentions in his preface, a dedication to the future emperor Titus.

> This is not a well-travelled path for most scholars, or one that minds are eager to wander. None of us has ever attempted it, and no one Greek has covered all of it. Most people look for attractive fields of research; those which are treated by others are said to be of immense subtlety, and are weighed down by the gloomy obscurity of the subject. Now all the subjects that the Greeks call *enkuklios paideia* ought to be dealt with but they are unknown or made confusing by over-complications, while others are so often discussed that they become tedious. It is a difficult thing to give novelty to the familiar, authority to the brand new, shine to the out-of-date, clarity to the obscure, charm to the dull, authority to the implausible, its nature to everything and all its own to nature. And this is why even if I have not succeeded, it is a brilliant and beautiful enterprise.

Pliny claimed to have studied around 2000 books by 100 authors, among them Catullus, Cicero, Livy and Virgil, resulting in some 20,000 digestible facts and observations (modern scholars suggest these numbers may have been greater still; he was either being modest or lost track). His nephew Pliny the Younger described him as a classical workaholic. Traveling through Rome, he would pay a companion to read to him as he walked. Having a bath—and more than one account describes him as a *compulsive* bather—he would dictate his latest entries, including this B-list of the healing properties of plants and fruits, nature in the service of man:

Brya: The pounded bark is given for the spitting of blood and for excessive menstruation, also to sufferers from coeliac disease. The leaves . . . with honey added are applied to gangrenous sores. A decoction of them is healing to tooth-ache and ear-ache. The leaves furthermore are applied with pearl barley to spreading ulcers . . . it is applied with chicken fat to boils. It is an antidote also to the poison of serpents except that of the asp. They say that if it is mixed with the urine of a castrated ox and taken in either drink or food it is an aphrodisiac.

Brambles: Nature did not create brambles for harmful purposes only, and so she has given them their blackberries, food even for men. They have a drying and astringent property, being very good for gums, tonsils and genitals. They counteract the venom of the most vicious serpents, such as the haemorrhois and prester; the bloom or the berry counteracts that of scorpions. They close wounds without any danger of gatherings. The same shoots, eaten by themselves like cabbage sprouts, or a decoction of them in a dry wine, strengthen loose teeth. They are dried in the shade and then burnt so that the ash may reduce a relaxed uvula.

Black Hellebore: A cure for paralysis, madness, dropsy without fever, chronic gout and diseases of the joints; it draws from the belly bile, phlegms and morbid fluids. For gently moving the bowels the maximum dose is one drachma; a moderate one is four oboli. It matures and clears up scrofulous sores, suppurations and indurations; fistulas also if it be taken off on the third day.*

* This is but a small sample: an edited summary from books 24 and 25, Loeb Classical Library edition, Harvard University Press, translated by H. Rackham, first published 1952.

Pliny hoped that all of educated Rome would benefit from his labors. He saw the path of learning as a moral expedition; similarly, we see how an encyclopedia may reflect both the period in which it was written and the moral guidance of its compiler. With *Naturalis Historia,* Pliny was expressing his belief that man and nature existed in productive harmony, and he was concerned with what we might now call an ecological balance: neither half should be unregarding or unprotective of the other. He was also celebrating Rome as the learned center of the universe (and defiantly Rome rather than Athens). He lived at a time of immense cultural and scientific confidence; knowledge, be it of the practical advances in mining or the orbital timings of the planets, was amassed and conquered in step with the conquests of the empire. Indeed, this was another encyclopedic goal: a sense of all being well with the world, a notion of order and stillness, perhaps even control. If you wrote it so, it would be so; nothing confirmed mastery in this eternal city as much as carved or written text. With this extended manuscript, everything seemed in one's command, the sun moving sublimely around the earth, Vesuvius unthreatening in the distance.*

BISHOP OF SEVILLE

If Pliny ever wondered how his text would be remembered, he would have gazed with satisfaction at the work of Isidore of Seville. Some seven centuries later, Pliny's *Naturalis Historia* would continue to form a cornerstone of learning in early

---

* Pliny's manuscript was reproduced many times, and more than 200 handwritten copies survive. It was no less popular by the time of the printing press: at the end of the fifteenth century there were fifteen different printed editions.

medieval Europe, and thanks to Isidore's *Etymologiae* (600–625 CE) it would remain influential throughout the Renaissance.

Matters both human and divine: Isidore of Seville considers his *Origins*

And we have further reason to be grateful to Bishop Isidore of Seville. In 2018, the *English Historical Review* called him "the patron saint of the Internet." Shortly after Isidore's death in 636, his pupil Braulio of Saragossa would remember "an excellent man . . . educated in every kind of expression, so that in the quality of his speech he was suited to both the ignorant audience and the learned."

Isidore produced an extravagant spread of reference works—books which catalogued the saints, analyzed the Scriptures, described each office of the Church and explained all current interpretations of the elements. Accordingly, Braulio claimed, we may fittingly apply Cicero's comment,

> Your books have brought us back, as if to our home, when we were roving and wandering in our own city like strangers, so that we might sometimes be able to understand who and where we are. You have laid open the lifetime of our country, the description of the ages, the laws of sacred matters and of priests, learning both domestic and public, the names, kinds, functions and causes of settlements, regions, places, and all matters both human and divine.

We know relatively little about his life. He was born in the middle of the sixth century, with Spain under Germanic Visigothic rule. His Catholic bishopric began in 600, and his close relationship with King Sisebut enabled him to follow both an influential political career and a humanist religious path. *Etymologiae* (sometimes called *Origins*) was composed in his *scriptorium* (writing house) and intended as "a grand tour of civilisation, starting with an outline of the formal curriculum of the ancient classroom and ending with a helter-skelter of mundane details about the objects to be found in a Roman garden or stable." It was that standard thing—a compendium of all knowledge in the known world. But its author never meant it as a reference work, and certainly not something to be dipped into in search of a single fact.*

After Isidore's death *Etymologiae* was divided by his pupil Braulio into twenty books, and the table of contents alone may leave us overawed, for here were the most important things in life:

* Then as now, humanism was a term open to interpretation. Isidore's theology included a book called *Against the Jews*, an argument designed to convert Jews to Catholicism, which included much criticism of Jewish rituals.

1. Grammar and its parts.
2. Rhetoric and dialectic.
3. Mathematics, whose parts are arithmetic, music, geometry, and astronomy.
4. Medicine.
5. Laws and the instruments of the judiciary, and times.
6. The order of Scripture, cycles and canons, liturgical feasts and offices.
7. God and angels, prophetic nomenclature, names of the holy fathers, martyrs, clerics, monks, and other names.
8. Church and synagogue, religion and faith, heresies, philosophers, poets, sibyls, magicians, pagans, gods of the gentiles.
9. Languages of the nations, royal, military, and civic terminology, family relationships.
10. Certain terms in alphabetical order.
11. Human beings and their parts, the ages of humans, portents and metamorphoses.
12. Four-footed animals, creeping animals, fish, and flying animals.
13. Elements, that is, the heavens and the air, waters, the sea, rivers and floods.
14. Earth, paradise, the regions of the whole globe, islands, mountains, other terms for places, and the lower regions of the earth.
15. Cities, urban and rural buildings, fields, boundaries and measures of fields, roads.
16. Earthy materials from land or water, every kind of gem and precious and base stones, ivory likewise, treated along with marble, glass, all the metals, weights and measures.
17. Agriculture, crops of every kind, vines and trees of every kind, herbs and all vegetables.

18. Wars and triumphs and the instruments of war, the Forum, spectacles, games of chance and ball games.
19. Ships, ropes, and nets, iron workers, the construction of walls and all the implements of building, also wool-working, ornaments, and all kinds of clothing.
20. Tables, foodstuffs, drink, and their vessels, vessels for wine, water, and oil, vessels of cooks, bakers, and lamps, beds, chairs, vehicles, rural and garden implements, equestrian equipment.

And then there were the subheads. To take just Book 1 (Grammar), we encounter Discipline and art; The common letters of the alphabet; The Latin letters; The parts of speech; Accents; Signs used in law; Epistolary codes; Schemas; Tropes; Meters.

In an introduction to the first full English version in 2006, the translators selected several bits of amusing and unreliable lore from each of the books, asides that may have caused a seventh-century Irish monk or an Italian poet from the thirteenth century to look up briefly from their work and wonder about the man who compiled them.*

From Book 1: Caesar Augustus used a secret (although hardly unbreakable) code in which he replaced each letter with the following letter of the alphabet, b for a, etc.

Book 3: The term "cymbal" derives from the Greek words for "with" and "dancing."

Book 6: Architects use green Carystean marble to panel libraries, because the green refreshes weary eyes.

Book 11: In the womb, the knees (genua) of the foetus are pressed against the face, and help to form the eye-sockets (genae).

---

* Translated by Stephen A. Barney, W.J. Lewis, J.A. Beach and Oliver Berghof et al. (Cambridge University Press, 2006) from the 1911 Oxford Latin version of the text by W.M. Lindsay.

Book 12: The ibis purges itself by spewing water into its anus with its beak.

Book 20: Wine (vinum) is so called because it replenishes the veins (vena) with blood.

And what of the title itself? Isidore was deeply interested in origin stories, of philosophies and disciplines, not least rhetoric and physics. And he was fascinated by the regions where things (metals, spices, birds) were first identified.

Pliny was not Isidore's only source. He found much to reproduce from the writings of Servius, Donatus, Palladius and Nonius Marcellus, as well as the Christian writers Jerome and Augustine. Unlike Pliny, Isidore's work for the Church precluded him from conducting much research of his own; he didn't travel much, and there are scant original narrative observations of the sort found in Tacitus. His work was an abridgement and a bridge, a link between late antiquity and medieval Christian scholarship, between the Greek and Roman Empires and those of the pagans and Visigoths. Isidore had a term for his method, something he considered a viable new trade: "compilator." He defined this as "one who mixes the words of others with his own, just as those making pigments crush many different [colors] in the mortar." He also saw himself as a gardener, selecting textual "flowers" as he went.

Consulting *Etymologiae* today we may revel in that combination of pleasures an old encyclopedia never fails to provide—illumination, bafflement and the invaluable impression of an age. Within Isidore's orchard we find:

Birds: There is a single word for birds, but various kinds, for just as they differ among themselves in appearance, so do they differ also in the diversity of their natures. Some are simple, like the dove, and others clever, like the partridge; some enjoy the company of humans, like the swallow, while others prefer a secluded life in deserted places, like the turtledove . . . Some make a racket with their calls, like the swallow. Some produce the sweetest songs, like the swan and the blackbird, while others imitate the speech and voices of humans, like the parrot and the magpie. But there are innumerable others differing in kind and behaviour, for no one can discover how many kinds of birds there are.

Bronze: The ancients used bronze before they used iron. Indeed, at first they would plow the earth with bronze; with bronze weapons they would wage war; and bronze was more prized, while gold and silver were rejected as useless. Now, according to Lucretius's *On the Nature of Things,* it is the opposite: "Bronze is despised and gold has attained the highest honor: thus time in its turning changes the positions of things, and what was prized becomes finally without value."

Ball Games: A ball (*pila*) is properly so called because it is stuffed with hair (*pilus*). It is also a "sphere" (*sphera*), so called from "carrying" (*ferre*) or "striking" (*ferire*). Among the types of ball games are "trigon-ball" (*trigonaria*) and "arena-ball" (*arenata*). Arena-ball, which is played in a group, when, as the ball is thrown in from the circle of bystanders and spectators, they would catch it beyond a set distance and begin the game. They call it the "elbow-game" (*cubitalis*) when two people at close quarters and with their elbows almost joined strike the ball. Those who pass the ball to their fellow players by striking it with the out-stretched lower leg are said to "give it the calf" (*suram dare*).

The influence of *Etymologiae* was wide, informing all the cultural centers of Europe before the Enlightenment. Almost

1000 manuscript copies survive, and it was among the earliest texts to have benefited from Gutenberg's printing press. Bede referred to *Etymologiae* extensively, and its author was immortalized more than 500 years later by Dante, whose *Divine Comedy* (*c.*1320) concludes with the dancing souls of solar illumination: "See, flaming beyond, the burning spirit of Isidore."

Isidore had once found a little time for his own poetry. Although its authorship has been disputed, he is believed to have composed several verses outlining his general philosophy of learning, perhaps even of life itself. Reading the lines below, one may imagine him looking around a cathedral library at Seville, or possibly a monastery scriptorium, surrounded by other learned men, intoxicated by the volumes stacked high upon the walls.

> These bookcases of ours hold a great many books. Behold and read, you who so desire, if you wish.
> Here lay your sluggishness aside, put off your fastidiousness of mind.
> Believe me, brother, you will return thence a more learned man.
> But perhaps you say, "Why do I need this now?
> For I would think no study still remains for me:
> I have unrolled histories and hurried through all the law."
> Truly, if you say this, then you yourself still know nothing.

BYZANTIUM

What a falling off was there. The relatively barren centuries between Isidore of Seville and the High Middle Ages were necessarily as hazardous towards the notion of encyclopedias as towards all other secular manuscripts, but our lack of cultural records in this period suggests that because nothing survived therefore nothing existed. What did survive was curiosity and desire, not least the desire to gather and interpret, and we must locate this innate human attribute in other places and forms.

Byzantine culture, declares the Byzantine professor Paul Magdalino, "was permanently encyclopaedic in the sense that it was continually collecting, summarising, excerpting and synthesising." Much of its Orthodox Christian output was a textual collation composed by kings for their heirs, and tutors for their pupils, and although the ninth and tenth centuries produced nothing of a cohesive nature that could be compared to Pliny or Isidore, it did construct plenty of moral and specialized compendiums.*

Our appreciation of these works requires a parallel effort of encyclopedism, bringing together the surviving excerpts of diverse works commissioned by Leo VI, Constantine VII and Basil II, a list covering law, ecclesiastical teachings and general history.

Emperor Leo VI the Wise (866–912) ruled from Constantinople, and if ever a medieval empire could be said to be sprawling, this was the one: his kingdom, the eastern half of the Roman Empire, extended from the shores of the Bosporus to cover much of the land surrounding the Mediterranean, including what is now Italy, Greece, North Africa and the Middle East, extending north to the Danube and east to Syria. But in the Macedonian Dynasty in which Leo governed, the empire was under constant attack (from Bulgarian and Arab armies; from maritime fleets capturing Sicily and Crete) and

* In Jason König and Greg Woolf (eds.), *Encyclopedism from Antiquity to the Renaissance* (Cambridge University Press, 2013).

his military talents were not equal to his literary and scholarly ones. Indeed, his written histories and treatises may have reflected a desire to instill some sort of order to his kingdom in such a persistent period of turmoil. Leo VI earned his moniker the Wise (he was also called the Philosopher): he attempted to codify all Byzantine law and trading regulations, and his poetry spoke of oracles and visions of the future.

The emperor married four times, in the face of much Church opposition. His illegitimate heir Constantine VII inherited his father's scholarly zeal, and his writing benefited greatly from his father's preparatory work. The finest example, and the one we may classify as encyclopedic, is now known as the *Constantinian Excerpts,* a large historical survey sourced from the ancient Greeks Herodotus and Thucydides, through Peter the Patrician (born 500 CE), to George the Monk (ninth century CE). Written in Greek and arranged originally into fifty-three volumes, each with the same preface explaining the intention of the writing that followed: to render historical information both more intelligible and accessible. Composed between 900 and 990, the project was thematic rather than chronological, utilizing at least twenty-six credited histories at no little expense: some 10,000 sheep had to be slaughtered and skinned to supply the parchment.*

The emperor and his proudly studious colleagues produced much else of an encyclopedic nature, not least a history of the empire from 817, the exhaustive agricultural manual *Geoponika* (with tips on how to grow flowers and plow a turnip field) and *De Ceremoniis,* a guide to court ceremonies and rituals.

* The estimation of András Németh, *The Imperial Systemisation of the Past in Constantinople* (in König and Woolf, above). Of the fifty-three volumes, only *On Embassies* survives in its entirety, alongside fragments of *On Virtues and Vices, On Ambushes* and *On Gnomic Statements.*

The concept of cohesive and comprehensive learning was something young Byzantine students learned at school: the curriculum, consisting mainly of grammar, rhetoric, philosophy and history was indeed called *"enkyklios paideia."*

The Dark Ages that fell upon Western Europe since the fall of Rome, with Church indoctrination all but eliminating the teachings of classical antiquity, was resisted in the East; in the loosest sense, the Barbarians at the gates were fended off as much with ancient Roman statuary and a belief in the retention of intellectual civilization as they were with swords and spears. It is likely that Constantine's historical encyclopedia was completed by Emperor Basil II some twenty years later around 990, and in this way did the imperial scribes safeguard and promote much of the knowledge that would resurface in the early Renaissance printing press of the fifteenth century.

C

CHALCENTEROCITY

On Wednesday, 14 January 1998, a man called Jeffrey Gibson sent an email to the Classics Listserv registered at the University of Washington in Seattle. He had a simple and modest request:

"I've probably asked this before, so please forgive duplicate postings: Is there an English translation of the *Suda*?"

Later that day, the list received a reply from Peter Green.

"The answer, alas is 'no.' Why? Were you thinking of filling the gap? A lot of people would be grateful, I suspect."

The following day Bill Hutton added, "Since translating the *Suda* would be a task requiring greater chalcenterocity than most individual classicists possess, perhaps we should make it a group project." Hutton thought it would be just the sort of thing the global academy did best: "Each of us could send in our favorite entries by e-mail."

An hour later Elizabeth Vandiver emailed: "Sounds good to me—I claim *ikria*."

This conversation went on for a while, years in fact. If one wasn't a classicist, and one came across this open conversation by chance, one might have several questions. Why did Professor Vandiver choose *ikria*? And what actually was the *Suda*?

Before any of these could be answered, there was another keen outpouring online; it seemed, in fact, that enthusiasm was boundless from all quarters of the United States and Europe.

"I cannot think of a better collaborative enterprise," wrote Professor Joe Farrell from the University of Pennsylvania, "nor of a better way to create and distribute the product than via WWW. May I suggest that there is also an opportunity to organize a number of graduate seminars around this objective? This would speed the work and lend excellent focus to the training of young scholars."

The next day, several other contributors began to consider how HTML text would be unified on the site, and how much time such a translation project would cost, and what sort of cross-referencing there would be. Almost immediately the project had a follow-up project with a name—Suda On Line—and someone proposed a logo reflecting its acronym: a shining sun.

"I think all these suggestions are terrific," wrote Kenneth Kitchell, a classics professor at Louisiana State University. "I would like to add one cautionary note, however. Such a project is likely to be done once and once only. Quality control is of great concern so that the project becomes a vehicle for fostering the dissemination of information and not mis-information."

James Butrica sounded another word of warning. "The original suggestion, for people to translate their favourite entries, is not going to work, since it would require too much supervision to make sure that everything got covered and some entries might languish untouched (not everybody is as interested in Iophon as I am, for example). But if each letter were taken by one translator, with additional translators for the letters like alpha that have many entries, it could be done in a relatively expeditious manner. *Si monumentum requiris . . .*"

And in this way was a monumental project born. It took sixteen years to complete (or at least to arrive at what its editors called a "usable standard"), and some of its founders, such as Professor Butrica, did not live to see its full online publication. The Internet was a very different place in 2014 to when the translation had begun, but a small community had managed to produce a work that spoke only of its best attributes—namely, the collaborative dissemination of information and ideas. And it was no small irony that the work of translation (coordinated by two of its founders, Bill Hutton and Elizabeth Vandiver, and based at the University of Kentucky) reflected the aim and methodology of the original cohort of writers who had worked on it more than 1000 years before. And this time it had footnotes and a bibliography, and was keyword searchable.

The *Suda* (or Fortress/Stronghold) was a vast tenth-century Byzantine Greek historical encyclopedia combining material on classical antiquity with biblical and Christian sources. It had been edited and published several times since the end of the fourteenth century, but it had never previously been fully available in English. It was compiled no later than 1000 CE, but its compiler or compilers remain unknown. The entries are arranged in alphabetical order, and appear as a combination of dictionary and conventional encyclopedia: grammatical points and philosophical concepts blend with biographies of ancient authors and lines from ancient texts. Sources range from Aristophanes, Homer and Sophocles, as well as Pliny's *Naturalis Historia* and other classical abridgements. More than

200 people worked on its modern peer-reviewed translation, an extraordinary display of scholarship and erudition producing 30,000 entries on history, literature and biography that might otherwise be lost to us.

What may we see through this looking glass? At random: that the ancient Greek word *Galeagra* (in its Latin transliteration) means "weasel trap, a device for punishment" and is accompanied by an unsourced quote: "As a finale they threw [him?] into a weasel-trap all shut up with iron bolts and rolled it on rough ground," which may refer to a specific cruelty practiced by Caligula.

We find that *Gallos* translates as "eunuch," as in the quip from Greek philosopher Arcesilaus that "Galli come from men, but men do not come from Galli." Another example cites a cunning military ploy: "He sent out youths whom he had prepared as Galli—with pipers, in women's robes, and having drums and figurines—against those besieging the territory."

And we learn that the verb *Gastrizesthai* means to be gorged or "nourished rather magnificently," but also to be hit in the gut. And that the noun *Galasinois* translates as "dimples," specifically the lines that derive from laughing (the philosopher Democritus was nicknamed Dimple when he laughed at the hollow ambition of mankind).

And of those special entries earmarked by the founding editors of Suda On Line in their first tentative emails, *Ikira* means "benches or planks," and may be used to define the earliest form of theatre seating. Iophon was an Athenian tragedian, the son of Sophocles. He is credited with some fifty plays, although authorship is disputed, and many of them may have been the work of his father. And what of Bill Hutton's consciously pretentious use of the word "chalcenterocity"? It derives from "chalcenterous," meaning the possession of "bowels of brass," a gender-neutral equivalent of balls of brass, or "possessing a tough, indomitable and possibly foolhardy nature."

CAMPFIRE TALES

We may ask what the monk of 1010 or the squire of 1050 was really learning here. Even if they could read Greek or Latin and had access to such a manuscript as the *Suda,* how much use was it to know that the Greek word *Angopênia,* which meant "woven vessel," derived from the honeycomb pattern in a beehive? Or that *Ankôn* denotes an elbow both in the biological and architectural sense (the latter describing a small room or enclosed area where a tyrant may throw someone undesirable)? This is indeed the ultimate expression of "knowledge in the round," as ancient tutors had intended for their school curriculum; it borders on trivia, and is no less fascinating for that.

We may logically ask the same question of all medieval collations. The Cambridge professor Peter Burke has noted that what may pass for knowledge today would carry quite another definition a few hundred years ago. One can make a valid distinction between "raw" information, something practical and specific, and "cooked" knowledge, something that has been processed and analyzed. Even this varies over time: early medieval knowledge would certainly incorporate witchcraft, angels and demons. We know that wisdom is not a cumulative accretion of facts, but something to be learned, perhaps through experience. But even an individual's gathering of knowledge may not always be progressive; increasing specialization may produce a more limited range of knowledge, and when encyclopedias are updated we may lose "old knowledge" to make way for new.*

We know of several distant manuscripts composed between 1050 and the first literary glimpses of the Renaissance and printing press in the fifteenth century. We may read these encyclopedias as vault-like *repositories* of information, an early inky storage and retrieval system, and perhaps a slightly desperate one. They were a form of intellectual harvesting, a resistance against the disintegration of wider learning (and the wider world) in the face of restrictive religious uniformity and the application of reason to faith. There was no room for skepticism. Writing and reading these rare volumes was almost a political act, although it's unlikely the studious compilers from *A–Z* would have seen it that way. The encyclopedist's notions of science (the cosmos, biology) were still linked largely to theology, and the category of "science" was mostly understood as practical craftsmanship. The wider world was almost a myth, with one's nearest cathedral city and Jerusalem the only two destinations worth consideration; the Age of Exploration that would later transform our geographical appreciation of the world was still several centuries away.†

Most of these Latin manuscripts survive in fragments alone, but of the handful that exist in their entirety by far the most appealing is the *Otia Imperialia* by Gervase of Tilbury—all 196 chapters of it. Despite his name (in the twelfth century Tilbury was a marshy manor on the north side of the Thames and possibly a former Roman village), Gervase spent his adult

* *A Social History of Knowledge* (Polity Press, Cambridge, 2000).

† The earliest universities in England, Italy, France and Spain (Bologna and Oxford in the eleventh/twelfth century, Modena in the twelfth century and Paris at the start of the thirteenth) evolved from cathedral schools and monastic schools, all of which followed the Latin Catholic theistic tradition.

life in Bologna, Naples, Venice, Arles and Rome; his education derived as much from experience as academia. A well-connected lawyer, once in the service of Henry the Young, the son of Henry II, he composed his great medieval text between 1210 and 1214 for his patron Otto IV of Brunswick, the Holy Roman Emperor. The translated subtitle suggests it was intended as an "entertainment" and "relaxation," although there was certainly also much instruction; the original title was *Liber de Mirabilibus Mundi* (*Book of the Wonders of the World*). One rarely read alone in the Middle Ages, and the manuscript was most likely read to Otto at night by his clerks as he struggled with insomnia.

The encyclopedia is divided into three parts. The first twenty-five chapters examine the world from Creation to Noah, beginning with the storied flow of the Ganges, the Nile, the Tigris and the Euphrates, "the four rivers that flow from Paradise." Gervase then examines the conditions necessary for the formation of clouds and rain. The second section, in twenty-six chapters, is concerned with history and topography, and the current rulers of the known world; and the remaining 145 chapters assume a more spiritual and mythological tone, describing folklore, miracles and the supernatural (or as Gervase has it, "marvels of every province, not every marvel, but some from each province"). One review of the project concludes that "it looks as though the author, in some hurry to present his book to the emperor, did not expand his notes as he had intended." We may balk at the contents of this dominant section, being so far removed from the more sober ambitions of Pliny and Isidore, but taken as a whole *Otia Imperialia* provides a comprehensive survey of the fearful world slowly emerging into a modern one. Gervase relied both on classical and oral traditions, his many biblical allusions combining with contemporary Christian theology and what one might call witches' tales (or what one eighteenth-century editor called a "bagful of foolish old woman's tales"); no one source was treated with more weight than another. Gervase himself stated in his dedication that many of his entries "may be dismissed as idle chatter, but they ought to be given a hearing, because they can provide no trifling instruction or warning with regard to many things."*

As was common with such a personal endeavor, there was also a prominent smattering of opinion on current affairs: Gervase supports a German claim to the throne of Constantinople and weighs in on papal abuse. In other news, "The Isle of Man is quite densely populated, and the way of life there is more refined than is the norm."

The first full English translation wasn't published until 2002. The volume runs to more than 1000 pages, and it opens with a summary of previous attempts: an earlier translator at the University of California "laboured strenuously" on the Latin manuscripts during the 1950s and '60s, but had his work "sadly interrupted" by his death. The first complete edition provides extraordinary insights into the medieval mind.†

From Part 2, a view of Asia: "It starts to the east with the region of paradise, a secure place, remarkable for its possession of every delight, but inaccessible to human beings because it is surrounded by a wall of fire reaching right up to heaven.

---

* "Gervase of Tilbury" by H.G. Richardson, *History*, 1961, vol. 46, no. 157. "The age of scepticism was not yet," Richardson observes. The *Otia* being billed as "an entertainment" now comes into focus: though convincingly told, Gervase did not necessarily believe all the more fanciful stories in his work, but included them as one might use Shakespeare to describe the monarchy—history as drama.

† *Otia Imperialia*, edited and translated by S.E. Banks and J.W. Binns (Clarendon Press, Oxford, 2002).

Within it is the tree of life: whoever eats of its fruit will remain in the same state forever and will never die."

A few pages on, a description of India: "There are . . . various kinds of monstrous creatures there . . . There are some, for instance, whose feet point backwards, and they have eight toes on each foot. Others have a dog's head and hooked claws; their skin is like the hide of cattle, their voice like the barking of dogs. There are . . . women who give birth five times, but their offspring do not live beyond their eighth year. There are also some creatures with no head: their eyes are set in their shoulders, and they have two holes in their chest to serve as a nose and mouth. There are others near the source of the Ganges who live just on the fragrance of a particular kind of apple. If they travel any distance they take some of these apples with them, because if they were to breathe bad unhealthy air they would die at once."

And just as you're thinking, "I'll have what he's having," consider the fate of Indian animals. "There are snakes so huge that their diet consists chiefly of stags; they even cross the ocean . . . The beast called the manticore is found in India too: it has a human face, a triple row of teeth, a lion's body, a scorpion's tail, and blazing eyes; it is the colour of blood, and has a voice like a snake's hiss; it feeds on human flesh, and can run faster than a bird can fly."*

Campfire tales, ghost stories, unsettling tales of inexplicable

* There is much debate in medieval scholarship over whether Gervase's work was intended as a textual accompaniment to the famous Ebstorf map, the twelve-foot-square, thirty-goatskin *mappa mundi* made sometime between 1234 and 1240 (and destroyed by the Allied bombing of Hanover in the Second World War). The controversy hinges on whether Gervase of Tilbury was the same Gervase as Gervase of Ebstorf. There is convincing evidence either way; the more extreme examples of fiery paradise quoted above, for example, are certainly redolent of some of the more fearful descriptions on the map.

occurrences—Gervase's *Otia* was full of them. His readers must have fallen upon such wonders as he describes, of mermaids and storm-inducing dolphins, not just with glee, but some degree of nodding familiarity. These were not tales of the gullible, but tales of the everyday. Not to believe them might be the greater sin.

About thirty manuscript copies of *Otia Imperialia* survive in their entirety, which is about twenty-eight more than *Speculum Maius,* the mid-thirteenth-century work of Vincent of Beauvais. There is a simple reason for this: size. *Speculum Maius* (*The Great Mirror*) was an immense gushing river of a work: eighty books in all, divided into 9886 chapters. There are more than 4 million words. It made Gervase of Tilbury's effort look like homework scribbled on a bus.*

Vincent of Beauvais is widely regarded as the most important educator of the thirteenth century. We know roughly when he died (1264), but not when he was born (somewhere between 1184 and 1194). He became a Dominican friar in Paris before 1220, and he became a "lector" (a specialized reader and educational adviser) in the monastery of Royaumont founded by Louis IX in 1228. He began writing his great encyclopedia under the king's patronage in 1235, and didn't put down his quill until twenty-nine years later; he almost certainly received help from a team of scribes, for no one could have realized this project on their own.

As was the pattern, *Speculum Maius* was a compendium, a collection of all writing its editor considered cogent, commendable and creditable. It was certainly comprehensive.

---

* Although there may be as many as 300 manuscripts with portions of the whole.

There are 171 chapters on herbs, 161 on birds and 134 on seeds and grains; about 900 chapters mention the lives of the saints, and about half this amount allude to chess. It was also contradictory: with about 350 cited sources, from Pliny the Elder to contemporary French scholars, from Cicero to Helinand of Froidmont, it would have been extraordinary had it not been. Entries disputed many things, not least whether a deer's tail was poisonous, and whether the black poppy was edible.

But what, in the grand scheme of things, did Vincent's *Great Mirror* reflect? It showed its readers everything of themselves. It shone a light both pagan and Christian, its author expressing a preference for neither. Vincent spoke of his work as valuable "for preaching, for lecturing, for resolving questions, and generally for explaining almost any sort of matter from every art." It also reflected the late-medieval desire for ordering, for the organized setting down of a universe. The work was divided into three parts: *Speculum Naturale* (science and natural history, including chapters on astronomy, anatomy, agriculture, light and color); *Speculum Doctrinale* (medicine, the mechanical arts, theology—based on the resurrection of man after banishment from Eden); and *Speculum Historale* (from Creation to the Last Judgment). A fourth section was added after Vincent's death and appears in printed versions from the fifteenth century: *Speculum Morale* was largely copied from the work of Thomas Aquinas, and was an attempt by Vincent's followers (and later printers) to attune the work to a more modern philosophy and Christian theology.

Vincent's own moral instruction continues to excite debate. He was a modest editor, claiming little credit for his vast encyclopedia (indeed apologizing for its shortcomings in its preface, a recurring theme), crediting instead the vast army of writers upon which he drew. But his modesty was inherently false: while he very rarely adopted the outspoken role of "auctor," or learned scholar expressing his own views, his selection from his sources was nonetheless pointed, politically and morally.

Vincent was particularly intrigued by the role of women, although he may not quite fit the role of medieval progressive some have assigned him. He made an educational distinction between the sexes, but it was very much the traditional one. "You have sons?" he quotes from the Book of Ecclesiasticus. "Train them and care for them from boyhood. You have daughters? Watch over their bodies and do not show yourself joyful to them." But Vincent also displayed a rare acceptance in the Middle Ages of the view that women might be worthy recipients of his collation of knowledge. In France he was exposed to several instances marking the ascendancy of women, not least the regency of Blanche of Castile, and the chivalrous concept of courtly love. There are sections in his *Great Mirror* highlighting specific crafts suitable for women (all non-physical, all domestic as one might expect), and he places much emphasis on the value of women reading (albeit for religious guidance). The education scholar Rosemary Barton Tobin has observed that while another of Vincent's works, *De Eruditione Filiorum Nobilium* (*The Education of Noble Children*), had the last ten of its fifty-one chapters devoted to young women, the instruction he suggests concentrates on the promotion of abstinence and the protection of chastity. Vincent opposed all forms of cosmetic beautification, for this would deflect focus from the soul. Moreover, Professor Tobin notes, a woman would always be required to uphold more virtuous standards than a man: "The girl is responsible for both her own behaviour and whatever interpretation others may place upon that behaviour. It is a severe burden which only adds to the heavier responsibility Vincent gives to girls as opposed to boys in the sphere of moral action."*

COOK'S TALE

But Chaucer was a fan. He once referenced "Vincent, in his Storial Mirour," and he may have drawn on his *Great Mirror* for *The Canterbury Tales*.†

Chaucer's great work is in itself encyclopedic, his twenty-four tales covering all manner of occupations and daily pursuits—the Physician, the Monk, the Prioress, the Friar, the Merchant. But his range of fictional forms also suggests a catalogue, spanning, in the words of one Middle English specialist, every possible style: "Romance, moral prose allegory, the comic and bawdy fabliau, penitential manual, beast fable, Breton *lai*, sermon, fictional autobiography, parody, dramatic monologue, tragedy, *exemplum*, satire and hagiography, to name but a few."‡

Professor Helen Cooper compares *The Canterbury Tales* to the compendiums of Vincent of Beauvais, not least in its fully rounded exploration of human character: strengths and weaknesses, reality and imagination, abstract thought and intellectual rigor. She believes the work was intended to be read as an entire literary expression of life, with some narrative cross-referencing, and to address one story alone would be to

---

* See "Vincent of Beauvais on the Education of Women" by Rosemary Barton Tobin, *Journal of the History of Ideas*, July-September, 1974, vol. 35, no. 3. Also Astrik Gabriel, *The Educational Ideas of Vincent of Beauvais* (Notre Dame, 1956).

† The line appears in the Prologue, *The Legend of Good Women*, *c.*1386.

‡ Ian Johnson of the University of St. Andrews.

miss the point, "like reading the Murder of Gonzago without *Hamlet*."*

The characters in the tales are broadly divided into three social groups—those who fight, those who work and those who pray—while the range of the stories would indeed have been familiar to anyone versed in the thematic groupings of a medieval encyclopedia, for they form a complete presentation of the world: the exotic world of romance and chivalry, the everyday practical world and the spiritual and cosmic world. And in a similar vein to many religious entries in early compendiums, the tales are morals: the stories test the extent to which the pilgrims live up to or fall short of an ideal. The main difference between Chaucer's work and the encyclopedia is that there is no attempt at universal or empirical "answers." Every character strives for their own truths.

* *The Structure of the Canterbury Tales* (Duckworth, London, 1983). As if to repay the compliment, Vincent of Beauvais includes a collection of fables in his *Speculum Doctrinale*, attempting to impose a coherence on them.

D

DAMASK SILK

The book you are reading now is a work of fact and opinion. Better than that, it is a collection of facts and opinions about books about facts and opinions. But now I want you to use your imagination. You need to imagine an encyclopedia in an unfamiliar language from a distant land more than 600 years ago. It is the biggest and most exacting encyclopedia ever made, too big to be printed. It is created, in fairy-tale fashion, for one megalomaniacal man, and it is named after him, the whole running to 22,937 sections within 11,095 manuscript volumes, each between 1 and 2 inches thick, all bound in the finest yellow damask silk.

Now open your eyes, for such a thing did exist. It exists still, in a recklessly truncated and scattered form, a mere speck of the original. It is mentioned in hushed tones by scholars of Chinese history and literature, as if its power is still a virulent force. And it has a wonderful name, the *Yongle Dadian*.

It is also known as *Yongle Dadian Vast Documents of the*

Yongle Era and *Grand Canon of Yongle*, and, in an earlier form, *Wenxian Dacheng*. When an analysis of the work was published in the *Journal of Library and Information Science* in 2010, its name was proving impossible to spell, as if it was jinxing readers from beyond the grave: occasionally it was the *Yonle Dadian*, once the *Yonele Dadian* and once even the *Yung Lo Da Dian*. Either way, it was the culmination of all Chinese knowledge—which, by immodest extension, meant all the knowledge in the world.

It was commissioned by the Yongle emperor Zhu Di, the third emperor of the Ming Dynasty, known also as Ming Chengzu, known also as the progenitor of the Age of Perpetual Happiness, additionally known as the fiercest of warlords. According to Pi-ching Hsu of San Francisco State University, the Ming emperor Yongle was a man of contradictions. He has been portrayed as both a sage-king concerned primarily with the everlasting well-being of his subjects and empire, but also as someone associated with quite a few "less happy" events, "including political scheming and mass murder."

The emperor was clearly an educated man, which explains his encyclopedia, but also an insatiable self-aggrandizer, which explains the size of it, and also his creation of the Forbidden City of Beijing. As an empire builder he was unsurpassed, extending Chinese influence during his rule (1402–24) to Vietnam, Korea and Japan, and expending much energy fighting the Mongols, while also reinvigorating domestic agricultural prosperity. And then there were the other things: killing his enemies, establishing a large spying network staffed by eunuchs, purging anyone who might question his legitimacy or expose his sexual appetites and scandals. But as Professor Hsu attests, the tyranny was punctuated with outward displays of being very kind to animals, not least wild horses and cats, and he showed particular affection towards an imported giraffe, believing it to be some sort of unicorn.*

And so it is with some relief that we return to his reference work. The *Yongle Dadian* was composed with an extraordinary sense of urgency between 1403 and 1408. Written by thousands of traveling scholars scooping up everything in their path, the contents were quantified in 1901 by the historian Luther Carrington Goodrich as

> thought, morals, poetry, frontier people (the Xiongnu and Hu for example), geography, surnames, government, law, the spirits, biography, divination, architecture (gates, bridges, halls, store-houses, walls, offices), villages, capital cities, history, burial customs, astronomy, botany, grain, military matters, Buddhism, Taoism, travels, bronzes, food and drink, caves, dreams, scholars, drama, sacrifices, clothing, mathematics, carpentry, post stations, shamans, literary collections.†

The compilers submitted their first draft to the emperor after seventeen months, but he disapproved, deeming it insufficient for his needs. No doubt happy to escape with their lives, the anxious scholars went back to plunder a further 8000 ancient texts, emerging with a much bigger encyclopedia of 3.7 million characters on 917,000 pages. This time the tyrant appeared content.

But one may reasonably ask the question: what was he

---

* *Journal of the American Oriental Society*, Oct.-Dec. 2002, vol. 122, no. 4.

† As quoted by Lauren Christos, "The Yongle Dadian: The Origin, Destruction, Dispersal and Reclamation of a Chinese Cultural Treasure," *Journal of Library and Information Science*, April 2010, vol. 36, no. 1.

so worried about? Why did his megalomania, his harvesting of everything, become so important to him? Powerful men and women are inevitably concerned with their legacies. It would be unusual if they amassed their immense power and wealth without simultaneously amassing cavernous amounts of guilt. It would be understandable, therefore, if they wished to leave something good behind, a reputation not wholly damning, something that may prompt future generations (their hand-washing descendants, say, or historians) to think better of them. A foundation, a grant or prize, the naming of a library; a benefactor "putting something back." Emperor Yongle had more to put back than most. But in this case I think he may just have been being an emperor; he wanted the best, the most, the ultimate. It wasn't knowledge for dissemination, or even knowledge for knowledge's sake—it was knowledge that no one else could have, a gift to himself wrapped in yellow damask silk. And of course the emperor's own entry in the encyclopedia would be a glorious textual shrine. But even if he had been persuaded to spread the knowledge around, the almost impossible size of the enterprise ensured that no one could afford to reproduce it and that no one got to read it.

The problem with having 3.7 million characters was that one needed an awful lot of wood carvers and a very large forest to turn it into something that could be printed and distributed. Scribes made a few copies of some of it, but the master copy was the only complete proof that such a thing ever existed. By logical extension, all that knowledge in the hands of one individual—wasn't that the perfect definition of intellectual tyranny? Wasn't that the exact opposite of what an encyclopedia was supposed to be?

The Chinese had been making encyclopedias—*leishu*—since the "Warring States" era between 474 and 221 BCE; even then, the historian Harriet Zurndorfer notes, there was "a dream of writing the world into a single text." In the dynasties that followed, the shape and intention of these manuscripts fell into several categories—the compendiums of everything known, the natural and philosophical histories, the factual texts designed for civil service examinations and all manner of specialist volumes. Then there were the *riyong leishu,* or collections of everyday practical information for those with limited literacy.

Unlike the *Yongle Dadian,* almost all of them were printed. For a snapshot of the vast range on offer one may consult the unique *Siku quanshu* (*Complete Collection of the Four Treasuries*), an imperial library catalogue compiled in the eighteenth century. The catalogue gave way to a physical library, combining 3461 separate works into a new masterwork of 2.3 million pages in 36,000 large folio volumes. Seven duplicates were made and distributed throughout the empire. It incorporated sixty-five *leishu* from a total of 217 consulted by the editors. These included volumes dating as far back as the Liang Dynasty (502–57), with ten from Tang (618–907) and twelve from Ming (1368–1644).

Wang Chutong, one of the *Siku quanshu* editors, then went on to compile the *Lianshi* in the 1790s, the first modern encyclopedia devoted entirely to the work and activities of women. Subjects covered marriage, physical appearance, weaving, poetry and the role of women across the social spectrum, from imperial princess to streetwalker. The work was edited by men, but as Dr. Zurndorfer observes, of the hundred contributors to the *Lianshi,* a large proportion were married to women with prestigious literary reputations. "One may infer that their appreciation of these women's talents spurred their involvement . . . and that the topics they pursued therein reflect that admiration."*

Given the circumstances surrounding its inception, perhaps it was inevitable that the *Yongle Dadian* would meet a tumultuous end. Initially stored in the Ming Dynasty capital Nanjing, it moved with the emperor to the new capital Peking (later renamed Beijing) in 1421, and for almost a century and a half it remained in the summer palace in the Forbidden City. When a fire almost destroyed the palace, two copies were finally made, one of them destined for the Beijing Hanlin Academy, China's largest repository library established in the 1720s. The fate of the other copies and fragments of copies is uncertain, but many were burnt when British and French troops sacked the Imperial Archive in 1860.

The last remaining copy, the one at the Hanlin Library, met a lonely and unceremonious fate. That manuscript, writes Lauren Christos, the Librarian at Florida International University, "over time fell prey to poor preservation whether through theft, rodents or insects, warfare or fire." The rodents didn't chew everything: of the original 11,095 volumes, about 800 were still readable in 1900. After the Siege of Peking in that year, and the fire that swept through the library, the number dropped to only 370, or 809 sections, the equivalent of having only entries for the letter *A*.†

* For more detail on the *Siku quanshu* and other Chinese encyclopedias see Harriet T. Zurndorfer in König and Woolf, above. The *Lianshi* had a medieval precedent of sorts: *Horus Deliciarum* was edited by Abbess Herrad of Landsberg *c.*1180, although it was as much a visual instruction as a textual one, the abbess painting or commissioning more than 300 miniature illuminations depicting philosophical, religious and scientific scenes. The original was destroyed in a fire in 1870, but copies remain.

† Other volumes are scattered around the world—Germany has five, Britain fifty-one, and the Library of Congress forty-one.

The loss of the text heralded the loss of an entire culture, for what is a society without an archive of its history and the memory of its people? In some quarters, the destruction of physical evidence of a group's culture is legally defined as genocide.*

And in time even the name disintegrated. Maybe it really was the *Yongle Dadian* or the *Yung Lo Da Dian*. Perhaps *Wenxian Dacheng* should still hold. We only have what we call it today, for tomorrow it is still not there.

DEVISE, WIT

> Devise, wit; write, pen; for I am for whole volumes in folio.

When the lovelorn Armado calls upon divine inspiration near the beginning of *Love's Labour's Lost,* the audience knows his quest is doomed. Here is the pompous Spanish braggart sure that he was the first man to fall in love, dropping his military pursuits to woo his intended with poetry. Alas he has neither the talent nor the learning to write the persuasive sonnet; he has only the pale prospect of parody.

For centuries, scholars have debated the learning of Shakespeare himself. We have little if any documentation of what he was taught at school, nor the historical volumes by his side as he wrote *Henry VI* in 1591 and *Henry VIII* in 1612, nor what informed his philosophical worldview as he framed the minds of Hamlet and Lear.

It's unnerving to learn that for much of the eighteenth century Shakespeare was regarded as an ignoramus. His plays

* The Convention on the Prevention and Punishment of the Crime of Genocide of 1948 was the first human rights treaty adopted by the General Assembly of the United Nations.

were castigated for their lack of chronological, historical and geographical accuracy, and his lack of bookishness was used by the academic elite as an assault on creativity. The modern view has changed. Though lacking a donnish background, we know that Shakespeare had access to several almanacs and encyclopedias, and there are numerous direct correlations between passages in his plays and the widely available volumes he may have had at his elbow.

He wrote on the cusp of Copernican comprehension; that is, the gradual acceptance that if the earth revolved around the sun, we should adapt our philosophical and dramatic approaches accordingly. The first English translation of Copernicus, *A Perfit Description of the Celestiall Orbes* appeared as part of the *Digges Almanac* of 1576, a popular digest that was almost certainly within Shakespeare's grasp.*

Another publication, a more general encyclopedia commonly known as *Batman upon Bartholomew,* is widely regarded as his most likely companion. It was published in 1582, when Shakespeare was eighteen, and immediately entered university libraries and educated homes. *Re*-published is more accurate, for it was a reprinting and modest update of a thirteenth-century work by the Franciscan monk Bartholomaeus Anglicus, popularized when printed by Wynkyn de Worde in London in 1495, and finally updated by Stephen Bateman (or Batman) in Shakespeare's time.† The whole was the traditional mixture of fact and fiction, and, as English professor Neil Rhodes points out, scholars have detected some possible direct borrowings: the encyclopedia mentions the effects of the moon's light as a cause of madness

---

* A fortuitous link: After Thomas Digges died, his widow went on to marry Thomas Russell, one of the trustees of Shakespeare's will.

† Another fortuitous link: *Batman* was dedicated to Henry Carey, patron of the theatre company Shakespeare wrote for in the 1590s.

(alluded to in both *Measure for Measure* and *Othello*); the geometric properties of the soul and our energy patterns (*King Lear*); and the concept of beast-like men (*The Tempest*). Other entries would be reflected in his sonnets.*

One more publication stakes a claim: Pierre de la Primaudaye's *French Academie,* first translated into English in 1586. This was primarily a modern work, its four volumes encompassing the creation, the cosmos, animals and plants, the human body and its diseases, and a Christian philosopher's guide to life. How did this show itself in Shakespeare's work? Convincingly. Professor John Hankins has traced elements of the *French Academie* in the "All the world's a stage" speech in *As You Like It,* and in Lear's speech that "When we are born, we cry that we are come / To this great stage of fools." The references to the unweeded garden and the sleep of death in *Hamlet* may also derive from Primaudaye, as well as the many references to the force and influence of "custom" in *Hamlet* and *Pericles.* Finally, Othello's speculations on Desdemona's supposed infidelity, and particularly the notion of the heart as a fountain, find several parallel sources in *French Academie.*

It's an exercise worthy of the best detectives. "None of this is conclusive," Neil Rhodes concedes, "but if Shakespeare did own an encyclopaedia—and in view of the enormous diversity of his subject matter it would have been a very useful companion—then this would almost certainly have been it." And beyond these forensics, one recurring theme in his plays—man as a microcosm of the workings of the universe—reflects the grand ambitions of every compiler of the modern encyclopedia: the world in a book.

---

* See Neil Rhodes's *Shakespeare's Encyclopaedias* in König and Woolf, above. Also J.E. Hankins, *Shakespeare's Derived Imagery* (University of Kansas Press, 1953).

DOGMATIC DELIVERY OF KNOWLEDGE

In his later years, Shakespeare would have known of the far-reaching educational proposals of Francis Bacon (1561–1626), and in his roles as attorney general and lord chancellor Bacon would have been known to those who saw Shakespeare's plays. Bacon's treatise *The Advancement of Learning* (1605) was a hugely influential work, an exuberant promotion of the idea that the health and wealth of human lives could be improved beyond measure by the application of intellectual pursuits. Bacon was a heavy-hatted cheerleader, leaving it to others to realize his ideology in practical form. But all future encyclopedists would have reason to be grateful to him.*

Nothing if not precocious, Bacon attended Cambridge University at the age of thirteen, where his acquisitions included a bow and quiver of arrows, a pair of pantofles and a dozen new buttons for his doublet. He read Livy, Demosthenes, Aristotle, Xenophon and Hermogenes. For nine months his education was interrupted by the plague. On his return to Cambridge, he impressed Queen Elizabeth with his gravity and maturity. When she asked his age, he announced he was "two years younger than Her Majesty's happy reign," the charm of which suggested to all present that he would go far in life.†

---

* Three decades later, René Descartes proposed a similar philosophy. *Discourse on the Method of Rightly Conducting the Reason, and Seeking Truth in the Sciences* (1637) argued that there was little that couldn't be improved or solved by the systematic breakdown and analysis of a complex problem. But Descartes had doubts about the possibility of containing such knowledge between hard covers. "Even if all knowledge could be found in books," he wrote in the 1640s, "where it is mixed in with so many useless things and confusingly heaped in such large volumes, it would take longer to read those books than we have to live in this life, and more effort to select the useful things than to find them oneself."

† And so it proved: a lord, a viscount, legal adviser to Elizabeth and James I,

The publication of his great educational proposal was initially overshadowed by the discovery a few days later of the Gunpowder Plot, but its influence endures. The *Advancement of Learning* opened with a double-length pull-out strip entitled Analysis, a visual aid for the treatise to follow. This praised "the excellency of learning" and criticized "the zeal and jealousy" of *divines* (self-appointed representatives of God), "the severity and arrogance" of politicians, and the slightly vaguer "errors and imperfections of learned men." Other targets included those who displayed a "distrust of new discoveries"; the "conceit that the best opinions prevail"; an "impatience of doubt"; a "mistaking of the end of knowledge"; and the "dogmatic delivery of knowledge."

A second pull-out section at the start of the second volume—the one concerned with how Bacon's improved theories of learning may be practiced—again presented a shorthand view of the text to come. Here the pluses—"the places of learning, the books of learning, the person of the learned"—were again outnumbered by obstacles, some of which prevail today: the "smallness of rewards for lecturers"; the "want of apparatus for experiments"; a "want of mutual intercourse between the universities of Europe"; and the "want of public appointment of writers or inquirers into the less known branches of knowledge."

And then, in the form of a family tree, came Bacon's

Bacon is best remembered by historians of science as the great promulgator of empirical (i.e., skeptical and methodical) research. His flamboyance of mind was reflected in his manner, and this was prominently displayed at his wedding to Alice Barnham. As Dudley Carleton, one of those in attendance, recorded in a letter in May 1606, "Sir Francis Bacon was married yesterday to his young wench in Maribone Chapel. He was clad from top to toe in purple, and hath made himself and his wife such store of fine raiments of cloth of silver and gold that it draws deep into her portion. The dinner was kept at his father-in-law Sir John Packington's lodging over against [adjacent to] the Savoy."

approximation of what such a compendium of knowledge should look like, with the branch devoted to Human Learning providing the most useful snapshot of the range and value of academic pursuits at the beginning of the seventeenth century.

The accumulation of learning, Bacon decreed, should be divided into History, Philosophy and Poesy. History is then subdivided into Natural History ("of creatures, of marvels, of arts"), Civil History ("memorials, antiquities, chronicles, lives and narrations"), Ecclesiastical ("history of the Church, of prophecy, of providence") and Literary ("orations, letters, sayings etc."). Poesy was concerned with poetry and the imagination ("narrative, representative, allusive"). Philosophy was split into science (physical and metaphysical), prudence (experimental and magical), body (medicine, athletics and the "sensual arts") and mind (human will and the "nature of good"), and reason (invention, judgment, memory and tradition).

Future encyclopedists would perceive in Bacon's summary a significant practical pointer for their own work, and certainly a confident mission statement—a reaffirmation that their occupation fulfilled a modern need.

The vastness of the realms of knowledge now made these categorizations, this streamlining, a necessity. *Encyclopaedia Britannica* was still 160 years away, but these considerations would still be valid when its publishers first met. Bacon lived at a time when our understanding of science and natural history was producing a revolution of the mind: the work of Copernicus, Galileo and Kepler heralded a new type of precision thinking, and their number would soon be swelled by Robert Boyle, Christopher Wren, Edmond Halley and Isaac Newton. The encyclopedia was about to turn from a mere storehouse of facts to a more contemplative whole, and it would provide the natural and facilitating companion to a complete transformation of how we viewed the world.

E

EPHRAIM CHAMBERS (GENTLEMAN)

By all contemporary reckonings, Ephraim Chambers should be much better known than he is. As Bacon inspired, Chambers practiced. He made the first modern encyclopedia as we know it, and his work lit the touchpaper for the Enlightenment.*

The title was a meal in itself:

CYCLOPÆDIA:
OR, AN
UNIVERSAL DICTIONARY
OF
ARTS and SCIENCES;
CONTAINING
The DEFINITIONS of the TERMS;

---

* The Chambers we may now associate with almanacs and other reference books was not him: that was Robert Chambers, operating about a century later.

And ACCOUNTS of
The THINGS signify'd thereby,
In the several ARTS,
Both LIBERAL and MECHANICAL,
And the several SCIENCES,
HUMAN and DIVINE:
The Figures, Kinds, Properties, Productions, Preparations, and Uses,
Of Things NATURAL and ARTIFICIAL;
The Rise, Progress and State of Things
Ecclesiastical, Civil, Military and Commercial:
With the several Systems, Sects, Opinions &c. Among Philosophers, Divines,
Mathematicians, Physicians, Antiquaries, Critics &c.
The Whole intended as a Course of Ancient and Modern LEARNING.
Compiled from the best Authors, Dictionaries, Journals, Memoirs,
Translations, Ephemerides, &c. In several Languages.
In TWO VOLUMES
By E. CHAMBERS Gent.

This groundbreaking work, published in London in 1728, came about because its creator believed that the world contained too many books.

Chambers lived in London during a golden age of publishing. Book stalls clogged the Strand and lined the Thames, the ports were full of travelers' tales and enticing maps, and printing presses hammered through the night in Clerkenwell and Westminster to meet demand. New copyright laws had recently been passed to restrict piracy, but it was a hopeless task. London was rapidly overtaking Paris as the largest city in Europe, its population growing from 630,000 when Chambers arrived from his birthplace in the Lake District in 1714 to around 730,000 when he was buried in Westminster Abbey in 1740. An appetite for knowledge had resulted in what Chambers saw as too much print and too much choice (he liked to quote Ecclesiastes: "Of making books there is no end"). Although he would probably have called it something else, he was experiencing an early form of information overload.

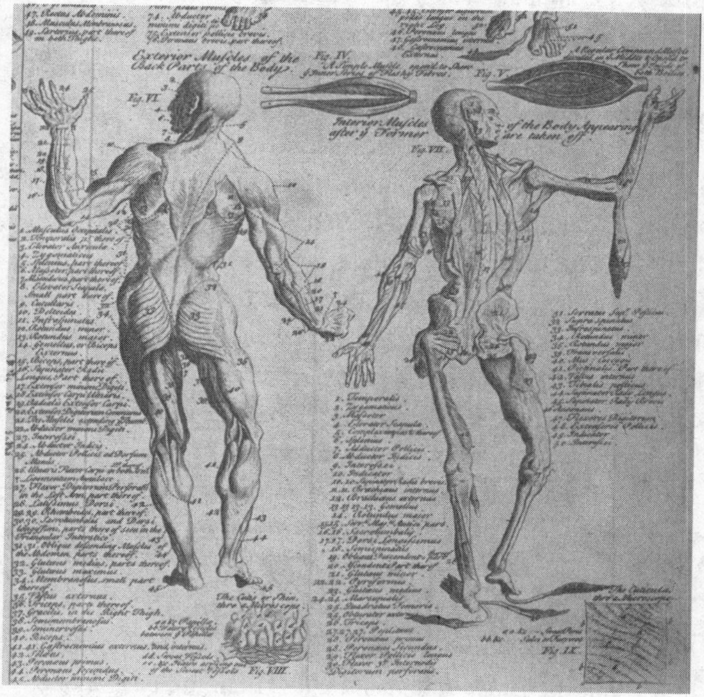

A gathering of arresting things: *Cyclopaedia* demystifies the human body in 1728

His solution was simple: he proposed a work that resembled a "commonplace" book—a gathering of relevant, significant and arresting things—that would "answer all the Purposes of a Library except Parade and Incumbrance." He produced two massive folio volumes, each almost unliftable, some 2500 pages combined, two guineas the set. The enterprise was financed by subscription but sold well beyond its initial supporters: Chambers's group of printers—he needed seventeen to manage the whole vast project—rewarded him with £500 for his success, about £60,000 today. The books are about the size of regular-issue Ten Commandments, and their influence on contemporary learning was not much less. Indeed, not long after its publication, Chambers claimed, with no apparent pause for modesty, that his work was simply "the best Book in the Universe."

But like all groundbreaking projects, there were predecessors, inspirations and rivals. Chambers's volumes represented the last of a trio of quite similar works, but the fact he was published last, and with the greatest fanfare, ensured not only the greatest sales but also the most enduring impact. They followed Antoine Furetière's three-volume *Dictionnaire universel,* published at The Hague in 1690, and *Lexicon Technicum,* compiled by the clergyman John Harris and published in several editions between 1704 and 1710.* This also claimed to be a universal guide to the arts and sciences, and appeared, like Chambers's work, in alphabetical order. Harris's *E*'s began with:

> **EARTH:** The surface of the whole Earth, Mr Keil, in his *Examination of Dr. Burnet's Theory,* makes to be 170981012 *Italian* Miles, and the *Italian* Mile is little less than the *English* one.
>
> **EARTHQUAKES:** Mr Boyle thinks that *earthquakes* are often occasioned by the sudden fall of Ponderous Masses in the Hollow Parts of the Earth, whereby those terrible Shocks and Shakings are produced.

---

* John Harris hoped his *Lexicon* would provide more than mere reference; he longed to have composed "a Book useful to be read carefully over." But in its first year of publication, Jonathan Swift was able to satirize (in *A Tale of a Tub*) what he saw as the plethora of "index learning," a trend towards abridgement and summation, which Swift considered a poor substitute for actually reading an entire work. (Without using the phrase, he accused them of dumbing down.)

Eccentricity: In the *Ptolomaic Astronomy*, is that Part of the *Linea Apsidum* lying between the Center of the Earth and of the Eccentric; ie that Circle which the Sun is supposed to move in about our Earth, and which hath not the Earth exactly for its Center. And the Ancients found this must be supposed, because the Sun sometimes appears large, and then it is nearest to us, and sometimes smaller, and then further off.*

Ephraim Chambers acknowledged *Lexicon Technicum* in his preface, while also raising its shortcomings: he called it (and its predecessors) part of "an inferior class of books," while his own was "superior to what had been known in any former work." (This was a common enough trait among early encyclopedists: calling rivals out in the manner of professional wrestlers.) In his preface he admitted he was more compiler than author, but he claimed much originality in his selection, writing that he was "far from having contented myself to take what was ready collected," but had "augmented it with a large accession from other quarters." In this he compared himself to a bee, gathering the pollen as he hopped from flower to flower, producing nectar "for the publick Service." (And in this he echoed Isidore of Seville's estimation that he was planting textual "flowers.")

He extended this theme to the heart of the project itself, including an entry on Plagiary, arguing that compilers such as he could not be accused of "author theft" because "what they take from others they do it avowedly, and in the open Sun. In effect, their Quality gives them a title to every thing that may be for their purpose, wherever they find it."

---

* Is it necessary to observe that our understanding has advanced, and that the Earth is not hollow, and nor does it enjoy the sun revolving around it? See below for the rather more accurate interpretation in Chambers's *Cyclopaedia*.

Examining the monumental volumes almost 300 years after publication, I was struck by one feature in particular: they are remarkable material objects. The stamping of the ink on coarse pages creates an impression on the fingertips. Turning the giant leaves, the reader may feel, as I did, a considerable sense of power and good fortune. Here is the world, all its natural science, theology, cartography, philosophy. And here is a distinct advance from some of its more fanciful predecessors, the ones with the hokum about witches' brews and faith in magic. Here, indeed, is an attempt at purposely filtered fact that would stand the test of time three centuries later.

Volume 1 opens with two extraordinary frontispieces. The first is a large opening fold-out copper engraving, a wide vista in the style of Hieronymus Cock. About eighty people in long robes are engaged in various forms of scholarship in an open-air classical forum, with pillars and statuary framing mechanical instruments and measuring devices. The message is clear: these people (about a quarter of whom are women) are mastering a great many of the activities you are about to read about, be they practical (astrological calculation, weighing); artistic (heraldic design, architectural planning); or theoretical (a lot of people debating, many with their arms open). Others are examining two large globes, perhaps wondering where to travel next.*

The second frontispiece is a complex chart of Knowledge, laid out, as with Bacon's work, like a family tree. This is Chambers's statement of intent, a diagram serving as both contents page and higher theory. It identifies forty-seven subject or theoretical groupings from the arts and sciences,

---

* The engraving is by "G. Child of Covent Garden." Chambers had learned his geographical knowledge of the world from the great map and globe maker John Senex, with whom he apprenticed not long after arriving in London in his mid-thirties.

and attempts to wrestle the limitations of an alphabetical listing back on to thematic ground.

At the top of the tree sits the phrase: "KNOWLEDGE is either . . . ," which then splits into two choices: "Natural and Scientifical" or "Artificial and Technical."

These split again, into "Sensible, Rational, Internal or External," and there are more subdivisions towards the foot of the tree, the more precise subject categories we may recognize as specialisms (and perhaps careers) today: Meteorology, Hydrology, Mineralogy, Zoology, Phytology, Geometry, Ethics, Music, Pneumatics, Mechanics, Astronomy, Agriculture, Rhetoric and many others. And then there are detailed notes, wherein each of these subjects is further explained. Meteorology, for example, regroups the encyclopedia's various entries on the history of air and atmosphere, including Ether, Vapour, Cloud, Rain, Shower, Drop, Hail, Dew and Damp. Alluringly, Geometry encompasses separate entries entitled Perpendicular, Parallel, Triangle, Square, Polygon, Cycloid, Quadratix, Prism, Planisphere, Analemma and Parabola.

Who was this overwhelming book intended for? In Chambers's words, for anyone wishing to reclaim the mind "from its native wildness." It was for those wishing to shrink rather than expand their library, an early desire for downsizing. Chambers wasn't alone with his wish. In 1680, the German polymath Gottfried Wilhelm Leibniz detected a "horrible mass of books which keeps on growing . . . disorder will become nearly insurmountable." There is a connected dilemma: not only so many books, but nowhere to put them all, and an inequality of access that ensured only the well educated could afford to consult them. Leibniz, incidentally, had read so many of these books that he was referred to by King George I as "a living dictionary," a phrase we might more commonly translate as "a walking encyclopedia." By the time Ephraim Chambers picked up his quill in the early eighteenth century, this phrase was already a mild insult, a term for an insufferable know-it-all. In classical Greece, and even in the Middle Ages, it was possible to imagine that the feat of committing a whole book's worth of factual content to memory was both desirable and possible. With the emergence of the *Cyclopaedia* it was clear that this was no longer the case.

Chambers dedicated his book to the newly crowned King George II. The nature of his fawning tribute may partly account for his work's impact. He "lay at Your Majesty's feet . . . an attempt towards a survey of the republic of learning." He believed that Great Britain now enjoyed a reputation for scientific and artistic expression that was once the province of Rome in her Augustan age; Rome would soon envy our own. To underline this British mastery, Chambers stressed the difference between "Your Majesty's subjects and the savages of Canada, or the Cape of Good Hope." He claimed his readers had recently been ennobled by a monarch "inspired with a generous passion to devote his cares to the welfare of mankind"; and the author was one of the countless many "conspiring with unexampled ardor and unanimity to all his glorious views."

Among his *E*'s, Chambers includes:

Earnest: Money advanced to complete or assure a verbal bargain, and bind the parties to a performance thereof. By the civil law, he who recedes from his bargain loses his earnest.

Earth: (extract) The orbits of all the planets include the sun as the common centre of them all: the earth . . . is not in the centre of any of them.

The earth's orbit being proved to be between those of Venus

and Mars, it follows that the earth must turn around the sun. For, as it lies within the orbits of the superior planets, their motion would indeed appear unequal and irregular; but they would never be stationary or retrograde without this supposition.

Empalement: A cruel kind of punishment wherein a sharp pale or stake is thrust up the fundament and through the body. It was frequently practised in the time of Nero; and it continues to be popular in Turkey.

And . . .

Encyclopaedia: The circle or chain of arts and sciences. The word is compounded of the *in, circle* and *learning*: the root being child, infant. It is sometimes also written *cyclopaedia*. Vitruvius in the preface to his 6th book calls it *encyclios disciplina*. See Cyclopaedia.

Padding back some 100 pages one finds:*

Cyclopaedia: The word *cyclopaedia* is not of classical authority, though frequent enough among modern writers to have got into several of our dictionaries. Some make it a crime in us to have called the present work by this name; not considering that names and titles of books, engines, instruments etc are in great measure arbitrary, and that authors make no scruple of coining new words on such occasions.

The word "encyclopedia" wasn't used in the title of a book until the Croatian polymath Paul Skalich published *Encyclopaedia, seu Orbis disciplinarum tam sacrarum quam*

---

* The only way to be sure is to count them, as the pages are not numbered.

prophanarum Epistemon (*Encyclopaedia, or Knowledge of the World of Disciplines*) in Basel in 1559. It was a minor work.*

By 1750, when the word was used in a prospectus for a French publication, it was still such a novelty that its meaning had to be explained, and not entirely satisfactorily: "The word 'Encyclopaedia' signifies the interrelationship of the sciences." Then as now, the word could be spelled either way.

* The word "encyclopedist" is believed to have been first used by John Evelyn in 1651 in reference to Johann Heinrich Alsted's *Encyclopaedia Septem Tomis Distincta*, a seven-volume set once again claimed by the compiler to be "the totality of knowledge."

F

FABULEUX!

Denis Diderot was born in Langres, northeastern France, on 5 October 1713, and from this day the world was fated to change just a little.

As with the first *Britannica*, his story begins with a problematic nose. Denis Diderot had four sisters, the eldest named Denise. Denis sometimes referred to this sister as "a female Socrates," such was her power of thought. Her early years passed without incident, but in her middle years she developed a little spot on her nose. The spot turned into a larger pimple, and the pimple alas grew larger and turned cancerous. The cancer consumed her face, and then her chances of finding a husband. She wore false noses made from wood and glass, and is reported to have remained astonishingly cheerful throughout, drawing strength from her Christian faith. Denis Diderot's daughter concluded that her aunt "possessed the rare secret of finding heaven on earth."

The way he described his birthplace, Denis Diderot had

found a similar haven. Returning there from Paris in middle age, he wrote to his lover Sophie Volland of "a charming promenade, consisting of a broad aisle of thickly verdured trees leading to a small grove . . . I pass hours in this spot, reading, meditating, contemplating nature, and thinking of my love." A century later, with his legacy secure, a statue of Diderot was erected in the square facing his childhood home. The sculptor was Frédéric Auguste Bartholdi, the man who designed the Statue of Liberty.

Upon what was this eminence founded? Initially it was a printed advertisement he wrote towards the end of 1750. Diderot offered a new product—new in length and scope, new in rigor and expertise, new in ambition and cost. It was the first encyclopedia that could lay claim to changing the world.

The prospectus was mouth-watering, but to appreciate it fully we should compare it to another prospectus issued five years before. This one was called a "dictionary," but was actually a modified French translation of Ephraim Chambers's *Cyclopaedia*. It was to have five volumes, each of approximately 250 pages. The reader was promised beautiful vignettes, and the text was to be composed and designed "by good masters," not least the principal editorial force behind the project, John Mills, an Englishman with good French, and his German colleague Gottfried Sellius. The volumes were due to be published between 1746 and 1748, at a total cost, when purchased as a set, of 100 livres.

But it didn't quite happen. Subscriptions trickled in, but Mills claimed he was cheated out of them by the publisher André le Breton, who counter-claimed that Mills's French wasn't up to the job after all. The two came to blows, Le Breton beating Mills with a stick, and when the issue came to court a judge found that Le Breton had every right to do so. Other editors were then enlisted, but only when Denis Diderot arrived on the scene did the project take on a new and more exacting shape. Indeed, his own prospectus of 1750 now promised a world far larger than that of Mills and Sellius, for it would eventually come not in ten volumes but seventeen.

It contained a "genealogical tree of all the sciences and all the arts" similar to the ones in Bacon's treatise and Chambers's work, and it stressed the interrelationships of knowledge, noting

> the connections, both remote and near, of the beings that compose Nature and which have occupied the attention of mankind; of showing, by the interlacing of the roots and branches, the impossibility of knowing well any parts of this whole without ascending or descending to many others; of forming a general picture of the efforts of the human mind in all fields and every century.*

And the sell worked. The prospectus itself was the subject of approving purrs in the journals; the *Edinburgh Review* suggested the work would be the most complete in any language of any age, and subscribers couldn't sign up fast enough. By April 1751, only six months after the prospectus appeared, there were already 1000 purchasers for a work whose cost had risen to 280 livres (approximately £6000 today), with the final number reaching 4000. For that they got an intention, neatly summarized by Diderot's own definition of the word "encyclopedia":

> The goal of an Encyclopédie is to assemble all the knowledge scattered on the surface of the earth, to

* As it turned out, the actual text of the *Encyclopédie* differed substantially from that outlined in its preliminary tree of knowledge. The tree now appears to be more of an idealized vision than a battle plan.

> demonstrate the general system to the people with whom we live, & to transmit it to the people who will come after us, so that the work of centuries past is not useless to the centuries which follow, that our descendants, by becoming more learned, may become more virtuous & happier, & that we do not die without having merited being part of the human race.

But it was something more as well. As Diderot's biographer Arthur M. Wilson recognized, its readers would soon find that what "purported to be a book of reference . . . was in fact a sort of political tract."

The timing was perfect. In 1957, Arthur Wilson composed a vivid reminder of the cultural scene into which Diderot pitched his work two centuries before. "It was the world of wigs, smallclothes and three-cornered hats; of panniers and beauty patches and pancakes of rouge laid on delicate cheeks."* Wilson found that each subscriber to the *Encyclopédie* made up a world which included

> . . . the minuet, danced in rooms gleaming with gilt and shimmering with mirrors; the world of the harpsichord, the recorder, and the viola da gamba; of the musket, the frigate, and the balance of power . . . the time when immense French and British colonial empires were in the making and were providing stakes for great colonial wars . . . a time when the Church patently expected to continue confining men's thoughts within a narrow orthodoxy, and privileged classes patently expected to continue to enjoy their privileges. Yet it was also a time when the merchant, banking and professional

* *Diderot* (New York, Oxford University Press, 1957). Smallclothes were knee britches.

elements of society were everywhere rising in esteem and wealth.

And beneath it all lay the disruptive rumblings of coal, steam, machine and revolution. The world was moving at an irrepressible speed: at the time of publication George Washington had just turned eighteen; Jacques-François de Menou, the first president of the Jacobin Club, had just been born. If you were an encyclopedist at this time you were probably encumbered with two emotional states: delight that there was so much remarkable new material to include in every edition, and horror that there was so much remarkable new material to include in every edition.

The first volume of the first edition appeared in Paris in 1751, the seventh volume by 1757, and the complete seventeen-volume letterpress set was for sale by 1765 (with 71,818 articles and 3129 illustrations). Then there were the plate sections and supplementary updates, which ran to another sixteen volumes by 1780. All of which needed a two-volume index. Printers throughout Europe began to share the load, with editions appearing in Geneva, Amsterdam and Lucca. This last printing in 1758 provided a foretaste of what was to come: the *Encyclopédie* was progressive in its approach to a modern world, and it was inevitable that some would see it as transgressive. A papal condemnation regarded it as a threat to religion and morality, and called for a ban and confiscation. It wouldn't be the last time that the project was seen as a danger to tradition; the *grandes* of the *Ancien Régime* were in no doubt of its power to influence and excite.*

The contents of *Encyclopédie* are best considered in terms

* While this was an enormous enterprise, weighing in at an estimated 40 tons, it was still only about one-twelfth of the size of the Chinese *Yongle Dadian*.

of its writers and editors, the latest erudite souls who put themselves forward to quantify the world. We must start (again) with Denis Diderot, who not only edited the bulk of the volumes, but also wrote and commissioned many of their leading articles.

That he was destined for a life of the mind is best illustrated by an incident from his romantic youth. Living in Paris with friends from Provence, he was aghast when the girl he loved was wooed by his friend's proficient dancing. He resolved to become as good as he was, so secretly took lessons with a dancing master in the Rue Montmartre. He gave it up soon after, but then returned for another shot. The same thing happened again; infuriated by his lack of progress, he quit but then tried once more. "What was lacking in me?" he asked himself in his memoir, having given up for good. "Lightness? I wasn't heavy on my feet, far from it. Motive? One could scarcely be animated by one more violent. What didn't I have? Malleability, flexibility, gracefulness—qualities that cannot be had for the asking."*

But the attainment of broad intelligence? That could be achieved by anyone with application and modest funds. His father was a master cutler, his knives and scissors much in demand. According to one surgeon, his scalpels were "very greatly perfected: better in the hand, they cut more cleanly, and the lancets with the mark of the pearl were sought out by all the doctors teaching medicine." His father wanted Denis to become a priest, and sent him to a Jesuit school. And Denis took it seriously, at one point (when he wasn't failing in his dancing) fasting and wearing a hair shirt. At university in Paris he read

---

* Translated from Denis Diderot, *Oeuvres Complètes,* edited by Jules Assézat and Maurice Turneaux in twenty volumes (Paris, 1875–77).

theology and law, but appeared so unsatisfied with both that his father stopped sending him financial support. He got married, unhappily, to a woman named Anne-Toinette Champion, who was latterly described as "beautiful, but shrewish."* Diderot took up with other women, most passionately with Sophie Volland, and by the early 1740s he had abandoned all religious beliefs and embarked on a literary career, first translating famous works from English to French, and then his own books, one of which, with its promotion of atheism, so scandalized the Church that it led to three months in prison.

His polymathic learning and a good relationship with the publishers of the earlier incarnation of the *Encyclopédie* brought him to its editorship in 1747. According to the scholars Frank and Serena Kafker, Diderot confounded as many contributors as he inspired, "for he could be a tardy correspondent, a slipshod copyreader, and a colleague who sometimes made promises he did not keep." In spite of this, Diderot managed to take them with him; they assumed the grand scheme would be worth the personal slights.

Diderot wrote (or contributed to) more than 6000 entries, tackling almost every subject (although many of these were translations from Chambers and other sources, not least specialist medical textbooks). In the first *A* volume alone he composed articles on giving birth (Accouchement), steel (Acier), agriculture, a boring machine for the manufacture of cannons (Alésoir), the Arabs, silver (Argent) and Aristotle. There exists hardly any record of his day-to-day notes or correspondence with his editors or writers, but certainly we know he did not

* *The Encyclopedists as Individuals* by Frank A. Kafker in collaboration with Serena L. Kafker, Voltaire Foundation at the Taylor Institution, Oxford, 1988. Much of my own summation of the contributors to the *Encyclopédie* comes from this fascinating book.

edit alone. From 1747 to 1758 he was partnered by Jean Le Rond D'Alembert, the illegitimate offspring of aristocratic parents (he was abandoned in a wooden box on the steps of the Parisian church Saint-Jean-le-Rond). Like Diderot, D'Alembert was another one of those men whose agile mind found it impossible to settle on a single profession.

A revolution in style: Diderot and D'Alembert glimpse the future

Trained as a barrister and doctor, D'Alembert was also a skillful musician and mathematician; he was clearly suited to the breadth of learning required to edit a tremendous reference work. And perhaps he felt he had something to prove: Frank and Serena Kafker have observed that while he had a sharp wit and a talent for mimicry, he also had "a high-pitched voice, a tiny build and rather plain features." The relationship of the two editors was productive but fiery. The Kafkers defined their characters as equally "touchy, self-righteous, given to emotional outbursts, and convinced of his intellectual excellence."

D'Alembert wrote daringly on mathematics, physics, music and astronomy, and his professional connections resulted in the commissioning of many fruitful entries. He was keen to use the *Encyclopédie* to advance contemporary and original thought. Indeed he saw it as a weapon, and his most controversial article almost brought down the whole enterprise.*

The entry entitled Genève contained rather more than just a brief history of that city-state; its length alone suggested there was mischief to come. The whole of England was afforded three-fifths of a column, Denmark merely seventeen lines; but for Geneva, D'Alembert wrote four double-columned pages. His tone was admonishing. He criticized the city's legislators for refusing to allow the staging of plays for "the fear of the taste for display, dissipation and libertinage that companies of actors communicate to the youth." In Geneva, D'Alembert argued, freedom of expression and loose morals were suppressed lest a whole generation grow up to sweep away their opposite. He had learned of this suppression when visiting Voltaire, and the philosopher and playwright certainly influenced the complaint. For good measure, D'Alembert also accused Calvinist ministers of hypocrisy and deception, and criticized what he saw as tuneless singing at church services.

His opinion of the city wasn't all bad—he approved, for instance, of certain Genevese penal leniencies (the refusal to put criminals on the rack among them), but he must have known that his article would cause offense. The local elders banned

* Both D'Alembert and Diderot acknowledged a significant philosophical debt to Francis Bacon's *The Advancement of Learning*; specifically, their taxonomy of knowledge "tree" in the preface was directly inspired by the pull-out "Analysis" in that volume. D'Alembert credited Bacon as an inspiration who had "silently in the shadows, prepared from afar the light which gradually, by imperceptible degrees, would illuminate the world." The entry in *Encyclopédie* by Abbé Jean Pestre entitled "Baconisme" referred to Bacon as a "grande génie."

the *Encyclopédie* in the city, and an angry meeting called by the Council of Geneva stopped just short of an official protest to the French government for fear of reprisals. The controversy hastened the breakdown of D'Alembert's relationship with Diderot, whose imprisonment a few years before left him in no doubt how swiftly the old regime—the unenlightened anti-intellectual elite—could censor and punish when threatened.

And there was still one more strong-willed individual in the mix, the *Encyclopédie*'s stick-wielding chief publisher André-François le Breton. Le Breton was born in Paris and entered the book trade by chance at the age of seventeen. A disputed inheritance landed him with the responsibility of publishing his grandfather's important *Almanach Royal,* a who's who of European nobility. This was a cash cow, and demonstrated to Le Breton how a successful reference work could set one up for life. He greatly expanded the *Almanach*'s coverage and sales, and he began looking around for other big projects.

We have seen how his plan to translate Ephraim Chambers's *Cyclopaedia* fell apart when he clashed with his editors, and it was a precursor of things to come. He then teamed up with three other publishers and appointed a new editor, Abbé Jean-Paul de Gua de Malves, but once again he quarreled over money and the quality of the work. Malves was dismissed, clearing the way for Diderot and D'Alembert to take on their decisive roles.

The new prospectus created a rush of subscriptions and doubled the editors' ambitions. The original plan to complete the new encyclopedia in three and a half years swiftly began to look unfeasible, as did the initial print run. The order of 1625 copies of Volume I in 1750 had increased to 4225 by Volume 4 in 1754, and Le Breton and his colleagues were getting rich. But the money—some half a million livres in receipts in the first four years—inevitably encouraged piracy, and the publishers fought hard to restrict unauthorized editions throughout Europe. Those in charge of the libraries at universities and other institutions abroad, alongside the wealthy educated elite, had recognized the emergence of something both *fabuleux* and *incroyable*, and the publishers of pirated copies, such as the one widely available in London within a year of the original, claimed a moral and economic obligation for their actions: one syndicate found "a view to serve their country by encouraging arts, manufactures and trades, and keeping large sums at home that would otherwise be sent abroad." Their set cost half that of the French edition.*

Le Breton faced another problem. The popularity of his encyclopedia was partly down to its boldness, and yet this also threatened its very existence. Church and State were nervous of its broad-minded acceptance of religions other than Catholicism, and wary of political views that veered from conservative norms. The most vituperative disapproval arrived from the Bishop of Montauban a year after publication. "Up until now," he wrote, "Hell has vomited its venom drop by drop. Today there are torrents of errors and impieties which tend towards nothing less than the submerging of Faith, Religion, Virtues, the Church, Subordination, the Laws, and Reason."

Such orthodox opposition increased each year, with the encyclopedia condemned by eleven general assemblies at the Sorbonne. D'Alembert's article on Geneva had sounded the loudest alarm for the editors in 1757, and two years later the progressive views in other volumes caused the Parliament of Paris to ban publication entirely and demand the recall of existing volumes. Further, it demanded that Le Breton refund

---

* The details are vague, but it appears that Le Breton and his fellow publishers sent a conciliatory party to London to halt publication by offering cut-price editions of their own. This would logically suggest advanced levels of French literacy among English readers.

all its subscribers. Faced with financial ruin and political embarrassment, the publishers canvassed influential royals, and after a brief interval managed to resume printing and distribution in secret. At the publication of the final volumes in 1772, the set was selling for 980 livres, more than four times its asking price when it appeared twenty-one years before. And such was the demand that people were willing to pay even more.

But Le Breton had struck what Denis Diderot regarded as a deal with the devil. Behind the editors' and contributors' backs he toned down the contents of about forty controversial articles just as they went to press. According to the Kafkers, Diderot "flew into a justifiable rage, never forgave Le Breton, and afterwards treated him with contempt." He found him "miserly, touchy and boring," and his wife was "a bundle of contradictions." The Parisian police weren't delighted with Le Breton either, imprisoning him for a week for disregarding instructions not to publish. If Le Breton ever cared that he would henceforth be regarded as one of the century's great cultural villains he didn't show it, and indeed he laughed all the way to *la banque*. He died one of the wealthiest publishers in Paris, with net profits from the encyclopedia estimated at more than 2 million livres (approximately £65m). And he left an educational legacy of sorts: if anyone doubted the potential rewards from producing a studious but daring multi-volume reference work, the *succès de scandale* of the *Encyclopédie* would have set them right. It remains the preeminent storehouse of mid-eighteenth-century knowledge, and a remarkable glimpse of the enlightened world at the dawn of revolutions cultural, mechanical and political. That it partly facilitated this advance there can be no doubt.

FACULTÉ

Our use of the word "superior" derives from the Old French *superiour*, meaning "upper," and no adjective better describes Diderot's own impression of himself, nor the moral position he assumed his nation held over others. In his mind, even years before the Revolution would attempt to reinvent the traditional calendar and clock, France stood alone and above. His hauteur turned knowledge to prejudice, and there is no better example than his entry on "Human Species" from 1765, a starkly abstract and almost comically ignorant analysis of the inhabitants of foreign lands.

His survey begins in the north, where Eskimos and other tribes are classed as

> degenerate men, of small stature and bizarre shape . . . most are no taller than four feet, the tallest four and a half. The women are as ugly as the men, their breasts are quite considerable . . .
>
> All of the homely people are boorish, superstitious and stupid. The Danish Lapps consult a fat black cat. The Swedes call the devil with a drum . . . They have almost no idea of God or of religion. They offer their wives and daughters to strangers. They live underground; they get light from lamps in their night, which lasts for several months. The women are dressed in reindeer skin in the winter and bird skin in the summer. In the latter, they defend themselves from the stinging of gnats with a thick smoke which they maintain around them. They are rarely sick. Their old people are robust; except that the whiteness of the snow and the smoke weaken their vision, and there are many who are blind.

The Chinese, by contrast, "have their limbs well proportioned, are tall and fat, with a large, round face, small eyes, long eyebrows, lifted eyelids, small and flattened noses, sparse and clustered beards . . . in general these people are soft, peaceful, indolent, obedient, superstitious, slaves, and ceremonial."

Indian customs are considered "bizarre . . . The Banians eat nothing that has lived. They fear killing an insect. The Nairs of Calicut are on the contrary, all hunters; they can only have one wife, but their wives can take as many husbands as they like. There are men and women among the last who have monstrous legs."

And so on into Europe, where "In general, the Greek women are more beautiful and more lively than the Turkish women . . . The Spanish are thin and fairly small. They are finely made, have handsome heads, regular traits, beautiful eyes, well-arranged teeth . . . Men are more chaste in cold lands than in warm ones. They are less amorous in Sweden than in Spain or in Portugal, and therefore the Swedes have fewer children."

The most detailed, fascinated (and to us horrific) analysis is reserved for Africa, an anthropology that would have enthralled the contemporary reader quite as much as it repels the modern one.

> The odor of these Negroes of Senegal is less strong than that of other Negroes. They have black, crinkled hair like curly wool. It is by their hair and their color that they principally differ from other men . . .
>
> Negresses are very fertile. The Negroes of Gorée and of Cape Verde are also well made and very black. Those of Sierra Leone are not quite as black as those of Senegal. Those of Guinea, although healthy, are short lived. It is a result of corrupt morals.

> The inhabitants of St. Thomas Island are Negroes similar to those of the neighbouring continent. Those of the coast of Ouidah and of Arada are less black than those of Senegal and of Guinea. The Negroes of the Congo are more or less black. Those of Angola smell so bad when they become hot that the air of the areas where they pass by remain infected for more than a quarter of an hour.
>
> Although in general Negroes have little intelligence, they do not lack feeling. They are sensitive to good and bad treatment. We have reduced them, I wouldn't say to the condition of slaves, but to that of beasts of burden; and we are reasonable! And we are Christians!

Elsewhere, the separate entry "Negroes" considered the commodification of humans in a civil manner, while leaving the reader in no doubt of its disapproval.

> People try to justify what is odious and contrary to natural law in this trade by saying that normally these slaves find the salvation of their souls in the loss of their liberty; that the instruction in Christianity given them, joined to their indispensability for the cultivation of sugar, tobacco, indigo, etc. mitigates that which seems inhuman in a trade in which men buy and sell others just like beasts for cultivating land.

Published in Volume 11 in 1765, some thirty years before the young Republican parliament partially abolished the slave trade in a few of its colonies (full emancipation only arrived in 1848), the entry describes the merits and costs of slaves as items in a machine catalogue, and suggests they were often willing participants in this bargain.

> Some, to avoid famine and poverty, sell themselves, their children and their wives to the most powerful kings among them who have the wherewithal to feed them . . . one can see sons selling their fathers and fathers their children or even more often those who have no family ties will place each other's liberty at the price of several bottles of spirits or of some bars of iron . . .
>
> The best negroes come from Cape Verde, Angola, Senegal, the kingdom of the Wolofs and of those of Galland, of Damel, of the Gambia river, of Majugard, of Bar, etc. In the past, a "pièce d'Inde" ["India piece"] negro (as they are called) from 17 or 18 to 30 years of age came to [cost] only thirty or thirty-two pounds in the merchandise appropriate for the country, which is spirits, iron, canvas, paper, maces and glass baubles of all colours, cauldrons and copper basins and other similar things that these peoples value a lot. But since Europeans have outbid one another, so to speak, these barbarians have known how to profit from their jealousy and it's rare that handsome negroes are still traded at 60 pounds and the Compagnie de l'Assiente has bought them at as high as 100 pounds per head.

And what of the lesser celebrated Encyclopédistes themselves? What sort of tribe were they?

They were as varied and intriguing as their scholarship and judgments. The article "Negres," for example, was written by Jean-Baptiste-Pierre le Romain, a cartographer and engineer who specialized in the topography of the West Indies. He wrote almost seventy articles for the *Encyclopédie*, the majority on the natural histories of plants, animals and minerals of the Caribbean. His productivity aside, he was among the least interesting of Diderot's cohort.

The Kafkers have assembled a huge personal dossier of

these men (women were not yet considered intellectually reliable enough for the task), and they are doubly pertinent in reminding us of the one ingredient the *Encyclopédie* lacked, the biographies of historical figures.* For with regard to this particular encyclopedia, it would be hard to imagine a more disparate, maverick or libidinous gathering of specialists.

There was Alexandre Deleyre, a clergyman who lost his faith and deserted his Jesuit church, and then edited and translated a collection of works by Francis Bacon. He wrote only two signed entries for the *Encyclopédie*, one a bold warning about the pitfalls of religious fanaticism, and the other an astonishing four-page article entitled Epingle, which concerned itself with the eighteen-step manufacture of straight pins. Though we may now regard this as slightly excessive, twenty-five years later it was used as an important example of the division of labor in Adam Smith's *The Wealth of Nations*. Deleyre was a champion of the Revolution, although his radicalism and pin obsession won him few friends at home. According to the Kafkers, his wife and daughter "found him almost impossible to live with—often sullen, given to fits of rage, behaving like a tyrant while hating tyranny in others."

There was Antoine Louis, the principal contributor on medicine. Louis wrote almost 500 articles, while still finding time to practice both medicine and law. His time at the autopsy table placed him in great demand as a witness in murder trials, and until the Revolution robbed him of his savings, he was one of the wealthiest surgeons in Paris. But the Revolution also saved him, as he played an important role in designing a new decapitating apparatus intended as more humane and less painful than its predecessors. Cleaner too. The machine, which

* A very limited number of biographies appeared only as brief mentions within descriptions of a subject's birthplace.

was built by a harpsichord maker, initially bore his name: it was known as the Petite Louison or Louisette, although it swiftly adopted the name of Louis's sponsor, the legislator Joseph-Ignace Guillotin.

Then there was Jean-Joseph Menuret de Chambaud, who also wrote for the *Encyclopédie* on medical affairs, and was ahead of his time on many issues. He lived in Hamburg and disclosed how environmental conditions could have a direct result on a population's health. He was a champion of the "vitalist" school of Montpellier, believing that exposure to the moon and the sun both had an effect on health and longevity, and he became (by buying the title) Consulting Physician-in-ordinary to Louis XVI. One of the things he taught the king was his text in the *Encyclopédie* entitled Manstrupation, which advised that masturbation was effectively self-rape, and the harm caused would lead to (unnamed) diminishing powers.

We should consider the fate of the majestically named Louis Necker de Germany, who probably never let anyone down in the cad department. At around the time he was writing an influential article for the *Encyclopédie* on friction in mechanics (entitled Frottement), Monsieur Necker was also engaging in friction with the wife of the Genevese clergyman Pierre Vernes. Vernes discovered their love letters and asked Necker to dinner, during which he shot him in the thigh.

Neither should we forget the entries on mechanics and economics made by Jean-David Perronet, who championed Newcomen's first steam engines in print at a time when most failed to recognize their significance. Perronet also wrote incisively about bridge construction (his entry entitled "Pieux, Pilots ou Pilotis," a description of deep-pile foundations in water, was the excitement of all France), but he built many bridges himself, including several over the Seine and Oise, and his great showpiece, Pont Louis XVI. He also found time to construct many relationships with married women, one of whom was the society favorite Madame Le Gendre, the younger sister of Diderot's mistress Sophie Volland, which made his relationship with his editor complicated.

The *Encyclopédie* boasted a couple of father-son teams, and none were more objectionable than the Barthez clan. Guillaume Barthez de Marmorières wrote on sheep rearing and beekeeping: his "Mouche-à-Miel & Miel" apparently drew much acclaim, as did his summary of shepherds as ignorant and lazy. But his son Paul-Joseph Barthez was the really foul one. He wrote twenty-two articles on such varied subjects as fainting, evil spells, the relative strength of man and animals, anatomy and the problematic topic (to him) of women. Who were these strange creatures? They were "The female of man." His entry surveys the literature: "Hippocrates stated positively that a woman cannot become ambidextrous. Galen confirms this and adds that this is because of her natural weakness . . . The Anatomists are not the only ones who have considered woman to be, in some manner, a failed man; platonic philosophers have a similar idea." Barthez Jr. then quotes Livy, who has suggested the female "is an animal both powerless and indomitable," and criticizes both the Christian and Jewish religion for their subjugation of women, and notes what a rough deal they receive in the East, where the "domestic servitude of wives . . . has made them contemptible." But then he emerges, seemingly, as something of a female champion: "We have so severely neglected the education of women among all of the refined peoples, that it is surprising that we can identify so many whose erudition and written works have made them renowned."*

---

* A modern searchable translation to English is still under way. *The Encyclopedia of Diderot & D'Alembert Collaborative Translation Project* (Ann Arbor: Michigan Publishing, University of Michigan Library, 2020). https://quod.lib.umich.edu/d/did/.

Alas, his own life suggests a less respectful attitude. "Not only was Barthez ugly," the Kafkers attest, as if such an attribute may infect his intellectual prowess, "he was also hot-tempered and belligerent." His qualities as a physician were dubious, he made enemies of many, and "he was rumoured to be a materialist, a cynic, a scoundrel and a lecher." In 1783 he was accused of raping an underage girl, and he is thought to have paid off the victim's father. You may be relieved to learn that Barthez did not fare well in the Revolution. His house was stoned, he lost most of his income, and he was forced to flee. But it did not all end badly. Towards the end of his life his honor and professorship was restored by Napoleon, who may have recognized a kindred spirit.

And finally, but most famously, are the contributions to the *Encyclopédie* made by the writer-philosophers Voltaire and Jean-Jacques Rousseau, rivals in literature but both equally eager to promote the dissemination of new ideas. Voltaire wrote more than forty largely uncontroversial articles on literary theory and grammatical definitions, but he also offered his thoughts on Elegance, History and Taste, which had something to offend everyone.

On Elegance he asserted that "There are languages in Europe in which nothing is rarer than an elegant speech. Rough endings, numerous consonants, auxiliary verbs needlessly repeated in a single sentence offend the ear." On History he regretted that so much writing about the past was based on fable to the exclusion of truth ("hence the origins of all peoples are absurd"), and he found it equally absurd that during the time of Ancient Egypt the sun changed where it rose and set "four times."

Throughout, Voltaire was his didactic, blustery self. But it was a particular feature of the *Encyclopédie*—and something that consistently distinguished it from its predecessors—that opinions were freely expressed as philosophical and moral truths. In this way, opinion replaced the superstition and myth of earlier encyclopedias, and the promulgation of progressive ideas enabled its subscribers to feel they were part of a movement rather than just a readership.*

Voltaire seemed to be writing with sore experience when he tackled the question of French Taste:

> A depraved taste in food consists in choosing those dishes which disgust other men; it is a kind of sickness. A depraved taste in the arts consists in enjoying subjects that are revolting to men of good judgment. Such taste leads us to prefer the burlesque to what is noble, and to prefer what is precious and affected to simple and natural beauty: this is a sickness of the mind.

And on the question of Happiness—the attainment of which was a key concern of the French Enlightenment in particular—Voltaire observed:

> What we call happiness is an abstract idea, comprising a few ideas of pleasure; as he who has only a moment's pleasure is not a happy man; just as a moment of sorrow does not make an unhappy man. Pleasure is more rapid-moving than happiness, and happiness more fleeting than felicity. When we say I am happy in this moment, we are abusing the word, and this only means that I am pleased [*j'ai du plaisir*]: when we have a bit of repeated pleasures, we

---

* In one sense, of course, the study of the past is *all* opinion, and new learning and modern interpretations may counter much of what has gone before. Voltaire acknowledged as much when he claimed in his entry on History that "There is the *history* of opinions, which is hardly other than the collection of human errors."

can in this space of time, say that we are happy, and when this happiness endures a little longer, it's a state of felicity; sometimes one is very far from being happy in prosperity, just as a person sick with nausea eats nothing of a large feast prepared for him.*

Rousseau's contributions were principally concerned with the technicalities of music, including entries on tone, rhythm and the chromatic scale. But his major essay for the encyclopedia concerned political economy, and it has dated well:

> It is . . . one of the most important concerns of government to prevent the extreme inequality of fortunes; not by taking away wealth from its possessors, but by depriving men of all the means to accumulate it; not by building hospitals for the poor, but by guaranteeing that the citizens will not become poor. The unequal distribution of inhabitants in our country, some crowded together in one place, while other areas are depopulated; the support given to the arts producing luxuries and to the purely industrial arts at the expense of the useful and laborious crafts; the sacrifice of agriculture to commerce . . . and finally venality pushed to such an extreme that public esteem is reckoned at a low cash value; and even virtue is sold at a market price: these are the most perceptible causes of opulence and poverty, of private interest substituted for public interest, of mutual hatred among citizens.

* This entry is popularly attributed to Voltaire, though its authorship is unconfirmed.

FLAUBERT, GUSTAVE (a diversion . . .)

A brief diversion to consider the case of Gustave Flaubert. The novelist appeared to be equally entranced and revolted by the notion of encyclopedias—their design, their intentions, their overwhelming suppression of wider reading. In *Madame Bovary* a minor character vainly recommends one as a cure for grief. In *Bouvard et Pécuchet* the notion of the encyclopedia appears to overwhelm the entire book.

Flaubert knew *Bouvard et Pécuchet* was his swansong, and he spent a great many years on it. He claimed to have read 1500 books as background research, but that was just too many books: he died in 1880 with the novel unfinished. The story is simple enough: the eponymous protagonists meet by a canal on a hot day in Paris and start a friendship. They are both copyists (old-fashioned scribes, medieval-style) and in many ways they are copies of each other. They are the same age, and are both vaguely dissatisfied with their lot. Several volumes of *Roret's Encyclopaedia* lie scattered around Pécuchet's Paris apartment, an indication of the narrative to come.*

When one of them inherits they decide to leave Paris and move together to Normandy, where they will better themselves by reading, traveling and learning important skills, an attempt to absorb all human knowledge—philosophical, agricultural, historical, medicinal, geological and theological. They will dismiss almost everything as flawed, contradictory

* Nicolas-Edme Roret's richly illustrated multi-volume set specializing in natural history was published in Paris in the first half of the nineteenth century. After his death in 1860, Roret's name continued to appear on a large range of "encyclopedic manuals" including watchmaking, chocolate manufacture and dance.

or impossible, and they will alienate those around them. They have become the embodiment of the "walking encyclopedia," but they have rejected almost all of its elements.

Mais oui, it's a satire, and an occasionally funny one, and it's plausible that the person Flaubert was really satirizing was himself. In a letter to a friend, Flaubert wrote that he intended his novel to be "a kind of encyclopaedia made into a farce . . . I am planning a thing in which I give vent to my anger . . . I shall vomit over my contemporaries the disgust they inspire in me."

Julian Barnes has called Flaubert's novel "an encyclopaedia of human endeavour" and quotes Cyril Connolly's phrase that it is "the Baedeker of futility." Flaubert himself proclaimed, "The book I am working on could have as a sub-title *Encyclopaedia of Human Stupidity.* The undertaking gets me down and its subject becomes part of me." Indeed, the pedantry expressed by Bouvard and Pécuchet is something he shared. Flaubert liked exactitude, although he "thundered against" platitude. He was reclaiming Stendhal's complaint that "an idiot who knows a date can disconcert the wittiest man."*

The grand sweep of knowledge, Bouvard and Pécuchet concluded, was just too difficult to grasp in its entirety, and was never complete or agreed upon, making any attempt to acquire even the smallest amount quite fatuous. And the same for history in particular. They consult a professor who confirms, "It is changing every day. There is a controversy as to the kings of Rome and the journeys of Pythagoras . . . It is desirable that no more discoveries should be made, and the

* Quotations taken from the introduction to the English translation of *The Dictionary of Accepted Ideas* by Jacques Barzun (New Directions, New York, 1967). See also "Flaubert, C'est Moi" by Julian Barnes, *New York Review of Books,* 25 May 2006.

Institute ought even to lay down a kind of canon prescribing what it is necessary to believe!"

Flaubert's notes for the unfinished portion of the book, discovered after his death, suggest that his anti-heroes would eventually return to their urban copying duties. In a lovely circle, they may have been obliged to copy the wisdom amassed during their doomed rural experiment, which they may have called a *Dictionary of Received Ideas,* the name of the volume Flaubert had been composing for years independently of his novel. Inspired by the trite musings of an elderly relative, it was certainly more than a dictionary; it was a battle cry against herd thinking and mediocrity, a collection of corrupted (but funny) aphorisms and other instructions from a world that had rejected original thought in favor of inanities. It wasn't published until 1911, and if today it strikes readers as coarse and cynical, not to say sacrilegious, then the author has achieved his intention.

A few of Flaubert's *F*'s:

Factory: Dangerous neighbourhood.

Farm: When visiting a farm, one must eat nothing but wholemeal bread and drink nothing but milk. If eggs are added, exclaim: "Heavens, how fresh they are! Not a hope of finding any like these in town!"

Felicity: Always "perfect." If your cook is named Felicity, then she is perfect.

Feudalism: No need to have any clear idea what it was, but thunder against it.

Fiction: Inevitably featuring "eponymous protagonists."

Flat (Bachelor): Always in a mess, with feminine garments lying here and there. Smell of cigarettes. If you hunted around, you would find the most extraordinary things.

Foreign: Contempt for everything that isn't French is a sign of patriotism.

Forgers: Always work in cellars.

Funeral: About the deceased, say: "To think that I had dinner with him only a week ago."

F

Furniture: Always fear the worst for your furniture.*

Responding to Flaubert's list, in 2013 the novelist Teju Cole produced updated entries of his own for the *New Yorker*.† These included:

Paris: Romantic, in spite of the rude waiters and Japanese tourists. Don't simply like it; "adore" it.

Germans: When watching football, "Never rule out the Germans."

Magisterial: Large book, written by a man.

FRANCKENSTEIN'S MONSTER

In Germany in 1731, Jacob August Franckenstein became the first editor of the magisterial *Grosses vollständiges Universal-Lexicon aller Wissenschafften und Künste*, an undertaking of sixty-four volumes published over eighteen years. Each folio was about two inches thick, and ran to some 284,000 entries on 63,000 pages; the estimated word count was 67 million. There

---

* Translated by Jorn Barger, 2002. Barger also compiled a thematic grouping of Flaubert's dubious advice. Categories included: Things to Make Fun Of, Things to Thunder Against, Things to "Wax Indignant" About, Things to Despise and Things Nobody Knows.

† See *New Yorker*, 27 August 2013. https://www.newyorker.com/books/page-turner/in-place-of-thought.

were also four later supplemental books, but the authors ran out of alphabetical steam when they reached "Caq."

The work remains one of the largest European encyclopedias ever produced. Just the title deserves a shelf to itself: *The Great Complete Encyclopedia of All Sciences and Arts Which So Far Have Been Invented and Improved by Human Mind and Wit: Including the Geographical and Political Description of the Whole World with All Monarchies, Empires, Kingdoms, Principalities, Republics, Free Sovereignties, Countries, Towns, Sea Harbours, Fortresses, Castles, Areas, Authorities, Monasteries, Mountains, Passes, Woods, Seas, Lakes . . . and also a Detailed Historical and Genealogical Description of the World's Brightest and Most Famous Family Lines, the Life and Deeds of the Emperors, Kings, Electors and Princes, Great Heroes, Ministers of State, War Leaders . . . ; Equally about All Policies of State, War and Law and Budgetary Business of the Nobility and the Bourgeois, Merchants, Traders and Arts.**

Unusually for an encyclopedia, it would carry biographical entries for living people (there were almost fifty entries for the name Wagner). And there would be a spectacular amount of idiosyncrasies and prejudices. Mermaids, for instance, were still a decidedly genuine thing. The Bible was hard fact. The reading of novels was regarded as harmful to the young. The entry on women was entitled Frauenzimmer—a term archaically describing a wench, and later the contents of a woman's room—explained, with the weight of a news bulletin, that women have achieved remarkable things in the arts and sciences, sometimes equaling the accomplishments of men.

* Commonly, and with some relief, the lavishly titled project soon became known as either *Universal-Lexicon* or *Zedler's Encyclopedia*, after its publisher and principal life-force Johann Heinrich Zedler. Zedler almost went bankrupt producing the encyclopedia in its early days, and he spent much time in litigation protecting its copyrights.

The articles were either surprisingly short or unpredictably long. Leipzig, where the encyclopedia was based, and where Dr. Franckenstein was a law professor, received 155 columns, whereas Berlin got two. Shakespeare received less than a column (there were two columns per page), while J.S. Bach, alive at the time, received no mention at all in the original publication, and got less than a column in a supplemental volume, despite being heralded as a composer of "undying fame." In contrast, the philosopher Christian Wolff (1679–1754), a leading figure of the German Enlightenment, was granted an astonishing 175 pages (while Plato only merited eight). Why the anomaly? One of the editors to succeed Franckenstein, Carl Günther Ludovici, was a leading Wolff scholar, and it may be assumed he just couldn't help himself.*

We may revel in many other enthusiasms. Ananas, for example, the exotic pineapple, was one of the best things in the world. It was a "thoroughly delightful American fruit," with an "excellent taste" and "pleasant smell"; it had medicinal qualities too, boosting fertility and vitality, relieving nausea, ameliorating gout and arthritis, easing the passage of kidney stones. It even helped with "insanity."

The authors Peter E. Carels and Dan Flory have observed that the medical entries were also peculiar in their detail. A surgeon inadequately trained in hand amputation, for example, could consult the encyclopedia for the right tools for the job, and learn where their assistants should stand in relation to the patient, and discover the precise amount of time of sawing required for the bones of the lower arm (about the same as it takes to read the Lord's Prayer). The process of conducting

---

* Lest this coverage appeared inadequate, Wolff was also mentioned extensively in separate articles on geometry, color theory, lexicography and medicinal horticulture.

a mastectomy was described in a similar step-by-step style. There was also peculiarly naive advice on physical etiquette, including an earnest entry on how to manage the need to urinate or fart during a social gathering (the key was patience and suppression).*

We may recoil from some of the other excesses. "Juden" traces a history of Judaism from biblical days, claiming that God rejected the faith after the crucifixion. The *Universal-Lexicon* was fearful of anything contradicting the Lutheran church. Jews were deceitful and treacherous, and "our sworn enemy"; redemption was only possible through conversion.

If we accept that such a comprehensive storehouse of knowledge and opinion was representative of more than just a succession of opinionated editors—and certainly this is what the *Universal-Lexicon* became as it claimed its authoritative two yards among the libraries of Europe—then mid-eighteenth-century Germany appeared poised between two worlds. It was a relatively peaceful time, a period as yet unshaken by political or industrial revolution. The Age of Enlightenment was an attractive proposition to a cadre of leading writers and philosophers consistently pegged back by the Church and State. Their encyclopedia provides a fascinating panorama of human comprehension and opinion, and in this alone it shared much with the *Encyclopédie*.

But we would have to wait almost thirty years, and look once again to Scotland, for the next great step towards the next great encyclopedia of the modern world.

* P.E. Carels and D. Flory, "Johann Heinrich Zedler's *Universal Lexicon*" in *Studies on Voltaire in the Eighteenth Century*, vol. 194, Voltaire Foundation, Oxford, 1981. See also: Jeff Loveland's comprehensive and illuminating *The European Encyclopedia: From 1650 to the Twenty-First Century* (Cambridge University Press, 2019).

G

GERMINATION

Encyclopedias are not like rose bushes, for which pruning is everything. They are usually the opposite, more like Japanese knotweed, spreading wildly and germinating freely, invasive and persistent in all countries where a foothold is possible.

When the second edition of *Encyclopaedia Britannica* completed its publication in 1784, sixteen years after the first, it had greatly increased its scope and cost, and had grown from three volumes to ten. It was issued in 181 installments, usually weekly, between 1777 and 1784, a total of 8595 pages (although some of the pagination was erratic: page 7099 was followed immediately by page 8000). The cost per issue had risen from 6 pence to 1 shilling, while the cost of the total set a year after completion was 12 pounds, more than four times the first edition. To afford it all, a skilled London carpenter would have to save everything he earned (and go without food) for fifteen years.*

Its increase in size was due partly to the addition of biography, primarily of dead writers, artists and churchmen. The majority were Britons, with a heavy bias towards the Scots. Isaac Newton received one of the longest entries at almost three pages, while Pythagoras received a single column (he "made his scholars undergo a severe noviciate of silence for at least two years; and it is said that where he discerned too great an itch for talking, he extended it to five"). One of the few living subjects was George III, who appeared briefly in entries on his ancestors. And women were no longer just the female of man; they too now received biographical reverence, not least the literary lights Eliza Haywood, Aphra Behn and Laetitia Pilkington. (Pilkington appears to have been astute at all manner of literary pursuits. Caught by her husband with another man in her bedroom one night, she explained that it wasn't what it seemed: the man had simply refused to let her borrow a book she wanted, but he was perfectly content to have her read it in his company until she reached a, well, happy ending.)

Most of the 1000-plus biographies were laudatory and moralistic, with rulers commonly praised for advancing the lives of their people (encouragement for the biographical expansion seems to have stemmed from the Duke of Buccleuch, one of *Britannica*'s most generous subscribers). Kathleen Hardesty Doig observes that when it comes to the entries on writers, most

* This detail and much other indispensable information about this second edition is to be found in the chapter "James Tytler's Edition: A Vast Expansion and Improvement" by Kathleen Hardesty Doig, Frank A. Kafker, Jeff Loveland and Dennis A. Trinkle in Frank A. Kafker and Jeff Loveland (eds.), *The Early Britannica: The Growth of an Outstanding Encyclopaedia* (Voltaire Foundation, Oxford, 2009). For an entertaining if somewhat outdated guide, see also: Herman Kogan, *The Great EB* (University of Chicago Press, 1958).

"lead exemplary lives while composing masterpieces," while the more arresting lifestyles of the ancients pass without censure, not least Nero's cross-dressing and Sappho's lesbianism. When it comes to religion, only Protestant ethics are commended.

What made this edition twice as expensive as its forerunner? Certainly its greater length, but certainly not its new editor James Tytler. The second edition had the same publishers, Andrew Bell and Colin Macfarquhar, and their replacement for William Smellie must have raised eyebrows in the literary world. For James Tytler wasn't an established part of it and not one of them; he was a pharmacist, a songwriter, and once served as a surgeon on a whaler ship. He edited and wrote pamphlets, although his intended masterwork, printed on his small, self-built press, *Essays on the Most Important Subjects of Natural and Revealed Religion,* was abandoned in mid-sentence on page 64. The closest he got to commercial publishing may have been his supposed authorship, just two years before, of a detailed guide to Edinburgh's prostitutes. But he came cheap, at 16 shillings a year, and he took to his new task with gusto.*

Tytler's tastes ran wide and happily odd. His work on the second edition was both authoritative and subjective, his opinions controversial and his technique slipshod. He compared the work to a navigator's compass, though a reader often ran aground. Some editorial decisions appear both baffling and appealingly romantic, not least the open-handed approach to the veracity of mythical creatures and beasts of the sea (mermaids were just the beginning). Other strange judgments we credit to the exciting times. The entry on Bastard informs that anyone who fathers

* Doig and colleagues question his role in the prostitute guide, although they concede "he may have been desperate." Bell and Macfarquhar's ambitions for the second edition required partners, and they agreed to print and promote it with eight other Scottish printer/booksellers.

an illegitimate child under a particular oak tree in Staffordshire will be safe from reprimand. And there was no way of knowing how much the steam engine, afforded seven pages, might prove more significant in the world than Fluxions, an impenetrable type of mathematical calculation, afforded six.

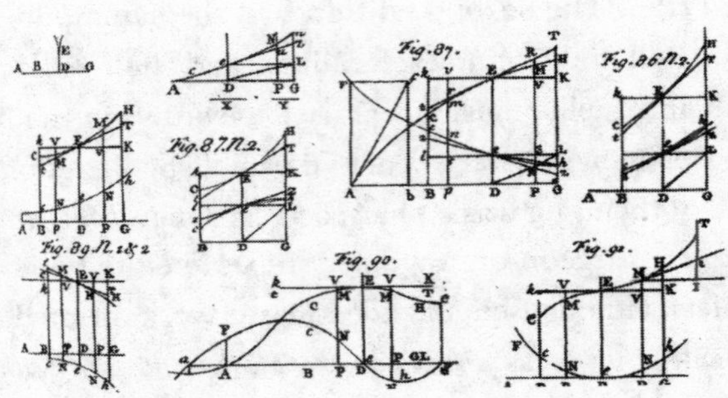

Fluxions, which received nearly equal billing to the steam engine in Tytler's second edition

In the realms of history and geography, his entries were notably expanded: America increased from thirty-one lines to twenty pages, Britain from five lines to eighty-one pages, and France from fifteen lines to twenty-six pages. But within those pages, written when the Revolution was either under way or complete, many American states are still apparently under colonial rule of the British, and Native Americans are depicted as lazy except when they're out for "revenge." The entry Colony explains that "the sad reverse that has taken place is well known to all our readers. For us to depict it would be a task equally superfluous and painful."

In a similar (and to the modern reader, shocking) tone, there are "inferior" people all over. Cypriots are lazy; the Hottentots are lazy and stupid; Highlanders are savage. The Chinese are in "misery" due to the corruption of their magistrates. Closer to home, in the entry on Leith, we learn that the commodities exported to the West Indies include wine, clothing, shoes and Negroes. Elsewhere, vivid exoticism is the key: the Congo contains ants that will surround men and beasts at night "and devour even to the very bone," while Mount Etna in Sicily contains a funnel with a "tremendous and unfathomable gulph, so much celebrated in all ages, both as the terror of this life, and the place of punishment in the next."

The new *Britannica* omits to credit its contributors, providing instead an extended bibliography (four times the length of the first edition's) prefaced by this explanation:

> To accomplish a task so arduous and important, neither labour nor expense has been spared. The best authors on each particular science have been collected and compared. Such as could be abridged without disadvantage have been epitomized with all possible care: others who were more concise and tenacious of their subjects have been more closely pursued and more faithfully retained. When topics have been obscurely or imperfectly treated, the utmost endeavours have been used to supply [amend] these defects, and upon such parts of science as the compilers have not found properly illustrated by other authors, original essays are inserted. Nor do these amount to an inconsiderable number.

Certainly there is much lyrical, useful and entertaining learning to be had. Among the *G*'s:

Galaxy: In astronomy, that long, white, luminous track which seems to encompass the heavens like a swath, scarf or girdle, and which is easily perceived in a clear night, especially when the moon does not appear. The Greeks call it Galaxy of Milk on account of its colour and appearance; the Latins, for the same reasons, call it *via lactea*; and we, the milky way. The ancient poets and even philosophers speak of the Galaxy as the road or way by which the heroes went to heaven.

Galileo (Galilei): The famous mathematician and astronomer, was the son of a Florentine nobleman, and born in the year 1564 . . . In 1592 he was chosen professor of mathematics at Padua, and during his abode there he invented, it is said, the telescope; or, according to others, improved that instrument, so as to make it fit for astronomical observations. Having observed some solar spots in 1612, he printed that discovery the following year in Rome; in which, and in some other pieces, he ventured to assert the truth of the Copernican system, and brought several new arguments to confirm it. For these he was cited before the Inquisition, and after some months' imprisonment was released upon a simple promise that he would renounce his heretical opinions and not defend them by word or writing. But having afterwards, in 1632, published at Florence his "Dialogues of the two greatest systems of the world, the Ptolemaic and Copernican," he was again cited before the Inquisition and committed to the prison of that ecclesiastical court at Rome . . . on this sentence he was detained a prisoner till 1634, and his "Dialogues of the system of the world" were burnt at Rome.

Gnomes: Certain imaginary beings, who, according to the cabalists, inhabit the inner parts of the earth. They are supposed small in stature, and the guardians of quarries, mines &c. See Fairy.

Fairy: In ancient tradition and romances signifies a sort of deity or imaginary genius, conversant on the earth, and distinguished by a variety of fantastical actions either good or bad. They were most usually imagined to be women of an order superior to human nature, yet subject to wants, passions, accidents, and even death; sprightly and benevolent while young and handsome; morose, peevish and malignant if ugly or in the decline of their beauty; fond of appearing in white . . .

One of the greatly expanded entries is on Gardening, occupying thirty-eight pages. The occupation has been newly "entitled to a considerable rank among the liberal arts," being "an exertion of fancy" and "a subject for taste." The author remarks that gardening is no longer confined merely to gardens, but may be applied to a park, a farm or a riding, and in all these areas it is a gardener's duty to improve beauty and correct faults. But beware of over-embellishment: Woburn Farm in Surrey is excessively ornamental.

There is much firm guidance. "Mere rocks, unless they are peculiarly adapted to certain impressions, may surprise, but can hardly please: they are too far removed from common life, too barren and inhospitable; rather desolate than solitary, and more horrid than terrible." Several English gardens are then appraised in detail, not least the rolling spread at Stowe in Buckinghamshire, and as each season is considered in turn there is much to delight the student of the obvious. In late summer, "maturity is always immediately succeeded by decay: flowers bloom and fade; fruits ripen and rot; the grass springs and withers . . . in the latter months of autumn, all nature is on the decline; it is a comfortless season . . ."

But Gardening is outdone by Pyrotechny. This explodes on to thirty-one pages, enlightened by four pages of Andrew Bell's copperplate engravings. We learn of the varying roles of saltpetre, brimstone, benjamin and spur-fire, and what combination is needed for water rockets, rains and spiral wheels. There is detailed instruction on mortars and fuses, while the step-by-step guide to making "crackers" (bangers) is crackers:

> Cut some cartridge paper into pieces 3½ inches broad and 1 foot long; one end of each fold down lengthwise about ¾ of an inch broad; then fold down the double edge down ¼ of an inch, and turn the single edge back half over the double fold . . . Then fold it over and over till all the paper is doubled up, rubbing it down every turn; this done, bend it backwards and forwards 2½ inches or thereabouts . . .

And so on for many, many folds before you could add the touchpaper and then visit your local hospital. And this is nothing compared to the complexities of making the homemade fireworks "Fixed Sun with a Transparent Face" or "Illuminated Chandelier." Editor Tytler almost certainly composed this lengthy entry himself, joining his contributions on Chemistry, Earthquake, Electricity, Heat and Hot-air Ballooning, the last a newfound passion.

Inspired by the recent ascent of the Montgolfier brothers, Tytler thought "How hard can it be?" In 1784 he secured financial backing for his first flight in a balloon 40 feet high and 30 feet in diameter. He fired up his coal-burning contraption in Comely Gardens in Edinburgh, and he was cheered off, according to one account, by "a crowd of cronies and backers, including a well-known golf caddie nicknamed Lord North." He flew for about half a mile before crashing onto a road. He went up again shortly afterwards and became entangled in a tree. Robert Burns immortalized him as "Balloon Tytler" in his *Notes on Scottish Song*. Back on the ground, Tytler made a modest contribution to the third edition of *Britannica,* but then sailed for America, where he pursued various schemes, not least excessive drinking, and one drunken night he ventured out into the snow, caught a deathly cold and died.

H

HAMILTON'S CHOICE

If you were a chief librarian at King's College in New York at the time of the American Revolution, and you had a budget to purchase just one major encyclopedia, something that would inform and inspire young and scrappy students such as Alexander Hamilton, John Jay and Robert R. Livingston, which one should it be? The *Britannica* was the obvious choice, but there were a few others. Perhaps you would prefer:

A New and Complete Dictionary of Arts and Sciences, Comprehending All the Branches of Human Knowledge, published in five volumes (3500 pages) between 1763 and 1764, edited by A Society of Gentlemen and published by W. Owen at Homer's Head in Fleet Street. This hoped to be "more universal and comprehensive" than any set published previously: "the smallest insect and plant find a place."

Or perhaps: *The New Royal Cyclopaedia or Modern Universal Dictionary of Arts and Sciences* edited by George Selby Howard, published in London in three folio volumes in 1788. This claimed to be modeled on "an entire and new improved plan," containing "all the latest discoveries and improvements" particularly "amphibiology, brontology, fluxions, longimetry, mensuration, phytology, stereometry and tactics." In fact it was largely and shamelessly a copy of an updated Chambers's *Cyclopaedia.*

Or maybe you'll be tempted by an Italian set. The profusely illustrated *Nuovo Dizionario* (1746-51) compiled by Gianfrancesco Pivati, perhaps, reflecting the changing fortunes of Venetian trade, or the French spin-off from the *Encyclopédie,* Jean-Henri-Samuel Formey's *Encyclopédie Réduite* from 1767.

But just a few years later, with King's College in New York recently renamed Columbia College, your choice would be much easier. It would be *Dobson's.*

This enterprise, published from 1789—all eighteen volumes and three supplements of it—may look a little familiar. It may look very like the third edition of the *Britannica,* and 95 percent of it was precisely that. The other 5 percent contained additions, corrections and amendments written to please an American readership, a fairly discerning lot: among the first subscribers (in addition to the librarians at Columbia and Yale) were Benjamin Franklin, Thomas Jefferson and Alexander Hamilton. George Washington was so keen on it that he bought two.

Suitably, Thomas Dobson began his bookselling career in Edinburgh. In 1784, in his early thirties, he moved with his wife and three daughters to Philadelphia and swiftly established himself as an importer of foreign titles "in good editions in the most elegant bindings," including Shakespeare, Swift, Pope and Sterne, and he built up specialist lists in medicine and children's books. Philadelphia was the most populous and cultivated city in America, and according to Dobson's biographer Robert D. Arner, it was the only place where a project as ambitious and risky as his encyclopedia could have any hope of success. It was home to the wealthiest merchants and lawmakers, as well as leading novelists and actors, and it was soon to be home to the federal government. Dobson saw his opportunity: not merely an imported *Britannica,* but a *Britannica* typeset, printed and improved in the very streets where it would be bought.*

Dobson's adverts in the local newspapers in 1789 promised a publication like none ever created on American soil. It would be printed in weekly installments of forty quarto pages over several years, the whole containing more than 400 copper plates. The work could also be purchased for $5 per volume. But the portents were not good. A year before, Dobson had announced the publication of a deluxe eight-volume edition of Edward Gibbon's *Decline and Fall of the Roman Empire* (in large-scale octavo, "handsomely bound, gilt and lettered . . . with an elegant head of the author, and all the maps"). The cost was $2 per volume, but his request for payment in advance did not attract enough customers to proceed.†

* For a compelling forensic account see Robert D. Arner, *Dobson's Encyclopaedia* (University of Pennsylvania Press, Philadelphia, 1991).

† A note on a printer's page sizes is overdue. Before the twentieth century, encyclopedias were usually printed in one of two sizes. The earliest, heaviest and most prestigious was folio, somewhere in the range of 12 × 19 inches. Quarto, which measured around 9.5 × 12 inches, became the more popular and manageable form. The terms refer to how many times a large original sheet of paper was folded: historically, a quarto volume was printed on sheets folded in half twice, with the first fold at right angles to the second, to produce four leaves (or eight pages). By the same process, an octavo book, a format still in use today for many modern hardbacks, has been folded in half again, producing eight leaves.

We are familiar with Shakespeare's First Folios, printed in 1623, although earlier and less reliable texts of his plays were widely distributed in quarto. Gutenberg's first printed books were also in quarto size. The earliest *Britannica* was in folio, while the ones most of us own or have consulted in libraries are slightly smaller than the traditional quartos, at 8.5 × 11 inches. Modern book sizes are complex things, with different terms applying in different countries. The UK's demy, royal, A, B and C formats will be less identifiable in the United States, while the US crown octavo and duodecimo will confuse Japanese printers versed in shinsho or bunkobon paperbacks. And of course manuscript and printing paper sizes—A3, A4 and foolscap etc.—are different again. If you want to be really bamboozled, may I recommend: wikipedia.org/wiki/Paper_size.

For his *Britannica*, Dobson once again insisted on an advance subscription model, but this time his effort would be assisted by a more persuasive prospectus and paid agents in Philadelphia, New York, Boston and Baltimore. He dismissed the alternative option of selling door-to-door, a method employed successfully just five years before by the book agent Parson Weems. Dobson regarded this method as short-sighted, as it "sinks the book in the public estimation and never fails to take the trade out of the bookseller's hands, who of course is no longer interested in it."

His prospectus in the newspapers was modeled closely on those of Bell and Macfarquhar in Edinburgh, and no wonder. Although he would never admit it, his undertaking was essentially piracy: American copyright law protected domestic publications, but those from overseas enjoyed no such privileges (and, it may be supposed, particularly not if they originated with America's former colonists). The only criterion was that any reprinted or translated publication was seen to improve the lot of American readers, and Dobson found no difficulty in such a claim. The first thing he did was remove the dedication to King George III. The illustrations—all those hundreds of copper engravings by Andrew Bell—were also copied, and sometimes slightly modified; frequently American engravers would scratch their names where Bell's had been, and Dobson misinformed American booksellers with his broadsides: "Every part of the Work will be executed by American artists." Dobson hoped that his *Encyclopaedia* (he dropped the *Britannica* just before publication) would soon be regarded as the most timely and reliable publication of a forward-looking nation. As Robert D. Arner defined it, "Dobson's *Encyclopaedia* brought Old World order and authority as well as the examples of the past to bear on unruly New World experience, offering a rebuke of democratic excesses that imperilled culture and learning." Further, it emphasized the primacy of the historical perspective, and although it had broken from England politically, the appeal of his *Encyclopaedia* "lay mainly in its promise of reuniting the American intellectual community with vital and sustaining European traditions and learning."

In Great Britain, the third edition of *Britannica* had received largely favorable reviews. After James Tytler's ascendancy in his balloon, its fervent new editor, the Episcopalian minister George Gleig, further added to *Britannica*'s reputation, achieving sales of 13,000 copies and net profits for its publishers of £42,000. Although many smaller enterprises would suffer financial jeopardy trying to emulate this success, there was now no doubt that encyclopedias could be lucrative affairs. One obvious indication: the arrival in the Edinburgh office of several writs for copyright infringement, the biggest from James Clark, who claimed that sixty-one pages in the third edition were copied verbatim, alongside his engravings, from one of his books on shoeing horses and preventing equine disease. The court found in his favor, but failed to order financial compensation.

Its key new ingredient—the greatly expanded recruitment of experts in their fields, something that would soon be taken for granted among all great encyclopedias—was widely appreciated. The *Eclectic Review*, for instance, found "considerable excellence," while the *British Critic* acclaimed a "great work." But the increased print run may have affected quality: judgment of the copper plates ranged from "as good as can be expected" to "execrable." And there was one memorable hatchet job: the *Agricultural Magazine* damned the entire work as "a trash viler than the vilest Scottish haggish."

In Philadelphia, Dobson's original print run was 1000 sets, but the early level of interest from subscribers doubled this. When purchasers got their first volumes in the early 1790s, they found the extraordinary range of entries that had impressed

British readers—including new treatises on Logarithms and Critical Philosophy (Kant) and the fifty-page article on the French Revolution, expressly written for the third edition—and additions designed to please American readers with their supportive post-revolutionary spirit. But the changes were small, and there were many notable omissions. While the article entitled President added the new executive, and Chronology added the date 1787 to include the formation in Philadelphia of the new Constitution, there was no mention of the Declaration of Independence and no biographies of Americans were added (not even the most obvious candidate, Benjamin Franklin).

Dobson's principal American contributor was the geographer Jedidiah Morse. He wrote about American Indians, the history of several states, and specific revolutionary battles. Inevitably, his interpretation of the war was rather different from the British one. The original view from Edinburgh was that "the beginning of every political establishment is contemptible," and went on to cast "the turbulence of some North Americans, and the blunders of some British statesmen" as the villains. Morse had a more positive outlook: in the past, in the Old World, new political institutions were marked by "the barbarous manners of savage tribes." But "very different were the circumstances which gave birth to this new republic." The causes of the revolutionary conflict were very different too. Gone was the British blaming of French emissaries for the uprising and the destruction of the "warmth of attachment to the mother-country." More significant, Morse added, was an American "abhorrence of oppression . . . love of liberty, and . . . quick sense of injury." Further, he claimed, the English found the cause of the conflict "in any source rather than their own misconduct."

While early installments of his work were well received by

readers, Dobson was struggling financially. Each of his letters to his subscribers contained increasingly urgent appeals for payment. The *Gazette of the United States* carried a notice in which he took the liberty of "representing to such subscribers as are in arrears, the indispensable necessity of punctuality . . . Though the importance of a few dollars may be but a trifle to the individuals, yet the accumulation of these trifles UNPAID leaves the publisher under very serious embarrassments."

And then disaster struck. In September 1793, with precisely half of his eighteen volumes published, a fire swept through his building destroying not only the volume in progress but the means of printing subsequent ones. His entire type foundry melted, with total losses exceeding $5000. Dobson praised the kindness of strangers for his swift recovery, not least the printer who donated an entire library of new metal type.*

The set was complete in 1798, and one of the earliest reviews appeared the following year. "The magnitude of the work far exceeds any thing ever before issued from the press in the United States," announced Charles Brockden Brown in his *Monthly Magazine and American Review.* Brown acknowledged both the great labor and hazard involved in such a production, and excused the errors and omissions as an inevitable consequence of having so many hands tackling such a large spread of topics. He particularly admired the cross-referencing, the "relation which the various objects of knowledge bear to one another," the distinguishing feature of an encyclopedia over a dictionary.

And then, as Professor Arner observes, Brown turned lyrical, finding inspiration in *Paradise Lost* to praise not only

* The fire was a personal tragedy for Dobson, but the yellow fever that swept Philadelphia and the eastern seaboard in these years was a broader one, which also had a large impact on his production schedule and sales.

Dobson's project, but encyclopedias as a concept. Nothing better exemplified the new American nation in aspiration and purpose:

> The Encyclopaedist conducts his reader to a lofty eminence, from which he is enabled to descry the boundless prospect that stretches before him; he points out to his view the accumulated labours, experience, and wisdom of ages; he assists him to survey the history of the human mind in its progress from rudeness to refinement, and to teach him to anticipate the glorious destiny which awaits the full development and exertion of intellectual energy in a more enlightened age.

I

INFORMATION OVERLOAD

Three new articles in the third edition of *Britannica* (1788–97) defined the far-seeing, near-seeing age in which it was published. Micrometer occupied nineteen pages, Microscope thirty-two and Telescope fifty.*

The entry for Microscope began simply enough: lenses, mirrors, Leeuwenhoek. We read of different makes—Withering's "Portable Botanic," Ellis's "Aquatic"—and what to look for: "The circulation of the blood may be easiest seen in the tails or fins of fishes, in the fine membranes between a frog's toes, or best of all in the tail of a water-newt." Copper plates showed more than thirty types of lens and calibration tool: "Place your object either in the needle G, in the pliers H, on the object plate M, or in the hollow brass box O, as may be most convenient."

---

* Between the first two sat the mysterious plant Micropus, a "bastard cudweed, a genus of the polygamia neceffaria order . . . the receptacle is palcaceous; there is no pappus; the calyx is calyculated; there is no radius of the corolla."

The pace of science and technology was accompanied by a thirst to absorb and interpret it. The editors of the *Britannica* would never want for new findings, for "research" was now the buzzword in specialist publications of the age. The cultural historian Peter Burke has identified several: *Recherches Philosophiques sur les Américains* by the Dutch philosopher Cornelius de Pauw (1768); *Asiatic Researches,* a journal from 1788; *Recherches sur les principaux paits physiques* (1794) and *Recherches sur l'organisation des corps vivants* (1802) by the French naturalist and evolutionist Jean-Baptiste Lamarck; *Researches, Chemical and Philosophical* by the Cornish chemist Humphry Davy (1799); *Recherches sur les ossemens fossiles* by the French palaeontologist Georges Cuvier (1812).*

The "second age of discovery" also announced big geographical finds—the West's exploration of the South Seas, the interiors of Africa, North and South America, Siberia and Australia—filling in the "dark" and blank spaces on the map and rendering them prime for plunder. As each new expedition enthralled members of the Royal Geographical Society in London and the Academy of Sciences in Moscow, so the explorers entrenched their reputations: David Livingstone, Alexander von Humboldt, Mungo Park, James Cook, Lewis and Clark. The hunger for discovery was accompanied by the desire to contain, own and exploit.

The encyclopedia was part of this control. History and maps enshrined ownership; the mighty book was a reader's mighty estate. Inevitably and immediately, an encyclopedia became a part of the society it aimed to reflect. *Britannica* was itself a land to be exploited: once blank, the pages were now filled

---

* See Peter Burke, *A Social History of Knowledge, Volume II* (Polity Press, Cambridge, 2012).

with new inky native wisdom (one early-twentieth-century advertisement promoted pictorial "scenes in foreign lands, costumes of strange peoples"). For as long as Britain claimed an empire, the multi-volume encyclopedia was colonialism in print. (Or, in an overworked term, knowledge was power.)

Scholarly archaeology, palaeontology and anthropology were also boosted in this sudden golden age, a period in which the notion of deep time itself was scrutinized. In 1750, the earth was widely considered to be only 6000 years old; geologists added millions to it. When astronomers joined the party, and the number turned to billions, the challenge for the encyclopedist was to explain not only earthbound philosophy but our place in the universe. (And we think *we* live in an Information Age.)

To accommodate all these new findings and acquisitions at the end of the eighteenth century, the study of storage and the concept of the archive became academic disciplines of their own, as did the art of knowledge-gathering and the categorization of new finds. The encyclopedia again mirrored these developments in both concept and design, having struggled with similar dilemmas for decades.

In one sense the encyclopedia had it easy: more information just meant more volumes. But where would you stop? When would a project designed to limit and encapsulate the growth of books itself know when to limit its expansion? Could something be too comprehensive? Would the *Ökonmische Encyklopädie*, printed in Germany from 1773 to 1858, eventually stretching to 242 volumes, be considered too ambitious for its own good?

The fact that it is not better known may provide the answer. The work was generally known as "the Krünitz," after its founder (and editor of the first seventy-two volumes)

Johann Georg Krünitz (glorious legend suggests he died while working on the entry Corpse). His was a grand general work, and much admired in its first years. But size wasn't everything, and it failed to find a large enough inexhaustible readership, its reputation rapidly eclipsed by a modest never-ending little effort called the *Brockhaus*, of which we shall learn more shortly.

J

JAHRBUCH

We have seen with the *Grosses vollständiges Universal Lexicon Aller Wissenschafften und Künste, Welche bißhero durch menschlichen Verstand und Witz erfunden und verbessert worden* how the Germans love a long title.

So it should come as little surprise to learn that the greatest German encyclopedia of the age had a name that also refused to roll off the tongue. But it was at least enduring. *Conversations-Lexikon oder kurzgefasstes Handwörterbuch für die in der gesellschaftlichen Unterhaltung aus den Wissenschaften und Künsten vorkommenden Gegenstände, mit beständiger Rücksicht auf die Ereignisse der älteren und neuren Zeit* was a title that lasted, in various forms, almost 200 years, from the beginning of the nineteenth century to 2006, increasing and decreasing in size and popularity, and second only to the *Britannica* in influence, regard and longevity.

The first six-volume edition appeared between 1809 and 1811, and its 2000 copies sold out within months. When a new and revised edition was published between 1812 and 1819, Europe's revolutionary wars and industrial expansion necessitated an increase to ten volumes and a print run of 3000. Its title was also revised, and inevitably lengthened, and was now almost a volume in itself:

Conversations-Lexicon oder Handwörterbuch für die gebildeten Stände über die in der gesellschaftlichen Unterhaltung und bei der Lectüre vorkommenden Gegenstände, Namen und Begriffe, in Beziehung auf Völker- und Menschengeschichte, Politik und Diplomatik, Mythologie und Archäologie, Erd-, Natur-, Gewerb- und Handlungskunde, die schönen Künste und Wissenschaften: mit Einschluß der in die Umgangssprache eingegangenen ausländischen Wörter und mit besonderer Rücksicht auf die älteren und neuesten merkwürdigen Zeitereignisse was edited and published by David Arnold Friedrich Brockhaus. To save time and energy, his great encyclopedia was—almost from its inception—known simply as *Brockhaus*. And in Germany the word "Brockhaus" is to encyclopedia what Roget is to thesaurus.

The spark came from the German scholar Dr. Renatus Gotthelf Löbel. In 1796, aware of the impact of both the *Encyclopédie* and *Britannica,* Löbel began work in Leipzig on a modest version of a new German encyclopedia, but died before the century was out. After several other editors and publishers took the helm, Friedrich Arnold Brockhaus acceded to the venture and, with the aid of his two sons, transformed it.

What set it apart? What would prompt the eleventh edition of *Britannica* (1910/11) to conclude that "no work of reference has been more useful and successful, or more frequently copied, imitated and translated, than that known as the *Konversations-Lexikon of Brockhaus*"? The answer, pertinently, lay in (part of) the title. This translated as "general German encyclopedia for the educated," and it announced a simple concept with wide appeal. Rather than the increasingly lengthy, philosophical and scientific entries of the *Britannica,* it offered a more popular approach to the attainment of knowledge: the "educated" of the title was inclusive, the volumes written to appeal to curious young adults rather than just the highly qualified. Further, the venture had an element of the newspaper to it: from 1857, supplements would appear every month, confusingly called the *Jahrbuch.* When the supplements appeared twice monthly from 1865, the name was changed to *Unsere Zeit* (*Our Time*). Never before had an encyclopedia created a sense of a living tutorial focused on continual intellectual improvement.*

Frequent new editions of increasing size were met with a corresponding increase in sales; the fifth edition was reprinted twice and sold more than 30,000 copies, a magnificent achievement, and soon its influence extended well beyond Germany. A translation of its seventh edition provided the groundwork for the *Encyclopedia Americana* (1829–33), the most successful American encyclopedia after *Dobson's.* In 1890, a Russian version was published in St. Petersburg, where readers could choose either the thirty-five- or eighty-six-volume set.†

* Not that Brockhaus didn't have competition. The generously illustrated *Konversations-Lexikon* produced by Joseph Meyer, for example, was a larger and more political work, and its size made it less nimble in adapting to changes and new events. The *Wunder-Meyer,* as it was known, was taken over by the Nazis during the Second World War. The two enterprises merged in the mid-1980s.

The word "Lexikon" translates formally as dictionary, but in the eighteenth century became applicable to anything in alphabetical order. *Konversations-Lexikon* came to denote the popular or accessible encyclopedia of things, rather than a catalogue of words.

† Unlike *Britannica,* the *Brockhaus* had always been a fairly modest publication, its size adapting to the perceived demands of its readership, which in modern times meant a reduction due to financial constraints and narrowing attention spans. The sixteenth edition of 1952–57, for example, the first to be published after the war, reduced the number of volumes from twenty-five to twelve, and the number went down again for the eighteenth edition of 1977–81.

The *Brockhaus* was based in the same building in Leipzig from 1808 to 1943, when it was bombed and partially destroyed by the British. It took four years to resurrect itself on a smaller scale in Wiesbaden, and the great project flourished again until the last full-scale print edition of 2006, by which time it had been partially destroyed by the Internet. It still thrives online, where one is greeted with the message "Willkommen in der Welt des Wissens und Lernens!"*

A popular approach: hounds, locomotives and English artistry in the expansive *Brockhaus*

In Edinburgh, the importance of the regular update wasn't lost on *Britannica*. Facing increasing competition, its publishers realized that the depth and quality of its entries, not to say its dependability, would only continue to appeal if it kept pace with the world around it. Revolution was everywhere:

* Welcome to the world of knowledge and learning!

technological, medical, philosophical, geopolitical. The answer would be supplements and yearbooks, but it wouldn't entirely solve the problem. Rival publications appeared more in tune with the times merely because they were new.

And at the turn of the nineteenth century there were a lot of them. One could choose between William Henry Hall's *New Royal Encyclopaedia*, *Kendal's Pocket Encyclopaedia*, the *Edinburgh Encyclopaedia*, the *English Encyclopaedia*, and the *Domestic Encyclopaedia*. All of them were smaller, cheaper and more hastily assembled than *Britannica*, and while envious of *Britannica*'s success, they claimed their brevity made them more suitable to the general reader.

But the biggest threat came from an updated version of an old friend and spur, the *Cyclopaedia*. This was no longer the concise two-volume folio edited by Ephraim Chambers in 1728; in fact, it was almost its opposite—a vast thirty-nine-volume quarto edition, with 32,000 pages and about 32 million words of text, with an additional five plate volumes and an atlas with sixty-one folding maps, making it almost exactly twice as large as Diderot's *Encyclopédie* and the 1810 fourth edition of *Britannica*. It appeared serially and alphabetically between 1802 and 1819, which meant—as with similar publications—readers learned a lot about the world's *A*'s and *B*'s years before they learned anything about its *Y*'s and *Z*'s; during its seventeen years of completion, this occasionally made a mockery of the extensive system of cross-referencing, with the reader of "Acorn: denotes the fruit of trees of the Oak kind . . . see Seed" having to wait years and many volumes before their inquiry was rewarded.

Its editor was Abraham Rees, a Welsh Presbyterian minister, a fellow of the Royal Society, a man determined to spread knowledge "far beyond the schoolroom, even the university." His new enterprise satisfied the desire for biography and contemporary history, while its sympathetic coverage of revolutionary Europe led to accusations of subversive sympathies. To counteract this, its editor went to sincere lengths to stress its Protestant leanings and Englishness, even referring to King Louis as "King Lewis." In other ways the volumes were exemplary examples of the Enlightenment: some of the most numerous and longest articles tackled the latest interpretations of the atomic system, the cosmos and the origins of the earth, as well as recent research in botany, zoology and natural history.

There were many engaging and surprising anomalies. Some of the alphabetical ordering, for example, was original: "New York" appeared as "York, New" and "St. Ives" as "Ives, St." Occasionally an entry starting with a letter earlier in the alphabet would invade a later one—entries beginning with I and J often appearing quite randomly, as if the editor had thought of a new addition when it was too late to reset the printing plates. And some of the editorial judgments were erratic, or at least acutely specialized, such as the sixteen pages of arcane tables devoted to the heliocentric tracking of the latitude and longitude of Jupiter, which required two pages of explanatory notes and made a rocket ride to the planet an easier option:

> From Table 1 of the epochs, take out the epochs of the mean longitude of the aphelion and node, with the Arguments II, III, IV, V, VI, VII, VIII, IX, and place them in an horizontal line. But if the given year not be found in that Table, take the nearest year preceding the given year as an epoch, and take out as before; under which, from Table II, place the mean motion in longitude, of the aphelion and node, with the Arguments.*

* The tables were published more than sixty years after John Harrison's horological establishment of longitude at sea.

Other entries now provide us with an intriguing glimpse into technological and scientific progress at the beginning of the nineteenth century:

Battery: In electricity, a combination of coated surfaces of glass, so connected together that they may be charged at once and discharged by a common conductor. Dr. [Benjamin] Franklin [. . .] constructed a battery consisting of eleven panes of large sash-glass, coated on each side, and connected in such a manner that the whole might be charged together. A more complete battery is described by Dr. [Joseph] Priestley, of which he says, that after long use he sees no reason for wishing the least alteration in any part of it. This battery consists of 64 jars, each ten inches long and 2½ inches in diameter, coated within 1½ inch of the top; and contains in the whole 32 square feet.

The most perfect batteries of modern construction since that of Dr. Priestley have been made in Holland for Teyler's museum at Haerlem by Mr Cuthbertson of Poland Street, London, then residing in Amsterdam [. . .] Teyler's second grand battery was finished by Mr. Cuthbertson in 1789. This is the largest and most complete battery that was ever made [. . .] 100 jars [. . .] the whole battery contains 550 square feet of coating and for convenience it is put into four separate cases.

Columbium: In chemistry, a new metal discovered by Mr [Charles] Hatchett in the year 1802, in a mineral which he had from the British Museum. The mineral, it appears, had been sent with some specimens of iron ore from Massachusetts in America to Sir Hans Sloane, in whose catalogue it is described as "a very heavy black stone, with golden streaks." Its lustre is vitreous, slightly inclining in some parts to metallic, moderately hard, and very brittle.

Railway: Tram or Dram-road, or Waggon-way, in Rural Economy, a track constructed of iron, stone, timber or other material. [. . .] Speaking of the great utility of canals in the carriage of various articles in [Shropshire], it is observed by Mr [Thomas] Telford, an able engineer, that another mode of conveyance has frequently been adopted to a considerable extent; which is that of forming roads by means of iron rails laid along them, upon which materials are carried in waggons, which contain from six to thirty hundred weight; experience, he thinks, has now convinced us that in countries the surfaces of which are rugged, or where it is difficult to obtain water for lockage, where the weight of the article of the produce is great in comparison with their bulk, and from where they are mostly to be conveyed from a higher to a lower level, that in those cases, iron railways are in general preferable to canal navigation.

When the project was complete, its preface announced that the publication was "very much to the relief of the Editor's mind." Writing in the godlike third person, Abraham Rees explained how neither expense nor energy had been spared in its construction, although "if he had foreseen the time and attention which the compilation and conduct of it required, and the unavoidable anxiety which it has occasioned, he would probably never have undertaken it." Further, he calls upon our sympathy, for "he has devoted almost twenty years of his life, measured not by fragments of time, but by whole days of twelve or fourteen hours . . . and in so doing impaired his health and constitution."

And even in the preface he admits an element of failure. Some of the details in his contributors' articles appeared to him "erroneous . . . they are actually controverted and contradicted in other parts of the *Cyclopaedia*." And he regretted its unanticipated length: "It would have been . . . more gratifying to the Editor to have compiled a Cyclopaedia in fewer volumes . . . as in all probability the sale would have been greater and the sum of money expended upon it would of course have been much less."

A similarly exhaustive task was nearing completion in France. Only this one was bigger—much bigger. The *Encyclopédie Méthodique* (1782–1832) was a vastly reorganized and expanded version of Diderot and D'Alembert's work, published and edited by Charles-Joseph Panckoucke, resulting in 203 volumes and over 100 million words.*

The *Méthodique* rejected an alphabetical arrangement in favor of "subject dictionaries" that might allow readers a broader educational view. In his prospectus, Panckoucke compared the formation of his work to a brick-by-brick reconstruction of a beautiful palace. The old palace was Diderot's; the new editor's contributor-contractors installed conservatories as far as the eye could see.

The greater length of the treatises ensured that the more controversial doctrines of the Enlightenment could be maintained with greater concealment from censors, although the extended number and the length of these entries did little to guarantee quality or a high subscription rate. Some contributors may have lengthened their entries to increase their fee, while others couldn't bear the thought of not including everything known on their subject. As for Panckoucke, its chief editor, it seemed as if he refused to actually edit. More was more. The ambition to create the ultimate work of reference must have been as frustrating as an attempt to reach the end of the Internet. Ultimate for whom? And how could this unique

* One may be reminded of Franckenstein and Zedler's comparably ambitious *Universal-Lexicon* from 1731, although that was a miserly sixty-four volumes published over eighteen years.

and overwhelming work possibly hope to keep pace with the nineteenth century? Abraham Rees had admitted as much in the preface to his own vast undertaking: "Science is progressive, and since the commencement of this work, its advances in several departments have not been inconsiderable."

The scope of the *Méthodique* resembled the conception of perfect cartography by Lewis Carroll and Jorge Luis Borges: for true accuracy, a map would have to be the same size as the area it covered, at the scale of a mile to a mile. Such exactitude was clearly absurd, as absurd as the encyclopedia of everything. The complete set of *Encyclopédie Méthodique* sold about 1500 copies.

As they aimed for an optimum size in the decades to come, all the editors of every encyclopedia reluctantly agreed on one thing: they couldn't win. A wider reading public, the expansion of trade and industry, cheaper costs of printing and more outlets for marketing hastened the growth of both the specialist encyclopedia and the two- or three-volume general set. Even the editors of *Britannica*, which ran to twenty-one volumes for both its seventh edition (1830–42) and its eighth (1853–60), confirmed to readers that their sets contained everything they needed to know rather than everything knowable. By its ninth edition (1875–99) it was edging towards a specialism of its own—the foregrounding of experts, particularly on scientific matters. Its twenty-five volumes became known as the Scholar's Edition, such was the academic style of its prose, frequently pitching itself beyond the capability of the general reader.

And underpinning all of this was a grander question, one we may argue still: what is knowledge, and how should it be presented in a book?

K

KNOWLEDGE

Knowledge confers majesty. The ownership of a large encyclopedia may suggest grandeur in the manner of a drawing-room globe or a hand-drawn map of aristocratic lands. At the beginning of the nineteenth century, possession of the *Encyclopaedia Britannica* had become a source of pride and privilege, of honor even. Such possession was often aspirational, an emblem of status, the Patek Philippe of the home library.

The fable is told, and it may even be true, of how Fath-Ali, Shah of Persia 1797–1834, took such pride in his acquisition of the eighteen-volume set of the third edition of *Britannica* at the beginning of his reign that he decided to change his title. The set had been transported from London by the British ambassador, traveling for many weeks with his arduous load, and its arrival so overwhelmed the Shah that he decreed he would henceforth be known as: "Most Exalted and Generous Prince; Brilliant as the Moon, Resplendent as the Sun; the Jewel of the World; the Center of Beauty, of Mussulmen and of the True Faith; Shadow of God; Mirror of Justice; Most Generous King of Kings; Master of the Constellations Whose Throne is the Stirrup Cup of Heaven; and Most Formidable Lord and Master of the *Encyclopaedia Britannica*."*

As the nineteenth century wore on, such a thing was increasingly seen. A well-bound set was now regularly purchased to furnish a room; the consultation of the volumes would be an occasional and secondary purpose.

K

But how was this knowledge best transmitted and absorbed? Writing in *Blackwood's Magazine* in 1824, the philosopher Alexander Blair argued that the concept of the large-scale encyclopedia had fundamentally failed, highlighting "an essential fallacy." He claimed that knowledge is advanced by individual minds wholly devoting themselves to their own part of specialized inquiry. This was "a process of separation, not of combination." He argued that previous attempts to display the "Circle of the Sciences" were based on the misconception that this unity could be grasped by individuals. His point was reinforced by the fact that the title "Encyclopedia" was being increasingly attached to studies of single subjects: *The Encyclopaedia of Wit* (1804), for one, and *An Encyclopaedia of Gardening* (1822) and *An Encyclopaedia of Music* (1825).†

Blair evidently regarded an encyclopedia as something that failed twice: it was too big to be read in its entirety, but too wide-ranging and inclusive in its content to do any subject justice, even if treated at some length as a treatise. This was not

* Mussulman is an ancient Persian term for Muslim. The story was proudly recalled by Herman Kogan in *The Great EB* (University of Chicago Press, 1958).

† As quoted in Richard Yeo, *Lost Encyclopaedias: Before and After the Enlightenment* (Book History, Johns Hopkins University Press, 2007, vol. 10).

an uncommon opinion. In their first half-century, the popular pioneering encyclopedias of Chambers, Diderot et D'Alembert, and Bell and Macfarquhar underwent a subtle shift in their proposition, moving from the realm of expanded dictionary into a much larger knowledge base. They were still far from Chambers's notion of many shelves of a library filleted into one publication, but they were increasingly designated items to be read rather than just referred to (more "this is all you need" rather than "this may fulfill a need"). The decades would change this pattern back again, and marketing men found it easier to sell the encyclopedia as a tool, an assistant, rather than an omniscient tutor. But at the beginning of the nineteenth century the debate about precisely how this knowledge was to be presented—indeed precisely what an encyclopedia was designed to be—was still fluid.

We have met the most famous debater before, but now his voice was louder. Samuel Taylor Coleridge was last seen berating the publishers of *Encyclopaedia Britannica* for presenting their installments in alphabetical order (this "huge unconnected miscellany . . . a worthless monster"). His dissatisfaction endured through the years, so that by 1817 it had expanded to a fully formed manifesto, and the manifesto brought forth a brilliant adventure called *Encyclopaedia Metropolitana*. In tone it wasn't that dissimilar from *Kubla Khan*, the epic fever dream he had published the year before, with its stately pleasure domes and caverns measureless to man. In his new vision Xanadu was now London, and the dream was a compendium of knowledge unlike anything that had appeared before.

Coleridge's grand project emphasized the systematic relationships within knowledge bases, presenting the sciences, the arts and other subjects as a rational and unified progression rather than a scattered constellation. This was the way to learn and document the world's learning, he argued, and to show how the soul of wisdom may exceed its circumstances.

His thoughts are first glimpsed in a letter he wrote to a friend in 1796. On his return from university studies in Germany he proposed to open a school "for 8 young men at 100 Guineas each . . . and perfect them in 1. The history of savage tribes. 2. Of semi-barbarous nations. 3. Of nations emerging from semi-barbarism. 4. Of civilised states. 5. Of luxurious states. 6. Of revolutionary states. 7. Of colonies."

When it came to his encyclopedia, the key word was *method.* He employed it in the way mathematicians and physicists do, and in the way Francis Bacon did before him: the methodical and systematic advance from one piece of information or thinking to another. "All things, in us, and about us, are a chaos, without Method," he wrote in his preliminary treatise. "There may be transition, but there can never be progress; there may be sensation, but there cannot be thought: for the total absence of Method renders thinking impracticable."

This wasn't entirely fanciful. The *Metropolitana* exists as fifty-nine parts, or thirty volumes (22,426 pages, 565 plates), issued between 1817 and 1845, the work of four editors and Coleridge as founding supervisor/cheerleader. The "divisions" of its contents page displayed both the variety and approach of its subject matter, but it also suggested quite a different type of publication to the *Britannica.*

In many ways it harked back to the ancient world. The "Pure Science" division included Logic, Rhetoric, Mathematics, Metaphysics, Morals and Theology. "Mixed and Applied Science" covered Mechanics, Pneumatics, Optics, Astronomy, Heat, Light and Sound; among the "Fine Arts" one would read about Painting, Heraldry, Music and Engraving. The "Useful

Arts and Natural History" featured Agriculture, Carpentry, Fortification, Anatomy and Zoology. These were lengthy, subdivided studies packed with academic fervor and exhausting thoroughness. They were not for random consultation on an inclement Sunday. If you bought the *Metropolitana*, you ended up with a big library of small books on major topics.

The entry on Numismatics, for example, stretched to thirty-one tight double-columned pages, about 30,000 words. Both sides of every coin of every reign were scrutinized, and every symbol of war or God or chariot race had a story and a purpose. A reader would discover symbols on Grecian coins derived "from the productions of the climate," including wines, melon and parsley; the diminution in the size of Roman coins (signaling a deflation of the currency); a pyramid indicating the relative value of coins in 300 BC and 200 BC (where one Sestertius equalled 2 Quinarius, and 20 Quinarius equalled 2 Tremissis); the use of abbreviations denoting high office (Trib Pot for Tribunitiâ Potestate, Pont Max for Pontifex Maximus); the differing value of brass, copper and silver coins in the age of Augustus—until every coin was appraised. It ended with a look at various coin cabinets and caskets, one for every level of collecting, and advice on how best to arrange a collection within them (here the alphabet was rejected as well, in favor of "a system more accordant with truth," specifically the truth of chronology and a tour of dusty locations where coins once circulated and buried hordes might yet be found: Gaul, Thrace, Macedon, Thessaly, Illyria, Epirus, Euboea, Zacynthus, Commagene, Phoenicia, Parthia and Zeugitania.

And this was letting the reader off lightly. Entries like these (and I've picked one of the most involving) appeared hewn from the side of rock cliffs, and they were not uninteresting once you hacked your way in (through the story of coins, some of the hubristic glory that was ancient Rome also emerged). But these huge essays run next to each other with hardly a breath between them, the surrounding pages distinctly lacking the occasional geographical or literary diversion one might encounter in other encyclopedias, the sort of thing that makes them as engaging as they were instructive.

In *Britannica*'s seventh edition, for example, published at the same time as the *Metropolitana* between 1830 and 1842, one overruns a search for James Mill's thoughts on the Freedom of the Press and finds brief insights into the Necropolis, Nepal and the Netherlands. In Volume 5 of the *Metropolitana*, by contrast, there are 165 uninterrupted pages on Meteorology and fifty-one on Engraving (followed by twenty more on Notes on Engraving). The authors were the sort of leading figures to command respect, but none of them considered concision a virtue. Fellows of the Royal Society, a conclave of bishops and reverends, the astronomer William Herschel, the mathematician and computing pioneer Charles Babbage, professors from St. John's, Cambridge and Oriel, Oxford—the great, the brilliant, the pedantic and the windy.

Admittedly, something unexpected happened in the *Metropolitana*'s fourth division. The last volumes suddenly turned alphabetical and catch-all, and more of a glossary. They contained a Complete Vocabulary of Geography, a Philosophical Lexicon, and a History of the English Language, seemingly an attempt to cover everything not considered in the essays that had gone before, perhaps a sop to everyone who had expected the sort of traditional encyclopedic dictionary they had grown used to.

Although possessed of extraordinary philosophical scope, Coleridge's vision was swimming so fiercely against the tide that today its memory, not to say its physical presence, has been largely washed away. It was widely read within the universities, but failed to leave a lasting impression on either the popular psyche or the popular market. Its critical reception was mixed. In 1862, the editor of the monthly magazine *British Controversialist* found it a "magnificent projection" that "dazzled . . . by its excursive brilliancy"; the treatises on Logic and Rhetoric "added greatly to the estimation in which the 'Encyclopaedia' began to be held." But a year later *The Quarterly Review* sniped that "the proposals of the poet Coleridge . . . had at least enough of a poetical character to be eminently unpractical." In subsequent years, the journal noted, a large proportion of the contents was "dug out of the ruins and re-issued in separate volumes by fresh publishers who acquired the property of the work, and thus distinctly recognised it as a mere quarry of valuable materials."*

Predictably, *Britannica* did not take kindly to the attacks on its principles and practice. The eighth edition (1853-60) contained a biography of Coleridge by the author and literary critic Thomas De Quincey, and the vitriol flowed unceasing. He was "capable of immense service to poetry," his verse imbued with "simplicity and lucidness." But his prose style, evidenced in both his literary criticism and (it was implied)

* Though no more readable now than then (and probably less so), the *Metropolitana* does have its champions today, not least those who credit the role it played in establishing a framework of applied science, a term that Coleridge was the first to use and popularize after acquiring it in Germany. The historian of science Robert Bud has noted that one of the encyclopedia's later editors, H.J. Rose, was also principal of the new King's College, London, where the many rational treatises on applied science found a practical application in numerous areas of engineering, including the railways and mining, as well as several areas of the arts and manufacture. It is likely that the *Metropolitana* was also employed as a useful educational tool within the nascent polytechnic movement; see Robert Bud, "'Applied Science': A Phrase in Search of a Meaning," *Isis*, University of Chicago Press, September 2012.

his groundwork on *Metropolitana*, was "disfigured by turgidity, and the affected use of words." His humor was "ponderous and unwieldy." Coleridge, De Quincey concluded, "lived on the future; and Coleridge's future was a bad bank on which to draw; its bills were perpetually dishonoured."

Coleridge's initial ambition, expressed in 1803, for a series of volumes designed to "set up the reader, give him at once connected trains of thought and facts, and a delightful miscellany for lounge reading" had long been abandoned. By the time its second edition was concluded in 1858, thirty-four years after its founder's death, the prospect of such popular appeal had been thoroughly replaced by text both earnest and exhausting, and the modern reader was looking for something else from their encyclopedias.

The publishers of *Britannica* were having their own problems keeping pace with a changing world. Nothing had transformed modern lives so much as electric light, elongating both working and leisure hours, improving safety, transport and entertainment; for our particular purposes, the encyclopedia could be printed more swiftly, sold more efficiently, and be read for longer. But an attempt to actually explain the scientific principles of light could still easily run aground on the triple hazards of old-fashioned alphabetical order, traditional publishing methods and the missed deadline.

In the 1870s, *Britannica* was still published piecemeal. The first volume of the ninth edition appeared in 1875, and the last, the twenty-fourth, only in 1888. The contributor specializing in acrobats had to write his entry more than a decade before the one specializing in yaks. And if you were writing about Light, it was no use submitting your entry after Volume 14 (Kaolin–LON), which had gone to press in 1882.

Both earnest and exhausting: a new volume of *Metropolitana* hits the streets

Unless your name was John William Strutt, the third Baron Rayleigh. Lord Rayleigh (1842–1919) was just too clever for deadlines. A student of Eton and Harrow, a professor and chancellor at Cambridge, a president of the Royal Society, and a recipient of many scientific medals, Rayleigh was expert in mathematics, hydrodynamics, viscosity, explosives, acoustics, photography and electromagnetism. He discovered and isolated the rare gas argon, for which he would receive the 1904 Nobel Prize for Physics.

Britannica invited him to contribute the entry on the physical properties of Light for its ninth edition. He was given a deadline, but more pressing demands caused him to miss it, and the volume was deprived of his insights (another man hurriedly and inadequately filled his shoes). But there was still hope that the Lord's expertise could be employed, and an enterprising editor ensured that Volume 17, MOT-ORM (1884), made space for an article from Rayleigh entitled Optics. But a similar calamity occurred: the Lord failed to get his act together. And then, as the twenty-third volume (T-UPS) approached, a few blank pages were set aside for Undulating Light, and the editor held his breath. But, oh dear again—no dice from his Lordship. With almost all hope lost, Rayleigh submitted his celebrated entry, Wave Theory of Light, for Volume 24 (1888), and the world learned that among the many suppositions regarding the propagation of light as a vibration, "the most famous is that which assimilates light to the transverse vibrations of an elastic solid. *Transverse* they must be in order to give room for the phenomena of polarisation." How illuminating that was, or how murky, only an individual reader could decide.*

This was another problem for *Britannica*: the transformation of knowledge into comprehension. Contributions from experts often failed to prove useful to a lay reader approaching the

* The Lord had the last laugh. When word got out that *Britannica* was planning a tenth edition for 1902 (the ninth edition reprinted with supplements), Rayleigh was asked to write about Argon. No one in the world knew as much about this noble gas as he did, except perhaps his fellow professor and co-discoverer, Sir William Ramsay. So it would have been a travesty had anyone else composed the *Britannica* entry about such an inert subject. Rayleigh conjured around 3000 words, frequently referring to his original research published in academic journals. He explained how he had isolated argon from other gases in the air, and how he and Ramsay had presented their discovery to an astonished Royal Society in 1895. Equally astonishing was the fact that he managed to get his unique account to the editor of *Britannica* early enough to appear in Volume A-AUS.

subject for the first time, and while few entries came as close to the thicket of specialist detail that marked the *Metropolitana*, many faced their own problems of readability. *Britannica*'s ninth edition was a towering masterwork of the British ivy-walled university, but its mastery did not initially extend to dirtying itself with the practicalities of sales or the popular market. Men like Lord Rayleigh, even if they met their deadlines, were writing for their peers, and this was not an attribute likely to expand the readership. But then something happened to transform *Britannica*'s fortunes: the arrival of two brilliant and shameless Americans intent on dragging the worthiest of institutions into the modern age.

L

LIBERATION?

In the last years of the nineteenth century, full-page advertisements appeared in *The Times* offering the twenty-four-volume set of *Encyclopaedia Britannica* for £27, less than half of the original asking price of £65. That was for the full morocco binding. The half morocco binding was only £20 (once £45), while the no morocco cloth-bound version was only £16 (originally £37).

What could you expect for a bargain like that? Prospective buyers were reassured that while the price had fallen dramatically, the value of what they were getting had not fallen at all, "not by one word." They would receive the same extraordinary fare as the people (pity them!) who had paid top whack: 30 million words across 22,000 pages, 338 full-page plates and 671 maps, and a separate 499-page index in a supplementary volume. Swinburne wrote on Keats; Robert Louis Stevenson wrote on the French poet and songwriter Pierre-Jean de Béranger; mathematicians descended from their lofty perches to explain complex proofs in impenetrable style. For just one guinea down, the purchaser would find the entire set "in every respect as desirable" as the one printed for libraries and other institutions, and on the same high-quality paper.

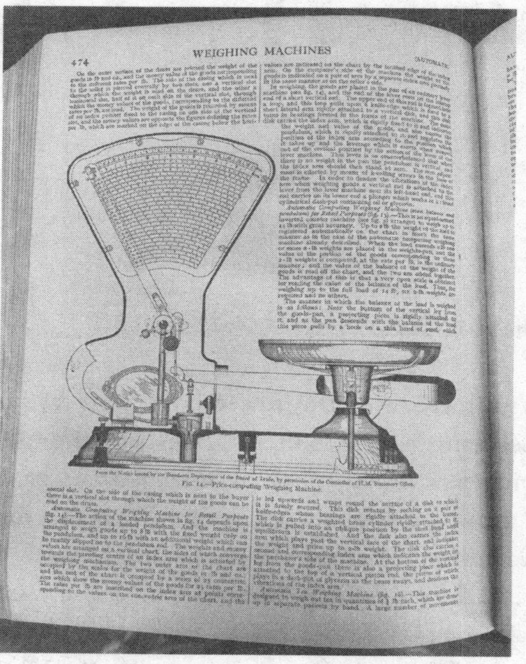

474 WEIGHING MACHINES

The world in the balance: *Britannica*'s classic eleventh edition from 1910/11

There was a catch, of course. The goods were newly printed but old stock. The bargain on offer was the ninth edition, the "Scholars edition" with all those brilliant but often too brilliant entries, parts of it twenty-three years old, repackaged and re-marketed by two businessmen who had no input into its editorial content and no time to read its pages.

But for *Britannica* there was no catch: the cut-price marketing push transformed the fortunes and future of the company, and brought profit to *The Times* after years of losses. Before the offer, and disregarding thousands of pirated editions, the ninth edition had sold about 5000 sets over ten years; *The Times* adverts doubled that in a few months. And beyond this, the businessmen, who were American and brought with them American concepts of the hard sell, transformed the entire notions of what an encyclopedia could be, who would buy it, and how they should pay for it.

From now on, the encyclopedia would no longer be just for the wealthy or well educated. It was no longer aimed at the contributors' peers. It was now to be sold to everyone with even a modest education who wanted to better understand the changes around them, and wished to improve the lives of their family. Comprehensive knowledge would become aspirational and affordable by installments, and the market for encyclopedias would move from the margins to the mainstream.

The cut-price adverts in *The Times* varied in length and appearance, becoming almost as much a fixture as its court reports. In return for this, and for its occasional editorial support, the newspaper received one guinea for every set of *Britannica* sold through its pages. It was a perfect match: each a fusty institution with enough authority to sink a battleship, each a cash-strapped knowledge base struggling to find its feet in a modernizing world. One of the advertisements stated "The *Encyclopaedia Britannica* is too well known to need description," but then proceeded to describe it for more than 5000 words.

> The *Britannica* is essentially the production of men who wrote out of the fulness of knowledge. The wonderful story of the 19th century is told by the men who made its

> greatness . . . for the men who fought against ignorance, and brought enlightenment to their generation, themselves tell how the light was spread.*

The adverts were the chief responsibility of Henry Haxton, a well-connected newspaper man from the Hearst stable and a literary showman of the Barnum school. He was happy to boost circulation with any stunt or scheme, but he was also a man of higher culture, an urban salon dweller, a great friend of James McNeill Whistler.

Haxton had been hired by Horace Hooper, a fellow American who saw *Britannica* as much as a trading commodity as a learning resource. Hooper was the product of the Chicago school of publishing, which bred a mindset of cheap books, knock-offs, multi-volumes, Bibles and the selling of reference works to everyone who wished to be thought truly American. Encyclopedias were synonymous with aspiration. If New York and Boston were the well-mannered boutique side of the book trade, Chicago was the cacophonous supermarket. Having successfully sold a great many lesser and pirated sets with less prestigious names, Hooper regarded *Britannica*

---

* Yet, despite reflecting all the greatness and progress of the world, the edition somehow managed to neglect half its people; the value of women to *Britannica*, both as subjects and contributors, would only slowly emerge and be recognized in the new century. There was one notable exception to this in the ninth edition (1888): the entry "Women, Law Relating to." It began: "The law as it relates to women has been gradual in its operation, but its tendency has been almost uniformly in one direction. Disabilities of women, married or unmarried, have been one after another removed, until at the present day, in most countries, the legal position of women differs little from that of men as far as regards private rights. Politically and professionally the sexes are still not upon an equality, but even in this aspect women have considerably greater rights than they once possessed, and the old theory of their intellectual and moral inferiority is virtually exploded. Those who defend their exclusion must now do so on other grounds."

as under-exploited, both in the United States and its home market. Resolving to fix this, he and his colleagues successfully negotiated reprint rights with A. & C. Black, the encyclopedia's Edinburgh-based owners, and they set about reviving a sleeping giant.

But Hooper and Haxton's bold manipulation of the ninth edition was just a precursor to their real achievement. Not the tenth, which consisted solely of supplements to the ninth and made no special claims for itself beyond its earnest continuance of a line, but the eleventh edition, arguably the most varied and robust popular encyclopedia ever made. It was so varied, indeed, and so enduring, that when Wikipedia opened for business ninety years later, it copied almost every word for its website, finding in it a solid base on which to build a digital revolution.*

Haxton's promotion for the eleventh edition was just as wordy as his previous campaigns. He outlined the depth of coverage ("history and race development . . . biography, law and physics . . .") and the timeliness of the work ("the Britannica will enlighten you on . . . prohibition, suffrage, tariffs, currency, waterways, transportation and government ownership!"). He called the new edition "a liberal education," and remarked on its universal accessibility: "In answer to the hundred questions which everyday come to your mind and your wife's and children's minds, it will give you more precise information than you can get from any other source."

The key theme of this edition was progress—of the world, of Great Britain's place within it, of the encyclopedia itself. The editors intended it as an altogether more engaging

* It helped that it was out of copyright.

publication than its predecessors, and almost imperceptibly a more humane one. It was an invitation to a conversation, a liberating force. It had a new publisher, the University of Cambridge, giving *Britannica* an even more noble cloak of respectability than it had achieved under the aegis of *The Times*. But under the editorship of Hugh Chisholm, a generous, clubbable man whose journalistic experience extended no further than editing the *St James Gazette,* it assumed a decidedly more energetic and less reserved academic approach, and certainly a less long-winded one, and adopted a warmer and more personable hue, so that its articles were far closer in tone to a genial discussion in a gentleman's club than a stern address from a lectern.

The eleventh edition is still widely regarded as a pinnacle, both of the encyclopedia industry and the publishing industry. One may begin with the layout, a clear double column per page with tight but wholly legible type. Then there was its self-confidence: to claim, as Henry Haxton had done, that it marked "the high tide mark of human knowledge" was not empty rhetoric; it was a belief extensively shared by its editors, and almost certainly by its readers. In his illuminating biography of the eleventh edition, Denis Boyles observed that it "has a personality that can't be easily overlooked; it's plausible, reasonable, unruffled, often reserved, completely authoritative." He goes as far as to call it "the last great English-language encyclopaedia. As a general reference work it's unrivalled, as unique now as when it was published."*

Writing in the *New Yorker* in 1981, the Dutch author Hans

* *Everything Explained That Is Explainable: On the Creation of Encyclopaedia Britannica's Celebrated Eleventh Edition, 1910–1911* by Denis Boyles (Alfred A. Knopf, New York, 2016).

Koning celebrated the Eleventh's seventieth birthday: its readership was once "simply and obviously every English-speaking educated person on earth, who . . . would expect to find and *would* find the final authority on everything."

Koning reasoned that the *Encyclopédie* of 1751 rang in the age of reason, and the eleventh edition rang it out. He believed it marked the last time that an encyclopedia could hope to map a circle of all human knowledge "with a single centre," for the world then "was a rational and ultimately a harmonious place . . . In 1910, Anglo-Saxon self-confidence and self-satisfaction were unshakeable."

With hindsight, and our studied suspicion of things empirical and colonial, *Britannica*'s pomposity seems absurd. We know that the enlightenment reflected in its pages—and the many subsequent decades of what Koning calls "almost official, almost religious optimism"—was doomed to be snuffed out forever on the battlefields of France and Belgium; the half morocco bindings crumbled like, yes, old books. But just four years before, Koning reasons, on the Oxbridge quads and in all the other learned stations of Britain and America, "all of humanity appeared to be on the threshold of being totally understood, described, improved, and then perfected." The encyclopedia was the natural repository for all this, the ultimate pure salon for the world. And even after the First World War, with so many uncertainties and dislocations, *Britannica* provided a leaning post, unstable as it was; in our minds, this was still the world we would defend in the next war, the twenty-nine volumes as good a domestic shelter as anything else.

The eleventh edition has 44 million words. My favorite ones concern the apple, for the simplest of reasons. It tells you something you didn't know, and it does so with an economy of expression, a lack of pretentiousness and an element of delight. Most importantly, it stands the test of time. Alongside historical description and practical instruction on grafting, propagating, fertilizing and harvest, about 2000 words in all, there is a genuine love for the subject. As with many of its most noteworthy articles, this one is signed, or at least initialled: A.B.R. It is the work of Alfred Barton Rendle, FRS, FLS, MA, DSc, Keeper of the Department of Botany at the British Museum.

A slice:

Apple: (a common Teutonic word . . . aphul, aphal, apfal, modern German Apfel), the fruit of Pyrus Malus, belonging to the sub-order Pomaceae, of the natural order Rosaceae. It is one of the most widely cultivated and best-known and appreciated of fruits belonging to temperate climates. In its wild state it is known as the crab-apple, and is found generally distributed throughout Europe and western Asia, growing in as high a latitude as Trondhjem in Norway. The crabs of Siberia belong to different species of Pyrus. The fruit is too well known to need any description of its external characteristics.

The apple is successfully cultivated in higher latitudes than any other fruit tree, growing up to 65° N., but notwithstanding this, its blossoms are more susceptible [to] injury from frost than the flowers of the peach or apricot. It comes into flower much later than these trees, and so avoids the night frost which would be fatal to its fruit-bearing. The apples which are grown in northern regions are, however, small, hard, and crabbed, the best fruit being produced in hot summer climates, such as Canada and the United States.

Apples have been cultivated in Great Britain probably since the period of the Roman occupation, but the names of many varieties indicate a French or Dutch origin of much later date. In 1688 Ray enumerated seventy-eight varieties in cultivation in the neighbourhood of London, and now it is calculated that about 2000 kinds can be distinguished. A large trade in the importation of apples is carried on in Britain, imports coming chiefly from French, Belgian and Dutch growers, and from the United States and British North America.

But the greatest delight is a list, a catalogue of apples arranged in order of their ripening. I found it bizarrely inspiring, almost moving, in its variety and obsession. The list made me hungry for the crunch. And it made me sad to think that when I next visited a supermarket, or even the keenest grower in Kent, I would find hardly any of them.

White Juneating: July

Irish Peach: Aug.

Devonshire Quarrenden: Aug.-Sept.

Duchess of Oldenburg: Aug.-Sept.

Peasgood's Nonesuch: Sept.-Nov.

Sam Young: Oct.-Dec.

King of the Pippins: Oct.-Jan.

Court of Wick: Oct.-Mar.

Sykehouse Russet: Nov.-Feb.

Fearn's Pippin: Nov.-Mar.

Reinette de Canada: Nov.-Apr.

Ashmead's Kernel: Nov.-Apr.

White Winter Calville (grown under glass): Dec.-Mar.

Braddick's Nonpareil: Dec.-Apr.

Court-pendu Plat: Dec.-Apr.

Northern Spy: Dec.-May

Scarlet Nonpareil: Jan.-Mar.

Lamb Abbey Pearmain: Jan.-May

This is just half of the dessert apples. There are nine varieties of pippin. In addition, the large number of "kitchen" (i.e., cooking) apples included the Keswick Codlin, the Lord Suffield, the Yorkshire Greening and the Bess Pool. How utterly enticing is this information? Just the thing, I'd suggest, to lighten the load between Appin, a coast district of Argyllshire, and Appleton, Nathan (1770-1861), American merchant and politician. (These days the entry would be preceded by App Store and followed by Apple Computer.) And it is just the thing to support the view that the eleventh edition may be the most life-affirming *Britannica* ever made, and the most amenable to a general open-me-anywhere read.

If it wasn't so unwieldy you might take it everywhere to recite to friends. This is particularly true of the biographical entries, the amuse-bouche of the encyclopedist's art. To open just one spread, pages 714-5 in Volume 12, provides seven entries from Gulf Stream to Gum. We learn that Gulfweed is the popular name for the brown seaweed observed by Columbus. We read of Sir William Withey Gull (1816-90), a clinical physician who believed in never giving his patients false hope, and the first to describe (in 1873) the disease now known as myxoedema, defining it as a "cretinoid state in adults." We discover the Larinae, Sterninae and Rhynchops grouping of Gulls, and read how, in 1878 Howard Saunders, of the Zoological Society of London, counted forty-nine species. And we encounter the remarkable John Gully (1783–1863), for five years the unlikely MP for Pontefract, Yorkshire. Why was he unlikely? Because he was first a sportsman, and for many years it seemed possible that he might never leave his varied fields of play alive:

> He came into prominence as a boxer, and in 1805 he was matched against Henry Pearce, the "Game Chicken," before the duke of Clarence (afterwards William IV) and numerous other spectators, and after fighting sixty-four rounds, which occupied an hour and seventeen minutes, was beaten. In 1807 he twice fought Bob Gregson, the Lancashire giant, for two hundred guineas a side, winning on both occasions. As the landlord of the Plough Tavern in Carey Street, London, he retired from the ring in 1808, and took to horse-racing. In 1827 he lost £40,000 by backing his horse Mameluke (for which he had paid four thousand guineas) for the St Leger. In partnership with Robert Ridskale, in 1832, he made £85,000 by winning the Derby and St Leger with St Giles and Margrave. In partnership with John Day he won the Two Thousand Guineas with Ugly Buck in 1844, and two years later he took the Derby and the Oaks with Pyrrhus the First and Mendicant, in 1854 the Two Thousand Guineas with Hermit, and in the same year, in partnership with Henry Padwick, the Derby with Andover. Gully was twice married and had twelve children by each wife. He appears to have been no relation of the subsequent Speaker, Lord Selby.

Sixty-four rounds; the Game Chicken; twenty-four children in all; *appears* to have been no relation. We not only forgive but celebrate the idiosyncrasies; these entries were far from algorithmic in their construction. The eleventh edition contained more biographies than any previous *Britannica*, many vivid with human foible and eccentricity. Hans Koning was both delighted and alarmed by the number of bizarre Germans included, not least princelings and captains of long-forgotten military campaigns, and the "amazing number of times" little towns popped up with names like Ingolstadt. No subject was too insignificant. Friedrich Rudolf Ludwig, for example, had a book of poems published posthumously in 1700, which were "for the most part dry and stilted imitations of French and Latin models," but not so dry or stilted that they were considered unworthy of mention. And inclusion began young: Christian Heinrich Heinecken was a talented student of history, and spoke Latin and French, and all by the age of three (alas he died at the age of four in 1725).

Of course there were weaknesses. There was a blindness towards issues we may now consider important (Freud and psychoanalysis), and a squeamishness around sex (which ensured there was no entry on Sex). Conversely, there was plenty of sober coverage of topics we would now regard as dubious (poltergeists and other paranormal activity, phrenology). We may attempt to pardon both omissions and errors with the catch-all explanation we use so often these days: those were different times, with different values and codes; ignorant historical errors of judgment will always be easy prey for those who come later.

In his introduction, the editor Hugh Chisholm carefully embraced the concept of controversy, something encyclopedists had previously been reluctant to do (despite their revolutionary leanings, Diderot and D'Alembert were careful not to specifically endorse contentious entries for fear of imprisonment; inclusion was endorsement enough). Chisholm welcomed debate, for "impartiality does not consist in concealing criticism, or in withholding the knowledge of divergent opinion, but in an attitude of scientific respect."*

But then we must face the entry entitled Negro. This is more than problematic; a prejudice so extreme that it can neither be explained nor forgiven, and yet remains visible, cold and hard, on library shelves (in my own beloved London Library indeed, not 10 yards from where I'm writing this, on an upper shelf, a shadow waiting to fall). It would be difficult to imagine assumptions more offensive. The entry will most likely leave you breathless, for it is history as written, and in 1911 it was believed to be both true and wise. It was written by Thomas Athol Joyce, the chief ethnographer at the British Museum.

Negro: (from Lat. niger, black), in anthropology, the designation of the distinctly dark-skinned, as opposed to the fair, yellow, and brown variations of mankind . . . The colour of the skin, which is also distinguished by a velvety surface and a characteristic odour, is due not to the presence of any special pigment, but to the greater abundance of the colouring matter in the Malpighian mucous membrane between the inner or true skin and the epidermis or scarf skin. This colouring matter is not distributed equally over the body, and does not

* In his memoir *Another Part of the Wood* (1975), Kenneth Clark wrote of how, in the eleventh edition, "One leaps from one subject to another, fascinated as much by the play of mind and the idiosyncrasies of their authors as by the facts and dates. It must be the last encyclopedia in the tradition of Diderot which assumes that information can be made memorable only when it is slightly coloured by prejudice." His use of the word "slightly" may now be considered understatement.

reach its fullest development until some weeks after birth; so that new-born babies are a reddish chocolate or copper colour. But excess of pigmentation is not confined to the skin; spots of pigment are often found in some of the internal organs, such as the liver, spleen, &c. Other characteristics appear to be a hypertrophy of the organs of excretion, a more developed venous system, and a less voluminous brain, as compared with the white races.

It was *of its time*, of course, and it serves to remind us what a time it was. It will come as little relief, or even surprise, that *Britannica* expressed similarly assured prejudices against Chinese, Afghans, Arabs and Native Americans. (Other judgments appear so naive as to be almost comical: Antisemitism, for example, was a "passing phase in the history of culture.") Some of these slurs appeared as a theoretical and political act, and chimed with the encyclopedia's entry for Civilization, which calls for the "betterment of the race through wise application of the laws of heredity."*

* Denis Boyles points out that the notoriety—i.e., blatant racism—of the Negro article has ensured that it is one of the eleventh edition's most widely read. There is no record of any conflict or objection from the encyclopedia's editors or fellow contributors at the time of sale, and any objection from readers may have been treated just like an objection to any other entry, and dismissed with the assuredness that populates the rest of the publication. (You may choose not to read on, but for factual context I've included some further representative extracts below.)

> "Mentally the negro is inferior to the white. The remark of F. Manetta, made after a long study of the negro in America, may be taken as generally true of the whole race: 'The negro children were sharp, intelligent and full of vivacity, but on approaching the adult period a gradual change set in. The intellect seemed to become clouded, animation giving place to a sort of lethargy, briskness yielding to indolence.'

> "It would be generally but not universally held, also, that the negroes in the United States progressed under slavery, that they were far better qualified for incorporation as a vital and contributing element of the country's

For many years after its launch, *Britannica*'s eleventh edition continued to be promoted as something between a knowledge circus and the latest time-saving gadget. Whereas once the *Britannica* was sold primarily on content—the caliber of its professors, the unique material between its covers—it was increasingly being marketed on price and value. "At the present price," an advertisement in the *American Magazine* proclaimed, it was "the cheapest book ever published." How so? Because it eliminated the need for a reference library of 400 to 500 books and would be "about one-seventh" of the cost. The set also eliminated sixteen "arduous" years of ordinary book buying. The entire set would be yours for $5 down, followed

---

civilization at the time of their emancipation than they were on arrival or than an equal number of their African kindred would have been. But probably the rate of progress has been more rapid under freedom than it was under slavery.

"The negroes in the United States have played and are playing an important and necessary part in the industrial and economic life of the southern states, in which in 1908 they formed about one-third of the population. But that life was changing with marvellous rapidity, becoming less simple, less agricultural and patriarchal, more manufacturing and commercial, more strenuous and complex. It was too early to say whether the negroes would be given an equal or a fair opportunity to show that they could be as serviceable or more serviceable in such a civilization as they had been in that which was passing away, and whether the race would show itself able to accept and improve such chances as were afforded, and to remain in the future under these changing circumstances, as they had been in the past, a vital and essential part of the life of the nation."

It is a particular misfortune of *Britannica*'s wide-ranging influence and authority that it may have both delayed and withheld the possibility of progress advanced in the paragraph above.

In 1970, a social studies teacher in New York called Irving Sloan published a survey of the treatment of black Americans in nine popular encyclopedias. He found considerable improvement in recent decades, including far more comprehensive and less prejudiced articles on the general history of the "Afro-American." But he also noted a paucity of individual entries on the achievements of black men, and very few for black women. See: https://files.eric.ed.gov/fulltext/ED090113.pdf.

by $5 per volume for 37 or 47 months, depending on your choice of dark-green sheepskin or dark-red full morocco (there was also a 31-month miserly cloth binding "regarded as entirely satisfactory by those who had to choose the cheapest form," and a version in "full limp velvet suede," price on application).

The Advertising entry in the eleventh edition, written by its advertising manager Henry R. Haxton, expressed a common concern: "In the French, and some English Newspapers, where an advertisement is often given the form of an item of news, the reader is distressed by the constant fear of being hoodwinked."

But in 1913, two years after it launched, Haxton wrote another advertisement celebrating his and his encyclopedia's success. Published in *The Times*, it certainly matched the product it was selling—a thicket of text explaining why this edition was superior to all its predecessors, and no feature was omitted. It was "the most successful book of our time." In the last two years, Haxton claimed, it had sold 40,000 sets, or 1,160,000 volumes, making it imperative "not to sell" the encyclopedia but merely to fulfill existing orders. But now, with only 10 percent remaining, the set was available once more! The reader had a choice of paper—either "heavy book paper," which brought each volume in at 2¾ inches, or English-made opaque Indian paper, which made the volumes only one inch thick: this innovation was "an inspiration of genius."

Inevitably, *Britannica* would make "*the* ideal Christmas present," and it was now so cheap that a clever reader would consider buying numerous sets as both an investment in knowledge and an investment in itself. "I bought two copies for the benefit of my two sets of grandchildren," Dr. C.W. Eliot, President Emeritus of Harvard, happily informed the campaign.

"I find them altogether admirable, and my grandchildren, who are at the most inquisitive ages, are of the same opinion."*

But not everyone thought highly of it. A review by Joseph Jacobs in the *New York Times* criticized the extent to which it relied on articles reprinted from earlier editions: he estimated that "not more than a fifth" of the content was absolutely new. Hugh Chisholm replied that the obverse was the case—not more than about one-fifth was retained from previous editions (he claimed that a quick survey of one volume found only 16 percent had appeared in the tenth edition). "I know it to be a fact that no previous edition has been so original in its matter, as compared with its predecessor, as that which I have had the honor of directing to its conclusion."

The most forceful and prolonged battering came from the critic and poet Willard Huntington Wright, who also wrote detective novels under the name S.S. Van Dine. Wright/Van Dine's entry in Britannica.com lists many of his titles, including his philosophy primer *What Nietzsche Taught* (1915) and *The Kennel Murder Case* (1933)—but there is one significant omission: *Misinforming a Nation* (1917). This was a 220-page assessment of how America had fallen fatally under the spell of the "assumed cultural superiority" of England, noting how everything English was consistently overvalued and overpraised on American shores. Wright's assault was fueled by what he saw as English contempt for Catholicism, coupled with an intellectual prejudice he perceived against all aspects of American beliefs and aesthetics. The majority of his ammunition was employed specifically against *Britannica*'s

* Dr. Eliot knew a good length of books when he saw one. He was the editor of the fifty-book set of *Harvard Classics*, known as "the five-foot shelf of books."

eleventh edition, "this distorted, insular, incomplete, and suggestively British reference work." Its framework was narrow and parochial, and he could find "no more vicious and dangerous intellectual influence" on young American minds; if accepted as in any way authoritative it would "retard our intellectual development fully twenty years." Wright barely drew breath. He also found that, far from being "universal," the encyclopedia was rather the home of "second- and third-rate Englishmen . . . given space and praise much greater than that accorded truly great men of other nations . . . The vocabulary of hyperbole has been practically exhausted in setting forth the dubious merits of this reference work . . . the ethics and decencies of ordinary honest commerce have been thrown to the wind."*

His complaints appear not to have affected sales. The eleventh edition was an extraordinary global success. It sold about 1 million sets, more than every previous edition combined. It won a famous army of fans, not least Ernest Shackleton, who took the entire edition on his two-year

* Willard Huntington Wright, *Misinforming a Nation* (New York, B.W. Huebsch, 1917). Wright was most likely reviewing one of the many American editions of the eleventh *Britannica* adapted for sale through many regional newspapers and department store catalogues. These would have included additional material pertaining to the United States, written by American specialists. It was telling that when *Britannica* was considered by one of its staff many decades later it was judged *too* American and certainly prejudiced against Britain. In 1988 the genealogist Charles Mosley, who worked for *Britannica* for several years, first as a subeditor and then as its London editor, wrote in the *Guardian* how the pro-American bias "amounts to more than impertinence." "The full horror of what an American editorial monopoly entails is seldom appreciated. The American editors who write short in-house articles are ignorant and parochial . . . The *Encyclopaedia Britannica* is a publication so contemptuous of Britain, the land of its birth, that it cannot be bothered to ascertain correct usage when speaking of The Thames." Mosley questioned its priorities when it came to biographical selections: he balked at the inclusion of globetrotting television journalist Alan Whicker, and mourned the lack of the Conservative cabinet ministers Lords Carrington or Whitelaw.

voyage aboard *Endurance,* and would report how it saved him and his crew, socially and psychologically, as they battled the Antarctic ice. They believed they were carrying the sum of human civilization along with them, a talisman in which they would themselves soon feature as heroes.

The eleventh edition was to be the last of its kind, the last to be so sure of itself, the last before the war. Many of its contributors died between 1914 and 1918, and with them died the superiority, the callousness and the downright brilliant know-it-all assertiveness of *Britannica*'s imperial tone. As Hans Koning concludes, one is "almost tempted to envy the writers . . . their doubtlessness" in this unthreatened world. The key word here is "almost." One re-examines the entry that observed how the Negro had "dark tightly curled hair . . . of the 'wooly' or the 'frizzly' type," or the lines that claim Haitians are "ignorant and lazy," "the Chinese character is inferior to the European," and the Afghan is "cruel and crafty"—and one begins to understand how the next generation of *Britannica* readers (those children who were once told they would be intellectually undernourished if they didn't consume its pages) might form their worldview.

LITTLE WOMEN

In 1926, Janet Courtney published a memoir called *Recollected in Tranquillity,* a title suggesting her career had hitherto been hectic. She had worked as a secretary at the Royal Commission on Labour, and as a clerk at the Bank of England, but her most interesting years occurred at the High Holborn offices of *Britannica.* She was a lynchpin of administration, a role that entailed discretion, sublimation and being underappreciated on a daily basis.

But in December 1910, at the launch of the eleventh edition, when she was still known as Janet Hogarth, she had a rare evening in the limelight, albeit in a tokenistic way, when she was called upon to give a speech at a banquet celebrating the role of women at the encyclopedia. The banquet was at the Savoy, the last in a sequence of four; the first three had been men only.

Hogarth adored her job and most of her colleagues. "There never was an office so gay, so self-confident, so crowded, so uncomfortable, yet so irresistible in its attraction." She was proud of her own entries in the new edition, most of them small and all of them unsigned, and prouder still of her achievements as chief indexer, a highly complicated assignment covering and cross-referencing 30,000 pages in less than a year, a half-million separate entries, a volume in itself.

She was introduced at the dinner by the editor Hugh Chisholm, who praised the number of women who had "lent their assistance" to bring the eleventh edition to publication. The number of contributors was still small compared to men, "but in the sections relating to social and purely feminine affairs their contributions were of the first importance."*

Rising to her feet after the meal, holding a cigarette, Hogarth observed how the lighting in the ballroom had been softened "to make us look our best." She said that the cleverest answer to the question "What are women put into this world for?"

* It was not immediately clear what these "purely feminine affairs" consisted of, but an American advertisement for the eleventh edition sold by Sears, Roebuck & Co. provides a clue. Beneath the subheading "The Britannica in Women's Affairs" we read that the encyclopedia "gives to the woman fundamental information on politics, on economics, child welfare, domestic science, on foods and their relative values, on hygiene, sanitation, home decorations, furniture, rugs and furnishings."

was "To keep the men's head straight." And she agreed that although the number of women was still small, at the launch of the ninth edition thirty-five years before "if anyone had suggested to the then editors and proprietors that women's share in the work should be not only acknowledged but proclaimed upon the housetops, the suggestion would have been regarded as absolutely revolutionary, if not positively indecent." But now, as the *Daily Telegraph* reported a few days after Hogarth's speech, *Britannica* had "given them the chance to demonstrate in this way their rightful place in the learned world."*

Up to a point. It was true that *Britannica* had always been a male preserve. Indeed, this had barely changed for more than a century since the first edition of 1768 (the one that had succinctly informed readers who chanced upon the entry Woman that they were the female equivalent of Man and should "See Homo"). But even now the improvement was marginal. In the tenth edition, compiled by almost 1800 contributors, only 37 had been women. In the eleventh, the figure was actually smaller at 35 women, although the total was also smaller at about 1500. A woman's "rightful place in the learned world" amounted to less than 2.5 percent. As the historian Gillian Thomas points out in her biographical study of those 35 women, *A Position to Command Respect*, far from being "proclaimed upon the housetops," as Hogarth claimed,

* Hogarth changed her name to Courtney upon marriage in 1911, after which she found her work increasingly stressful. She served as assistant editor on *Britannica*'s twelfth edition after the war, but regretted not being able to devote more hours to the work. "Men really need not be so frightened," she wrote in 1926. "They will never find the labour market flooded with married women. It is not an easy matter to combine professional work with matrimony. No doubt there is greater security, but there is also the added strain of another person to consider."

"the vast amount of women's work on the eleventh *Britannica* was invisible and unacknowledged."*

Gillian Thomas attempts to rectify this by recognizing the many women who acted as "literary devils" on *Britannica*—a term encompassing ghostwriting, researching long articles that would be credited to men, and writing small articles that usually went uncredited. These included Agnes Muriel Clay, a tutor in classics at Oxford; Agnes Mary Clerke, a classical scholar at Trinity College, Dublin, and the author of four books on astronomy; Pearl Craigie, classical scholar at University College, London, a popular novelist and playwright; Agnes Mary Duclaux, poet and literary critic, whose contributions to the *Times Literary Supplement* introduced English readers to Proust; Alice B. Gomme, a founder of the Folklore Society; Margaret, Lady Huggins, a leader in spectrography and honorary member of the Royal Astronomical Society; Flora, Lady Lugard, "Colonial Editor" of *The Times*; and Alice Meynell, poet and essayist.

The women shared differing and unpredictable political views. One, Lady Emilia Dilke, was a committed trades unionist, while Agnes Clay was involved in the Association for the Education of Women. Others, including Pearl Craigie, Mary Ward and Janet Hogarth, were supportive of the Anti-Suffrage Movement, arguing that women should stay above the fray of demeaning politics, fearing that a woman's influence in the home and education of children would be adversely affected.

---

* *A Position to Command Respect* by Gillian Thomas (Scarecrow Press Inc., Metuchen, New Jersey and London, 1992). In her introduction, Thomas recalls her father frequently referring to the eleventh edition to settle arguments, the green volumes behind a glass-fronted bookcase. Though her father, like the volumes, was regarded as rather old-fashioned, *Britannica* "still seemed an oddly comforting piece of cultural furniture"; he had bought the set on an installment plan "as a young man intent on self-improvement."

But not all their contributions were anonymous. The more unusual their specialisms, the more they received personal acknowledgment. Alice Gomme wrote on Children's Games; Mary Ward wrote on Spain; Jessie Weston on Arthurian Legends; Flora Shaw tackled the British Empire; Victoria, Lady Welby explained Significs, a precursor to the study of semiotics. It was primarily in areas of the traditional university syllabus that their work was ignored, not least in the fields of classics, mathematics and science.

The content of the eleventh *Britannica* was, predictably, also very male-dominated. There was no entry for Marie Curie, for example, despite the extensive coverage given to radioactivity elsewhere; her work, and her Nobel Prize for Physics, was covered only briefly in the entry about her husband Pierre Curie. Elsewhere, historical events seemed to have been placed in what Thomas calls "a hall of distorting mirrors." The story of Mme. Roland, a popular hero of the French Revolution, appears only within a biographical entry for her husband Jean Marie Roland. While she occupies almost three-quarters of the text, "the heading and the story's frame implies that the reader's attention ought to be devoted to her husband, even though the article itself can find little to say about him."

The strangest entry was the one entitled Women. This is signed simply *X*, the only lengthy article in the whole edition with this credit, and it is thought to have been written by the editor Chisholm himself. It runs to seven pages (compared to ten on the subsequent Woodcarving), and betrays signs of wrangling. Much of the article is devoted to the legal standing of women in a historical and matrimonial context, and the issue of education, where it manages to be both chivalrous and patronizing, describing the "temperate, calm, earnest demeanour of women" as a credit to school and university teaching, something that has "awakened admiration and respect from all." Women are said to have "invaded" other professions, including journalism, law-copying, plan-tracing and factory inspection, where nonetheless they are found to be "hard-working, persevering and capable" and quite able to "hold their ground"; a woman may also succeed as a queen and regent. The other main topic concerns women's suffrage, something *Britannica* appears to be largely against. The word "suffrage" and the subject of "the vote" seem initially so unpalatable that their appearance is replaced by "the movement for the abolition of the sex distinction in respect of the right conferred upon certain citizens to share in the election of parliamentary representatives."*

L

There was another reason why the entry entitled Women was subject to wrangling: an error in carpentry. The bookcases for the eleventh edition had been ordered and built a year before the completion of the set, and when it was clear the edition would run to one more volume than originally planned, Hugh Chisholm faced a dilemma. According to Gillian Thomas, he issued instructions to keep entries beginning *W-Z* down to a minimum. But Janet Hogarth, the contributor and chief indexer, recalled how Chisholm once tried to justify cutting the entry on Women in its entirety.

> I vividly remember a winter afternoon when he called me "into counsel" as he called it, in the editorial sanctum,

---

* In the 1950s, Herman Kogan wrote that *Britannica*'s Walter Yust, the editor of the fourteenth edition, was apparently surprised when informed by the historian Mary Ritter Beard how few were the biographies of women compared to men. Of roughly 13,000, fewer than 800 described the lives of women. Yust asked Beard for a list of omissions, and she obliged. Subsequent progress was slow.

> which . . . meant that whilst I sat meekly by the fire, he walked up and down, expounding to me that the then position of women as an integral part of the human race made it unnecessary to write about them as though they were a race apart! I cordially but respectfully agreed, and we decided that only a few columns, chronicling the suffrage movement and certain educational advances need be inserted.

More than any other publication, the storage of encyclopedias has always been an issue. But storage can also be an affectation, and from the time in 1860 when the eighth edition offered a £3 revolving mahogany bookcase to house its twenty-one volumes, spinning furniture became as much a status symbol as the books it was holding.

By the time of the eleventh edition, it had become an important selling point for the set, with three different designs. The first was a mahogany single-tier open case topped by a narrow "consulting table," while the other two came in "Jacobean Oak" with glass fronts, one of sturdy and compact design with the volumes placed vertically in three rows, the other of a more precarious build resembling a grandfather clock, with all the books stacked horizontally flat on top of each other. They were all "free," the way a mobile phone may now come free with a thirty-six-month contract, and only available "while stocks last," which almost certainly meant "while demand lasts."

By 1930, the bookcases had become a dominant feature in the advertisements. "Presented Free with each set is a beautiful bookcase-table, made of solid brown mahogany," proclaimed one, with everything in the accompanying photograph just as solid: a dad smoking his pipe in a chair by the edge of the bookcase, his wife on the edge of the chair consulting the *Britannica*, the long bookcase center stage with a lamp and vase on it, and behind the bookcase two very engaged children, a boy and a girl, each busting their buttons to get their hands on their mother's volume.

A few years later, a family in Port Washington, New York, posed on two sofas with the *Americana* in a bookcase between them. "*The Americana* made a real improvement in the homework of our fifteen-year-old daughter Kathleen in just a few months," reported Mrs. Raymond Saunders. "When people ask us if we use *The Americana* much, we just point to the bookcase, for at least one volume is always out of place and being used by one of the children." And Mrs. Howard W. Colburn of Goodwater, Alaska, concurred. "My oldest boy even learned how to work his algebra problems from the article on algebra."

M

METHOD

We do not have the guidance notes given to contributors for the Eleventh Edition of *Britannica*, but we do have them for the next major set, published eighteen years later in 1929.* It's a revealing document, part style sheet, part commissioning form, part sincere editorial cheerleading. And as a statement of intent it provides a rare insight into encyclopedic purpose early in the twentieth century.

Produced at *Britannica*'s London headquarters in High Holborn in the spring of 1927, it began by justifying why a new "epoch-making" edition was necessary. "It is planned to perform a service for the average intelligent man or woman that has never been done before. It has been attempted only in part, and then inadequately and intermittently."

The proposed service was the continuation of a familiar

* This was the fourteenth edition, the first complete overhaul since the First World War. The twelfth and thirteenth editions consisted of supplements to the eleventh.

policy: the further broadening of accessibility, the further diminution of the ivory tower. The editorial policy was "a result of careful study . . . extending over a period of more than a year," the twelve-page leaflet began.

> The last few generations, and more particularly the last half century, have seen an increase in knowledge beyond all precedent. While the man of to-day does know more than his forebears of one or two centuries ago, he is relatively much more ignorant. The reason is simple. There has been no organised attempt to present the results of modern research in a form that would be comprehensible to him. This is an age of specialisation, and with a few exceptions specialists have been content to write for other specialists rather than inform the public. Consequently a vast section of what is known to-day remains a sealed book to the average person. This situation is one that has caused lively concern to many students of our contemporary life. It is a situation which the new edition of the *Britannica* will be designed to meet.*

To bridge the gap between the average reader and modern knowledge, the editors drew up a fifteen-point plan. In summary:

1. Write every article so that it can be understood "by anyone of average intelligence and education." The editors acknowledged that such a task may present "a severe limitation" on the text,

---

* This was the perennial battle. Intriguingly, *Britannica* had first acknowledged the difficulty in the preface to its first edition in 1768, announcing that "any man of ordinary parts, may, if he chuses, learn the principles of Agriculture, of Astronomy, of Botany, of Chemistry, *&c.*" Comparing its contents to previous encyclopedias and dictionaries, its editor noted his competitors' "folly of attempting to communicate science under the various technical terms."

and that many subjects will be difficult to treat in simple language. "That problem is one which the contributor must face . . . there are books even on relativity which present that difficult subject so that an intelligent man can grasp it."*

2. Be interesting, be lively, be picturesque. "Do not antagonise, do not repel the reader by a dull, forbidding style."
3. Write for "a leisured audience" and help the reader in the pursuit of their business or hobby. Seek to answer most of the common questions that arise in everyday living: the new readership will include many who are interested in "such ordinary practical details as how to repair a Ford or paint a house."
4. The new edition will be designed to grip the attention of the reader and hold it, no matter where he should open a volume. Illustrations will therefore be of the utmost importance, "second only to the text." Stand by for a further communication as to how you may assist the art department.
5. Articles should not be local but international, and should appeal to readers of English everywhere in the world. "The English author writing on, say, Wages, Trade Unions, Armies, Ships, should not confine himself to facts relating

* Recipients of this style sheet were referred to *The Humanizing of Knowledge* by James Harvey Robinson (George H. Dorian Co., 1924). One key passage: "Scientifically and philosophically trained writers apparently have no idea how *hard* their books and articles are for the general reader: how much is included that few can appreciate; how many statements are dark and unintelligible to those for whom the book is ostensibly designed." Robinson's work must have had a stinging impact in the *Britannica* offices, not least because the author was a contributor himself ("Civilisation"), and because it quoted select passages from the twelfth edition (essentially the eleventh with supplements). As with the contributions of Lord Rayleigh (see end of *K* above), the subject of light proved particularly problematic. "A stream of light coming directly from a natural source has no relation to space except that concerned in its direction of propagation, round which its properties are alike on all sides." *The Humanizing of Knowledge* concluded, "Like the lovers in Dante's Commedia, the simple inquirer is likely to read no farther that day."

to Great Britain, but should include also the United States, Germany, and such other countries that may be of importance in connection with the subject."

6. Any words or quotations in a foreign language should be translated.
7. Any important article should include not only a bibliography, but also an indication of whether the book in question is for the expert or popular in nature.
8. Don't exceed your commissioned length. It is the maximum, and it will greatly aid the editor if your entry is precisely that amount. "Otherwise, the editors will have to condense, a proceeding naturally not pleasing to the contributors, or return to the authors themselves for condensation."
9. Send in your entry promptly.
10. Do not use the ambiguous and excluding words "we," "us," "our" etc.

11. When writing at length, provide cross headings, subheadings and side headings. For example "a long article, such as France, Electricity, Philosophy, should be divided into its important divisions, eras, or what not" (for example: The French Revolution; The Rise of Napoleon; The Battle of Marengo). To make life easier for editor and reader alike, cross headings should occur every three to ten thousand words, followed by sub-headings at one to three thousand words, and then side headings of three to seven hundred words. Triple wavy lines, double wavy lines, and single wavy lines should distinguish between them.
12. If you must use technical terms, explain them to the non-technical.
13. Always give a person's name in full when used for the first time.
14. Send in your entry typewritten with a carbon copy. One

will go to the printer, while the other will immediately be placed in safe custody.

15. When you send in your article, also send in a *brief* summary of your degrees and other qualifications for inclusion in the contributors panel at the front.

Britannica's contributors were coordinated by more than fifty associate editors in London and New York, and they had assembled quite a line-up:

Cecil B. DeMille (Motion Pictures), Lillian Gish (also Motion Pictures), G.K. Chesterton (Charles Dickens), J.B. Priestley (English Literature), T.E. Lawrence (Guerrilla Warfare), John J. Pershing (the Meuse-Argonne Operation), Ralph Vaughan Williams (Folk Song), Gene Tunney (Boxing), Harold Laski (Bolshevism), Konstantin Stanislavsky (Theatre Directing and Acting), Alfred P. Sloan Jr. (General Motors), Helen Wills (Lawn Tennis), J.B.S. Haldane (Heredity), Erté (Modern Dress) and Orville Wright (Wilbur Wright). And several hundred professors from leading universities.*

* A few months after this book appeared in hardback, I received an email from Ray Ward, an enthusiast of both reference books and quizzes (in 2012 he won BBC Radio 4's prestigious *Brain of Britain* contest). He pointed out that *Britannica*'s claim to have so many famous experts as contributors may be rather fanciful. Several of those listed would be unlikely to write a balanced article, not least J. Edgar Hoover on the FBI. "More importantly," he asks, "did they actually write them?" Looking at the small print, he found that many of the celebrities were merely "associated" with the entries, which could mean almost anything. "I looked up Mount Everest and found the only initials appended to it were T.N. (Tenzing Norgay). . . . The entry was replete with geographical, geological, geomorphological, meteorological, climatic, etc., information, and the problem with attributing such material to Tenzing is that he was illiterate. He could sign his name, but that was about it. (The books published in his name were ghostwritten.) He perhaps contributed some information, but cannot possibly have been responsible for the whole entry." There were almost certainly other examples of the "expert" being paid for the use of their name and access to their work rather than writing the entry themselves.

Each of these figures was paid the same as less famous contributors: two cents per word, a fee that remained unchanged from 1926 to 1973. In 1926 George Bernard Shaw received $68.50 for his article on Socialism, while Albert Einstein received $86.40 for his piece on Space-Time. (Beyond the famous contributors, a great many of the important new articles were in the scientific fields, including the latest thinking about Vitamins, Carbohydrates, Muscular Exercise, Insulin, X-Rays and Stellar Evolution.)

Before they submitted their entries, the contributors received one last pep talk. Their commissioners vowed not to lessen "by one hair's breadth" the accuracy or authority of their submissions, nor the elevated scholarly position that *Britannica* enjoyed. But "may the editors once more emphasise the great importance of writing all articles in a style so interesting that the average reader who begins them will read to the end."

Britannica, after all, was for many families the only important educational book to be found in their homes: "Its influence in the diffusion of information is and has been profound," and there was a duty to honor that trust. The aim was definitive: the contributors would write "the most useful, the most instructive and the most enlightening work that has ever been produced."

The resulting twenty-four-volume fourteenth edition appeared two years later in 1929, and it would remain in print (with minor updates and new printings) for forty-five years. One didn't have to be as astute as its writers to surmise that the widening of the encyclopedia's appeal was driven by an equally expansive quest for an increase in sales. And something else too: an overdue attempt to improve the perception of the encyclopedia in the popular imagination.

N

NOVELTIES

This was no small task. The encyclopedia had an image problem, the weight of the object presaging both the density of its contents and the burdens of its makers. The industry didn't invite much clowning around, in other words. And it didn't help that the popular novel chose to focus on the arduous nature of its construction.

In the main, fictional encyclopedias are objects of duty, both to write and to purchase. Most often they are drudgery personified, cumbersome as furniture. Dickens set the tone, and Arthur Conan Doyle followed, and by the time Vonnegut and Borges got their hands on a set, the encyclopedia had become an absurd folly, a monument to human futility.

Imaginative fiction presented the antithesis of the multi-volume reference book, and it was no wonder that it took until 1910 for *Britannica* to define what a novel should look like, and how it got its name. The word derives from the Latin *novus*, meaning new. It is "the name given in literature to a study of manners, founded on an observation of contemporary or recent life, in which the characters, the incidents and the intrigue are imaginary, and therefore 'new' to the reader." Such a thing was "founded on lines running parallel with those of actual history."

The entry classifies the novel as "a modern form of literature," a sustained story which is not historically true "but might very easily be so." It has been made the vehicle for "satire, for instruction, for political or religious exhortation, for technical information," but these were side issues, for the main purpose of the novel is to entertain "by a succession of scenes painted from nature, and by a thread of emotional narrative."

The article was written by the poet, biographer and critic Edmund Gosse, a leading reviewer for the *Sunday Times*, a champion of neglected poetry and librarian to the House of Lords. He identifies key literary trends in France, Spain, Germany and Russia (where, since Gogol set the pace in the 1830s, the novel has been one of "resignation and pity, but wholly divorced from sentimentality"). The novels of China, by contrast, are predominantly moralizing and virtuous in intent, not least the sixteenth- (or possibly seventeenth-) century work *The Twice-Flowering Plum Trees*. Nearer to home, Gosse reliably singles out Congreve, Fielding, Richardson and Sterne as central to the early structure of the English form. His tastes run to the traditional, and he is scathing of the popular ambitions of most authors. The novel's presence in literary life only became "absolutely predominant" in the nineteenth century, after which, he writes, everyone seemed to have a go, able or not:

> The novel requires, for those who are content to be only fairly proficient in it, less intellectual apparatus than any other species of writing. This does not militate against the fact that the greatest novelists, always a small class, produce work which is

> as admirable in its art as the finest poetry. But the novel adapts itself to so large a range of readers, and covers so vast a ground in the imitation of life, that it is the unique branch of literature which may be cultivated without any real distinction or skill, and yet for the moment may exercise a powerful purpose.

Sixty years later, in 1974, *Britannica*'s appreciation of the novel was written by Anthony Burgess. Ranging over many forms of fiction, serious and less so, his approach is predictably more welcoming towards the modern and the experimental. But his own idiosyncrasies are no less apparent: he reasons that "it may or may not be accidental that the novels most highly regarded by the world are of considerable length," citing *Don Quixote, War and Peace* and *David Copperfield*. And his own work is seldom far from his mind. Among the novels Burgess selects for special mention in the category of Fantasy and Prophecy are Orwell's *Nineteen Eighty-Four* and *A Clockwork Orange* by Anthony Burgess, while the books he chooses for his discussion of the upending of classical myth are Joyce's *Ulysses* and *A Vision of Battlements* by Anthony Burgess.

His entry ran to a novella-ish 22,000 words and displayed great care for structure—passages on Plot were followed by Character, Setting, Narrative Method and Point of View. He found no distinction between "plot" and "story," as both propel the novel "through its hundred or thousand pages." A plot may be a very simple device, "a mere nucleus, a jotting on an old envelope," and he offers three examples. Charles Dickens's *A Christmas Carol* might have been conceived as "a misanthrope is reformed through certain magical visitations on Christmas Eve"; Jane Austen's *Pride and Prejudice* could be plotted as "a young couple destined to be married have first to overcome the barriers of pride and prejudice"; Dostoyevsky's *Crime and*

Punishment was “a young man commits a crime and is slowly pursued in the direction of his punishment.”

In 1974, when his entry was published, the reader may have detected a note of frustration in Burgess’s claim that the novelist “is always faced with the problem of whether it is more important to represent the formlessness of real life (in which there are no beginnings and no ends and very few simple motives for action) or to construct an artefact as well balanced and economical as a table or chair.” Burgess concludes that “since he is an artist, the claims of art, or artifice, frequently prevail.” He reasoned that the novelist is required to show much ingenuity. “The dramatist may take his plot ready-made from fiction or biography—a form of theft sanctioned by Shakespeare—but the novelist has to produce what look like novelties.”

The fictional encyclopedia has never been a mouthwatering proposition. In *David Copperfield,* the amenable but plodding clerk Tommy Traddles dreams of the legal profession but is struggling for funds. When David calls on him at home in Camden Town (they are old school friends), Traddles is working for a man “getting up an Encyclopaedia; he describes himself as a “compiler,” but it is clear he is a mere copyist. The work is perfect for him, he reasons, for he has “no invention at all; not a particle.” He supposed “there never was a young man with less originality than I have.”

About forty years later, in *The Red-Headed League,* Sherlock Holmes encounters Jabez Wilson, a pawnbroker described by Watson as “obese, pompous and slow.” He too is earning money by copying, on this occasion Abbots, Archery and Architecture from *Britannica,* but before beginning on the *B*’s he uncovers the true reason for his dreary and diversionary employment: his paymasters are not publishers but bank robbers, digging a tunnel that ends up at his pawn shop.

In the short story "Where I Live," from 1964, Kurt Vonnegut shifts the focus to commerce. His narrator describes a salesman trying to sell the latest *Britannica* to a baffled librarian in a run-down place on Cape Cod's north shore called Barnstable Village. The library has an edition from 1938, "backstopped" by a 1910 *Americana*, and the salesman observes that rather a lot has happened since those volumes appeared, including penicillin and a world war, and the town's children would surely fall behind without his updates. But the librarian can't make these purchasing decisions without consulting his trustees, and they are nowhere to be found. So the salesman wanders around, describing what he sees in the village, not all of it charmless, and then, one supposes, leaves the area in pursuit of better leads. At the end of the story the reader learns that the library has indeed provided shelf space to the new *Britannica*, and a new *Americana* too, both of which mention the Iron Curtain. "But so far, the school marks of the children and the conversation of the adults have not conspicuously improved."

In 1975, the Argentine writer Jorge Luis Borges introduced another salesman, this one selling Bibles. He knocks on the door of the narrator, but the narrator already has a lot of Bibles, including rare ones (both salesman and narrator are unnamed). The salesman says he also has one other book, something special, the *Book of Sand*. It is special because it's always producing more pages, and has unpredictable pagination (page 40,514 is followed by 999). The little primitive illustrations are equally mysterious, appearing and vanishing at whim.*

* Professor Richard Yeo has observed that real encyclopedias were very much a part of Borges's life. In an autobiographical essay, the author remembers the steel engravings in his father's *Britannica*, and how, after winning a literary prize in 1929, he bought his own second-hand copy of the eleventh edition (*Book History*, 2007, vol. 10, Johns Hopkins University Press).

The salesman reveals he is a Presbyterian Scot from the Orkneys, which may or may not be relevant (though it does throw up a link with *Britannica*'s first editor, William Smellie). A deal is arranged, the salesman departs, and the book becomes an immediate burden to its new owner, this "obscene thing that affronted and tainted reality itself." He decides to lose it in the vast Argentine National Library, a leaf in a forest, to be found only by chance.

This was the terror of the never-ending encyclopedia, and its resting place brought to mind another of Borges's stories, "The Library of Babel" from 1941, in which the library was itself a universe, a byzantine series of hexagonal chambers containing every book ever written on every subject in every language. The library is finite but the books are infinite, and most are gibberish, and it is the hapless librarian's and reader's task to locate and interpret those that aren't. Somewhere there may even be a librarian who understands the system in which these books are categorized, and somewhere in this labyrinth there may be one book with an index to all the others.

Borges's parable presented a desperate acknowledgment of the overwhelming inexactitude of words and knowledge, and the futility of trying to contain either. But within it lay an element of hope: somewhere there was that mythical person who could understand and explain it all, that figure on the mountaintop. It has always been the encyclopedia salesman's mantra that this person could be you.

Unless your name is Clarence Wilmot, the troubled figure at the beginning of John Updike's *In the Beauty of the Lilies.* Wilmot is a church minister in Paterson, New Jersey, who loses his faith. To feed his family he answers an advertisement in the local newspaper for door-to-door salesmen. It's going to be a tough job: it is 1913, and Paterson is reeling from a strike at the silk mill. Hardly anyone has any spare money for encyclopedias, and those who do don't want one.

And they especially don't want *The Popular Encyclopaedia*, a cruelly misleading title. *The Popular* costs three dollars and fifteen cents for each of its twenty-four volumes, and once you have the set, a "free" walnut-stained cabinet will also be yours, an heirloom for your children and your children's children, etc. For each volume sold, Wilmot gets a dollar, but Wilmot's three children are ever hungry. As he trudges around in the snow, he has doors slammed in his face "by frightened maids, on orders he could hear shouted within rooms curtained from view." At the few thresholds he does cross he finds he has been admitted merely to alleviate the householder's boredom. He unfurls his demo books and sample pages and reels off the stats: more than 30 million words, 25,000 entries from more than 1000 contributors, all the way from Aachen to Zwickau. Clarence Wilmot proclaimed that 85 percent of the authors were American, "in sharp contrast with an unnamed competitor, whose contributors and emphasis were preponderantly British."

Wilmot is occasionally welcomed into a home but then toyed with. On one visit his host marches him over to a study, and to the recently issued eleventh edition of *Britannica*, and although Wilmot protests that any true American would find far more to interest them in *The Popular*, and at a far better price, he is barely listened to. His mark—described by Updike as a bespectacled sallow retired accountant or clerk—tells him, "I don't envy you your task . . . trying to sell books of knowledge in a city where ignorance is up on a high horse."

Once or twice our man finds a sympathetic ear. "My English, not good," says one Polish immigrant. "Never can read. But my children, maybe. Already they speak good." Clarence tells the man, who was once employed at the mill, that his encyclopedia will ensure his children get high marks at school. But then comes the heartbreak, for both salesman and his prospect: "Not good time now, mister. Strike . . . come back when strike won . . . You a good man. I like your ideas. America the best country."

Clarence Wilmot then meets Mavis, an eager and willing buyer, but she is a friend of his family, and when she asks to examine his wares he takes pity on her. "Quite worthless really. A less expensive American imitation of a British encyclopaedia . . . An encyclopaedia, you might say, is a blasphemy—a commercially inspired attempt to play God, by creating in print a replica of Creation."

But Mavis won't let him go. She has heard encyclopedias are all the rage. They are, he agrees: they are in the air now, along with radiotelegraphy and flying machines. "Encyclopaedias began, more or less, with a Frenchman named Diderot . . . You don't want these books, Mavis."

There was one more reason Wilmot was reluctant to sell his friend *The Popular*. He believed that all the information within an encyclopedia "breaks your heart at the end, because it leaves you as alone and bewildered as you were not knowing anything."

Wilmot had a point, and Updike did too. His novel was published in 1996, by which time personal computers were in millions of homes (Apple was already twenty), and the problem of information storage and retrieval had met a viable solution. But in 1913, when Wilmot was doing his rounds, the idea of owning knowledge in a preordained manner was as daunting as it was attractive. It was necessarily a new religion, its editor a god, its contributors the clergy. One need look no further than *Britannica*'s eleventh edition to see how assured this new order was, and how it left no room for doubt or debate. We were long past that point where the Greeks aspired to compiling a "circle of knowledge" that could be memorized: faced with an encyclopedic gathering in twenty-four volumes, the reader may only acknowledge what they have *yet* to learn, how unspecialized they are, and how lacking even in general knowledge. And thus Wilmot's customers faced their inadequacies and fears, for there their volumes would sit, the hand-tooling pristine, the calfskin not yet creased, too solemn to even wink at us, the Tower of London in print, something always there, and therefore seldom accessed.*

So we approach this pass, just over midway in the alphabet: the encyclopedia as problem, as fallacy, something no longer suited to its environment. Perhaps it will rise again. But for now, there does appear to be an alternative to the multi-volume set of tightly bound knowledge.

A few years before Updike's Wilmot began plying his trade in New Jersey, two outrageously ambitious Belgians were conceiving an entirely different method of knowledge compilation and retrieval, an information system they hoped would provide access to all the world's learning in one place. The system involved a vast collection of 3×5 index cards, and, as preposterous as it may appear to us now, it once represented a daring and viable future.

---

* A publication called *The Popular Encyclopaedia* did exist, but it was a Scottish rather than American venture, a seven-volume set printed in Glasgow in 1841. And there was also the *Newnes Popular Encyclopaedia* published in London in the early 1960s in thirty-eight three-shilling parts. Neither was a model for Updike; rather, his particular *Popular* was a sort of compendium of the *World Book, Grolier, Americana* and *Compton's*.

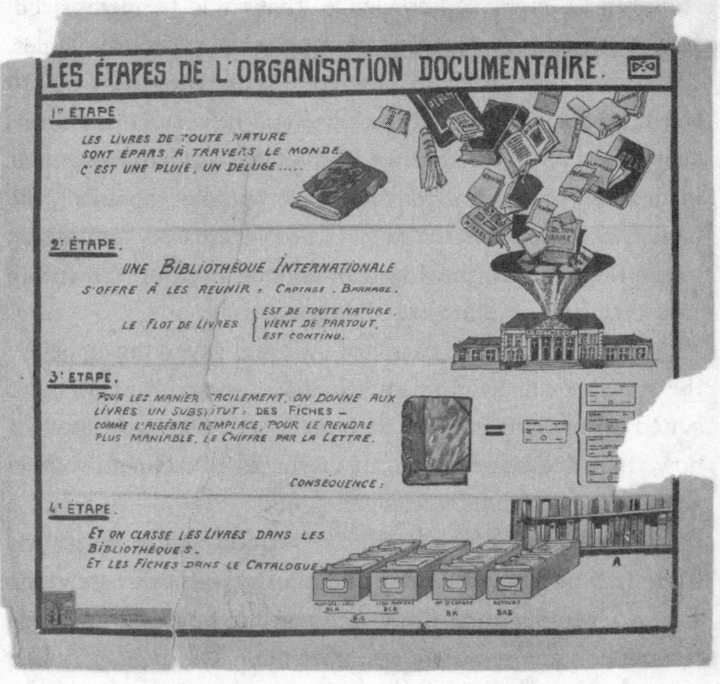

When filing was the future: four stages of classification at Paul Otlet's Mundaneum

O

OTLET, PAUL

In the pedestrianized center of the fortified city of Mons, western Belgium, lies the Mundaneum, a monument to a valiant dream. It consists of three floors of plans, photographs, a large globe, a reproduction of a "multimedia" desk known as the Mondothéque, and tall banks of wooden filing cabinets, beautiful in their worn patina and gentle disrepair—the physical remains of what its founder hoped would be "an encyclopaedic synthesis . . . embracing everything we know." Today it is a popular tourist attraction, and it was particularly popular during 2015, when Mons was the European Capital of Culture, and the curators popularized the notion that the Mundaneum was "like Google, but on paper."

One walks around in ceremonial reverence; you may feel you are performing an autopsy on a brain. The items displayed here were originally designed as both a conceptual and practical factory of knowledge compression, formed from a belief that traditional printed encyclopedias had run their course, and

that new electric communications systems should now bring the greatest knowledge to the greatest number of people, not least those who were responsible enough to act magnanimously with it. Its founders were Paul Otlet and Henri La Fontaine, two bespectacled bibliophiles with earnest demeanors and serious facial hair, Fontaine born in 1854, Otlet in 1868, each committed to the pursuit of peace and the rights of women, and both intrigued by the possibilities of creating something even the most intoxicated editor of *Britannica* would never dare envisage—a complete catalogue of the world.*

The pair met in the early 1890s while assisting on the compilation of the definitive book of Belgian jurisprudence. But like an encyclopedia, a definitive book of law would only remain so until the law changed. Otlet and La Fontaine were fascinated by what they saw as a formidable increase in the flow of information in all spheres of their lives, not least the new technological advances in production and transport, and their attendant philosophical theories about where they would lead. They saw the possibilities of global communication—the world expanding and shrinking simultaneously. And rather than being daunted by this inexorable expansion, they were excited by the potential to contain it. Summarizing his thinking in later years, Otlet spoke of the need for new instruments to comprehend humanity, "or the intellect will never know how to overcome the difficulties which overwhelm it, nor realise the progress that it glimpses and to which it aspires."

* A shy and introverted boy, Otlet began ordering things in his life from a young age; after school, while others played with hoops, he enjoyed reclassifying the books in his student library. When La Fontaine won the Nobel Peace Prize in 1913, he was acclaimed as "the effective leader of the peace movement in Europe." A losing battle, alas, and an ironically grisly one: the following year, in one of its first conflicts of the war, the British army would be forced into bloodied retreat by the Germans in—of all places—Mons.

The earliest and grandest public demonstration of this thinking was unveiled, to some scoffing, at the Paris Expo of 1900. Belgium once had an expanding and intimidating Victorian empire, not to say a grimly exploitative one, and now was the time to bring all its fragmented colonial knowledge home on a clean white card. The Expo was, after all, a good place for nationalistic boasting, and the stands that attracted the most attention were the ones with the greatest novelty. Otlet and La Fontaine certainly had that.*

They told everyone they met that even the best encyclopedias had their limitations, for they were part of an old order. They were cumbersome to update, and despite the best attempts of the smartest editors, it was almost impossible to make meaningful connections between topics or theories. But now there was a new way. La Fontaine and Otlet, accompanied by Leonie La Fontaine, Henri's sister, would attempt to incorporate the best encyclopedic principles with new communications technologies and global change. Not a minor quest, clearly—more like slaying a dragon. And it wasn't an ambition even the most far-thinking print encyclopedists would dare to entertain.

Their earliest physical manifestation of this was called Repertoire Bibliographique Universel, and today it might strike us as both quaint and overly familiar, for the original (*c.*1895)

---

* One could make the case, of course, that the Paris Expo was itself encyclopedic. As Alex Wright observes, the show was not yet the gaudy parade of corporate-sponsored glamour that such things would become. Certainly there was hoopla, and much excitement over new cinema technologies, escalators and food preservation (Campbell's soup cans made an early appearance), but this combined with a series of "august-sounding international congresses" to make it as much an academic convention as a trade fair. The novel topics for discussion would soon inform new pages in *Britannica* and *Brockhaus*: psychology, aeronautics, vegetarianism, homeopathy, alpinism and beverage-yielding fruits. See Alex Wright, *Cataloguing the World: Paul Otlet and the Birth of the Information Age* (Oxford, 2014).

resembled—in fact was—a stocky wooden filing cabinet divided into seventy-two small trays, each with a metal handle and a slot for a removable label. A visitor in a hurry might have thought they were promoting office furniture.*

To Otlet and the La Fontaines the filing cabinet more closely resembled a bank vault, each tray a safe-deposit box. For here were the connections between all the publications in the world, or at least their beginnings. The indexing was based on Melvil Dewey's American library decimal classification system of 1876, although Otlet and La Fontaine would soon come to see it as too limited for their needs.

They divided their topics in ways that would not have been unfamiliar to Ephraim Chambers compiling his *Cyclopaedia* in the 1720s. They used Dewey's ten category "schedules": 0—Generalities; 1—Philosophy and Psychology; 2—Religion and Theology; 3—Social Sciences; 4—[Vacant]; 5—Natural Sciences and Mathematics; 6—Technology; 7—The Arts; 8—Language, Linguistics and Literature; 9—Geography, Biography and History. The vacancy at 4 (achieved by combining Language and Literature) was an attempt at future-proofing, making space for an exciting new subject matter in the years to come. The new system also eliminated the Decimal from Dewey Decimal, enabling a more fluid interplay of relationships between topics: 51+53, for example, would connect mathematics and chemistry, while 63:30 would suggest statistics relating to agriculture.†

Behind this lay a system of what Alex Wright calls "brute-

* Leonie La Fontaine, a leading figure in the Belgian peace and women's rights movements, believed that the Mundaneum would advance both causes by connecting like-minded individuals throughout the world. She established the *Office central de documentation féminine* (1909), an early networking group.

† It was an early multi-disciplinary approach, but not too removed from what Coleridge attempted with his *Metropolitana*.

force indexing," a hard-hatted method of categorizing all human knowledge into four elements: facts; interpretation of facts; statistics; and sources. This sidelined creativity in favor of essential gutting. "The ideal," according to Otlet, "would be to strip each article or each chapter in a book of whatever is a matter of fine language or repetition or padding and to collect separately on cards whatever is new and adds to knowledge." Otlet is preempting the modern computer search engine. As Wright observes, "Umberto Eco's distinction between 'books to be read' and 'books to be consulted' seems relevant."

By the end of 1895, the Belgians had already amassed more than 400,000 entries in their catalogue, growing to 1.5 million at the end of 1897. By the time they presented their ideas at the Paris Expo in a series of lectures and displays, the figure stood close to 3 million, and they had received royal approval for the establishment of their Office of International Bibliography. Henri La Fontaine classified his aims as "nothing less than a question of creating a world depot, where all human ideas can be automatically stored in order to be spread afterwards among people with a minimum of effort and a maximum of effectiveness." Paul Otlet hoped to copy his card bibliography for distribution to leading libraries throughout the world, and hoped for reciprocal input as a result. Not for the first time, ambition was thwarted by the limitations of technology: rather than replicate their card system, the Belgians were obliged to reverse-compile it back into a very fat book, and then encourage recipients to cut out the strips of information on each page and stick them to cards themselves. (The book wasn't an encyclopedia; it was rather information about where information could be obtained.)

Otlet and La Fontaine were dismissed in the Belgian press as "solemn fools" wishing to turn a whole pulsating city into cards. But Otlet in particular seemed inured to ridicule, and swiftly expanded his thinking into many areas beyond the index card, all of them optimistic, some of them hubristic, others conceivably torn from the pages of *Amazing Stories* magazine. He was driven by the death of his son in the last year of the Great War, and he often declared that only by the global sharing of information could future conflict be averted. He was involved with the founding of the League of Nations, and resolved to devote his life to the formation of "a great human city, completely devoted to Peace."

We are fortunate to still have access to the vast amount of the visual demonstration material that Otlet and La Fontaine created in the course of their fifty-year passion (not to mention the index cards a visitor may peruse freely in their filing cabinets). Some of the graphic posters resemble vast and complex pyramids with tiny writing and lots of arrows, others seem to anticipate the pictorial spreads in a Dorling Kindersley book. A geopolitical atlas on boards takes its place next to a sketch of an ideal international museum, while a chart delineating the governing structure of the Union of International Associations hangs near a three-dimensional plan of the ideal "classification and presentation of didactic material." For years these items were gathered at the opulent Palais Mondial in Brussels, but when they were ignominiously displaced by a rubber trade fair in 1923, Otlet was forced to store them in a variety of unsuitable locations, including his home and the basements of buildings throughout Belgium. Only in 1998, fifty-four years after his death, did they take their permanent and honored place at the new Mundaneum in Mons.

What did the traditional encyclopedists make of all this? Not much. They certainly didn't appear to be threatened by Otlet and La Fontaine's new systems; most editors seemed too busy updating their editions. But the remnants in Mons are deeply prescient. Paul Otlet in particular was grasping towards a future of hyperlinked information retrieval. Inevitably one thinks of the Internet, although Otlet's vision was primarily tempered by a philanthropic and political liberalism. As his biographer Alex Wright concludes, his tireless endeavors are important "not just as a kind of historical curio, but because he envisioned a radically different kind of network: one driven not by corporate profit and personal vanity, but by a utopian vision of intellectual progress, social egalitarianism and even spiritual liberation."

That was the future, then. Its zenith, during the last summer before the war seemed inevitable, occurred at a gathering at the Trocadéro in Paris in August 1937. It is not unusual for today's historians of technology to look back at that five-day conference as the dawn of the Information Age, although back then it was just the plain old World Congress of Universal Documentation. Delegates from forty-five countries discussed acquisition, retrieval and storage, all the librarian's favorites, and there was a particular focus on the exciting potential of microfilm. Paul Otlet spoke again on his big subject, the potential of emergent technologies to benefit the scholarly exchange of information and, by implication, a peaceable global government—a United Nations before its time. Not everyone at the conference had such generous internationalist plans: a German delegation delivered a speech ominously titled "The Domination of Knowledge."

Other speakers included H.G. Wells, who had his own last-days-of-empire vision of how the world's knowledge might be colonized and controlled. Like Paul Otlet, the author believed that the answer lay in a universal network; knowledge alone, if properly organized and disseminated, could still save the world from itself.

Saving the world from itself: H.G. Wells consults his volumes at home in Kent

P

PANTOLOGY

Two months later, on the evening of 14 October 1937, H.G. Wells stepped ashore in New York to begin his first lecture tour of the United States. He was seventy-one. He planned seven talks in six weeks, and a few important diversions along the way, including meetings with Henry Ford in Detroit and President Roosevelt in Washington. A reporter at the dockside asked him about the possibility of war, but Wells predicted no conflict for two years, "because the nations are not quite ready."

And he had a scheme to prevent the war happening at all. Lasting peace could be achieved, and global prosperity enhanced, with a thing he called the World Encyclopaedia. It was an ambitious but attainable goal, he told his awed audiences in Boston and Chicago, "a sort of mental clearing house for the mind, a depot where knowledge and ideas are received, sorted, summarised, digested, clarified and compared." It would be nothing less than a vibrantly pulsing "World Brain." It was the epitome of pantology: a systemic view of all human knowledge.

Wells had been perfecting this idea since the First World War. But the skies had never been so dark: only now, he proclaimed, had the prospect of catastrophe turned a faintly fanciful notion into an overwhelming need.

A decade before his lecture tour, his photograph had appeared on the cover of *Time,* thick walrus moustache, self-satisfied countenance. His celebrity had begun with his science fiction novels—*The Island of Doctor Moreau, The Invisible Man, The War of the Worlds*—but in later years he had developed a reputation as a serious historian. His joint roles as public doom-monger and prophetic problem-solver had met much encouragement in the media, not least because he repeatedly railed against "the backward-looking stupidity" of the powerful.

In 1936 the *New York Times* visited him at his home overlooking Regent's Park, finding both "a divine cockney" and "the outstanding Utopian of this distracted generation." He was a workaholic with no time for theatre or opera when there were new treatises to write. Age had only strengthened him, or at least hardened him, and in the arena of cross-Atlantic public affairs he was still "too big to be ignored."

Previously Wells had forsworn the American lecture tour for reasons of inadequacy, specifically his weak voice. "The microphone is a great leveller," he announced, but it was just one of the things he regarded with a combination of wonder and terror. The aeroplane shrunk the world, but its bombs destroyed cities; the microphone was a useful boon to dictators.

"Our world is changing," he always began his lectures (the script hardly varied from city to city), "and it is changing with an ever increasing violence. An old world dies about us." The principal culprits were politicians, particularly those who had failed at Versailles and misdirected the League of Nations (they simply refused to acknowledge the extent to which scientific advance clashed with their own centuries-old values). The gap that appeared between the "futile amazement" of the Great War and the rapidly accelerating progress of the present was now a chasm, and he feared that our leaders were on the wrong and crumbling side of it.

And not only politicians, but educators too. He saw the most intelligent individuals in the world—university intellectuals, captains of industry, lawyers and doctors, conquerors of science—and observed their lack of connection with the requirements of modern society. He remarked how seldom their talents were designed to benefit the common good.

He had his solution: a world community linked by reason and enlightened thought. In one sense, he argued, such a thing already existed. "An immense and ever-increasing wealth of knowledge is scattered about the world today, a wealth of knowledge [that might] suffice to solve all the mighty difficulties of our age, but that knowledge is still dispersed, unorganised, impotent in the face of adventurous violence and mass excitement."

And so he proposed "a greater encyclopaedism . . . an intellectual authority sufficient to control and direct our collective life." He imagined "a permanent institution, untrammelled by precedent, something added to the world network of universities, linking and co-ordinating them with one another and with the general intelligence of the world." He referred to the great French achievements of Diderot and D'Alembert, and how he would use their spark to launch something vastly more elaborate.

> They served their purpose at the time, but they are not equal to our current needs. A World Encyclopaedia . . . would be in continual correspondence with every university, every research institution, every competent discussion, every

> survey, every statistical bureau in the world. It would develop a directorate and a staff of men of its own type, specialised editors and summarists. They would be very important and distinguished men in the new world. This Encyclopaedic organisation need not be concentrated now in one place; it might have the form of a network. It would centralise mentally but perhaps not physically.

His American lectures were a refined précis of an address delivered the year before at the Royal Institution in London. There he called his "oligarchy of professors" and other exceptionally competent people "a sort of modern priesthood," although religion itself would not play a part. Instead, like Plato, "they would make the philosopher king."

For the sake of argument, Wells placed himself in the role of "ordinary educated citizen."

> I will ask you to imagine how this World Encyclopaedia organisation would enter into his life and how it would affect him. From his point of view the World Encyclopaedia would be a row of volumes in his own home or in some neighbouring house or in a convenient public library or in any school or college, and in this row of volumes he would, without any great toil or difficulty, find in clear understandable language, and kept up to date, the ruling concepts of our social order, the outlines and main particulars in all fields of knowledge, an exact and reasonably detailed picture of our universe, a general history of the world . . .

After this, the student of knowledge could go deeper. The row of volumes would include a trustworthy reference to more detailed primary sources. In fields where there was controversy, "casual summaries of opinions" would be replaced by "very carefully chosen and correlated" arguments. Wells proposed that this World Encyclopaedia "would be the mental background of every intelligent man in the world."

Wells foreshadowed Orwell: "What a dreadful, dreadful world it will be when everybody thinks alike." But it wouldn't be so, he insisted, decrying a dictatorship of knowledge. That said, some uniformity of order would be required. "It may be worthwhile remarking that it really does not enhance the natural variety and beauty of life to have all the clocks in a town keeping individual times of their own, no charts of the sea, no timetables, but trains starting secretly to unspecified destinations." He prioritized a garden over a swamp.

He had an early outline of what his new venture should contain. It would begin with an account of the philosophies of the world "compared critically and searchingly." A history of languages would be interesting, followed by the origins and development of writing. Then it would be time for mathematical signs and symbols, accompanied by conceptions of time and space. After that, pure physics. After physics, chemistry and astronomy. Then the general science of life and biographies of scientists, pursued by health and medicine, "mental health as well as bodily health," followed by sport and pastimes. Greek and Roman history would now find its unexpected place, next to stories of outstanding men and women, next to education, religion and ethics. "Two huge parallel sections would give a double-barrelled treatment of economic life," the first covering production and economic organization, the second distribution and finance. Wells's leftist interest in the principles and laws of property would get a look-in here, accompanied by an economic geography and global atlas.

The final part would have a different tone, for it would deal with beauty, culture and the artistic life. In this category, "Aesthetic criticism would pursue its wild incalculable, unstandardised career, mystically distributing praise and blame" towards the cinema, radio, architecture and "the high mystery" of the novel.

It was quite a soufflé. Wells admitted there was a lot here already covered by the *Encyclopédie* and *Britannica*, but now was the time to "bring those gallant pioneer essays properly up to date." How much would such a thing cost, he asked himself. Only about half a million pounds annually, but "as much money to bring it into existence as would launch a modern battleship."

Wells thought it preposterous that one newspaper had reported that he was to write the encyclopedia himself, "all with my own little hand out of my own little head . . . at the age of 70!" Instead, he planned to write only "an infinitesimal" part. He suggested an "Encyclopaedia Society" to handle the administration. He hoped it would be written in English, but a team of translators should be on hand to make it accessible to everyone in the world. He imagined a bibliography of between ten and twenty thousand items. He hoped the vast enterprise would constitute a world monopoly with no serious competition, and thus income would be generated from its sale to repay the investment.*

* Another World Brain was conceived in Belgium in 1990, a far more conceptual notion than either Paul Otlet or H.G. Wells dared imagine, although it acknowledged the influence of both. The Principia Cybernetica, the child of Francis Heylighen, is based on the notion of evolutionary cybernetics, encompassing new networked forms of recorded knowledge, and lies outside the scope of this book. It remains an ongoing project, as does the Global Brain Institute in Brussels, and is well described by Alex Wright as an attempt to create "a grand synthesis of philosophical work . . . by breaking the entire spectrum of philosophical thought into 'nodes' in the network. These 'nodes' might include a chapter from a book, a paragraph from an essay, or even more narrowly targeted units of information." The plan, says Professor Heylighen, is

In London, Wells made it clear that while his ideas were yet to be executed, he was not "throwing casually formed ideas before you." Instead, "I am bringing you my best."

One of the earliest manifestations of his thinking, albeit not yet his best, surfaced in *The Work, Wealth and Happiness of Mankind* in 1932, in which he wrote of the need for an encyclopedia produced by a Committee of Intellectual Co-operation. A photograph in the book shows the Central Reading Room of the British Museum Library; the caption is "A Cell of the World's Brain"; the room is conspicuously deserted.

The section in the book devoted to encyclopedias is useful for the survey of volumes already in existence, an opinionated potted history not dissimilar to this one, although much more potted. Wells charges through the bases: the Great Library at Alexandria (which he calls a Museum), Aristotle, Pliny's *Natural History*. He praises Diderot and his "first encyclopedia of power," noting its cardinal importance in the intellectual movements of the time, not least the ideological content and impetus it lent the Revolution. "It released minds," he reasoned, and it set a precedent in recognizing diversity of opinion.

He is less impressed with later editions of *Britannica*. He welcomes part of it, singling out recent entries on Architecture, Pottery and Porcelain. But he wanted more of a debating arena, "on general ideas such as the idea of property, or the creative possibilities of financial or political reorganization." Wells wanted radicalization of thought, in other words, something that "would reach down to direct the ideological side of human education." Diderot's venture

to transform the Web "into an intelligent, adaptive, self-organising system of shared knowledge."

aside, this wasn't something modern encyclopedias were generally proficient at, or desired to be.*

But this is where his early ideas for the World Encyclopaedia slotted in. It would not necessarily be alphabetical, he suggested, for this would constrain its desire for continual updates. It would be philosophical and factual, discursive and organic, consistently liberal rather than predominantly reactionary.

And so it was that a few years later Wells's brief historical survey would rub up against the calamitously violent nature of the world, and germinate—or congeal, or coagulate—into his grand encyclopedic scheme on the eve of war. "You see how such an Encyclopaedic organisation could spread like a nervous network, a system of mental control about the globe, knitting all the intellectual workers of the world through a common interest and a common medium of expression into a more and more conscious co-operating unity and a growing sense of their own dignity, informing without pressure or propaganda, directing without tyranny."

It may appear, albeit fleetingly, as if Wells—like Paul Otlet before him—was planning the Internet. Or rather the ideal Internet, a force for intellectual good, guided only by the principled. He was closer, perhaps, to Wikipedia, and closer still to a child's view of the world, with a child's eternal optimism, and a masterfully naive solution to all our great dilemmas.

---

* Wells couldn't resist a dig at the airy specialists he saw as *Britannica*'s main contributors. "The rooms of these individuals are sometimes in the dignified colleges of universities, sometimes in carefully sought country retreats . . . These fundamental people are not very gregarious as a rule . . . some are negligently dressed and distraught in their bearing, but for the most part they look fairly well cared for." Wells found this species generally unobtrusive and ineffective. They were not sufficiently political, in other words, or forward thinking. "A single shipyard at work makes more noise than all the original thought of the world put together."

PYTHON, MONTY (a diversion . . .)

Eric Idle is at the door with malicious intent. He is smiling in that cheeky way he has, but don't be fooled: he is after your family silver. The door to the flat is answered by a slightly nervous woman played by John Cleese. The sketch is from November 1969, the first BBC series of *Monty Python,* the episode entitled "Man's Crisis of Identity in the Latter Half of the 20th Century."

The woman asks the man what he wants. He says he'd like to come in and steal a few things. The woman is suspicious: "Are you an encyclopaedia salesman?"

No, the man repeats, he burgles people.

The woman is doubtful; she still thinks he may be an encyclopedia salesman.

No, he insists, he's really not.

The woman wonders whether if she lets him in he'll then sell her a set of encyclopedias.

He can't make it any clearer: he'd simply like to come in and ransack her flat.

"No encyclopaedias at all?" she asks.

"Correct—none at all."

Still wary, she finally opens the door.

Once inside, the man says: "Mind you, I don't know whether you've really considered the advantages of owning a really fine set of modern encyclopaedias . . ."

The sketch shifts to Michael Palin sitting at a desk. That man, he announces, was a successful encyclopedia salesman. But not all of them are quite so successful.

Cut to: a clip of a man falling from a tall building.

And now, Palin says, here are two more unsuccessful encyclopedia salesmen.

Cut to: two more bodies falling from a tall building.

Palin: "I think there's a lesson there for all of us."

Palin took the lesson to heart. In the 1980s he published, with fellow Python Terry Jones, *Dr. Fegg's Encyclopeadia of ALL World Knowledge,* which, inevitably, had very little knowledge of the world at all. Dr. Fegg was a salivating monstrosity with a blood-soaked axe. His principal source of education was Parkhurst prison, where he spent time for grievous bodily harm. The previous title of his encyclopedia was *Bert Fegg's Nasty Book for Boys and Girls,* but this updated edition contained a lot more misinformation. The entries were generally not to be found in other publications: Aladdin and His Terrible Problem; the Patagonian Shoe-Cleaning Rat; Do-It-Yourself Teeth. The Patagonian Shoe-Cleaning Rat was not a fearsome thing, but rather a sad one: "This rat lives by hiring itself out as a shoe brush. Once it goes bald its career is at an end, and it has to rely on what it can make out of selling Patagonian Rat's Cheese (which understandably isn't very popular)."

By contrast, there was a certain frisson of danger to be found in the entry Parlour Game: Pass the Bengal Tiger. This game requires seven boys, seven girls, chairs, wrapping paper, tiger. One plays by passing the wrapped tiger around until the music stops, at which point a child unwraps a layer of paper (good luck to you!), and the loser is the child holding the now completely enraged mammal during the final unwrapping.

Q

QUESTIONING

For the child in the real world, the year 1910 began with a lot of questions. Do animals know when they are treated kindly? Is the country healthier than the town? Why does it rain so much in Scotland?

Because we once lived in simpler times, these things once had simple answers. They appeared in *The Children's Encyclopaedia*, which was known as *The Book of Knowledge* in the United States, a hugely successful and unpredictable enterprise that made at least a modest contribution to shaping young opinion between the wars, and thus adult opinion after it. (One could build a fair case suggesting that a junior encyclopedia would always be more influential than an adult one, given the impressionable age of its readers.) The answers are: we don't know, but it certainly does the human good; yes if you like pure air and sunshine, but no if you're more interested in better water and drainage systems; and Scotland is farther north than England, and so its colder climate condenses more water in the atmosphere (it also has a very broken west coast, and the water of the sea comes far up into the land).

Initially available as a fortnightly part-work between 1908 and 1910, and sold primarily on platform kiosks at train stations, the installments would build into that well-worn encyclopedic phrase "a treasury of knowledge," but it wasn't like most encyclopedias that had gone before. For a start, it wasn't alphabetical. It was a huge engaging hotchpotch of everything, and because it had no recognizable shape it was both surprising and barmy. It wasn't even thematic, it was just all over the place; it read as though its editor Arthur Mee had thrown his index cards out of the window into a high wind.

The contents page of Volume 1 lists nineteen "groups" of entries, although these too repel easy categorization. For instance, Group 2, "Men and Women," features articles on The First Flying Men, The Kings of Music, The Famous Men of Venice and The French Revolutionists. Or take Group 16, "Ideas," which features Movement, Justice, Courage and Truth, all the Marvel heroes in one. *The Children's Encyclopaedia* was a huge success: its publisher, the Educational Book Company, claimed sales of 800,000 in its first decade, a great many of these to schools and libraries.

The entry on Truth reveals another aspect of the project, a hard-line faith in God. It cites Montaigne's suggestion that we are born to inquire after truth, and "we should keep it constantly before our minds." But it is not enough. "He did not say that truth was hidden in a well. He said it was in the heights of the Divine. Truth is God, and in seeking truth we are seeking our creator."

This was heady stuff for a child who has just learned, in the same volume, about how to make their own sweets and a bag from a pair of gloves. And so the quest for truth became a game, "the greatest game of hide and seek that was ever invented. God had hidden his truth, and we shall never find it on this earth; but He has made the search for it so exciting and splendid." And on the following page—page 501 out of the 764 pages in Volume 1—you can build a toy to measure the wind (". . . put the washer on top of the wooden post . . .").

The encyclopedia, composed at the height of empire, was also committed to a proudly British way of life (all except the title, which changed from *Encyclopaedia* to *Encyclopedia* as it broke into the American market sometime in the 1920s). A section on the slave trade provides a distinct flavor of this—supercilious, even-handed, very sure of itself. The entry was called "The Good Explorers and the Bad Explorers of the Long Ago."

> The early explorers were of two kinds: simple priests who went with incredible daring into realms of benighted savagery to baptise men, women, and children whose very language they did not know; and Spanish and Portuguese slave-dealers who, by the middle of the seventeenth century, were carrying 10,000 poor wretches a year from Africa to Brazil alone, where, toiling like beasts of burden, the unhappy creatures, if exceedingly strong and equally fortunate, might live out seven years, but not more than seven.
>
> England, to her shame be it told, had her share in those slaves. In the century preceding the American Declaration of Independence, we carried three million African slaves to the New World; and threw another 250,000 into the Atlantic as they died in our ships. All the Negroes in the New World, and they number many millions now, are descended from the slaves stolen with cruelty and violence from the Dark Continent.

The children never tire: Arthur Mee molds young minds in the 1930s

This was the encyclopedia I had at school, a fact that now makes me feel slightly queasy, not least because the title of the editor's preface read, "To All Who Love Children All over the World." Arthur Mee's manifesto proclaimed that he wanted to cram a child's mind with everything relevant. His work would be written in words every child could understand, and the longest word in it would be "Encyclopedia." His grand project had not "come to steal away the joy of childhood and put a bitter grinding in its place." Rather, it was "a gift to the nation," and he hoped that every child who opened it would find something to engage him or her, not least upon gender-specific lines, "the mechanical interests of boys, the domestic interest of girls."

He signed off with a further list of questions. "What does the world mean? And why am I here? Where are all the people who have been and gone? Who holds the stars up there?"

Initially, and perhaps unsurprisingly with conundrums like these, Mee had no competitors. *La Petite Encyclopédie du jeune âge,* published by Larousse, hadn't been updated since 1853 and wasn't available in English. The hugely successful *World Book* from 1917 was a richly illustrated encyclopedia marketed to both children and adults, but it had little of Mee's peccadilloes or charm. The first proper rival emerged in the United States in the 1920s with the ten-volume *Compton's Pictured Encyclopedia,* heralded in its marketing as both more up to date than *Britannica* and more centered around classroom teaching ("It teaches happily . . . it informs accurately . . . *Compton's* keeps pace with annual progress"). *Compton's* would emerge as a significant mid-market rival to the highbrow *Britannica,* but this particular set was a general publication written for adults and much older children.

Britannica had its own plans to launch a junior version in

1914, but the war and its aftermath postponed the launch of *Children's Britannica* until 1934. It was "a proper encyclopaedia designed for you," the editor of the second edition Robin Sales wrote to its young readers in 1969, "but with a plan that will help you to use, when you are older, a grown-up encyclopaedia." Like the grown-up's *Britannica*, the articles were arranged in alphabetical order: in Volume 2, Badger was followed by Badminton, Baghdad and Bagpipe, taking one on a tour of the animal kingdom, the world of sports, an ancient Muslim civilization and the disputed origins of resonant woodwind in a few colorful pages. Likewise in the last volume: Walnut would be followed by Sir Robert Walpole, who would precede Walrus, who would learn to Waltz. And because the slim nineteen-volume set was just a stepping stone to greater things, there was detailed instruction on how to use the index, knowledge judged indispensable when confronting the full 40 million words later in life (the children's version contained 4 million). Thus there was no point being disappointed when you flipped the pages of Volume 8 to look up "goldfinch" and found no such entry. The clever boy and girl would rather go to the index, find that the goldfinch was considered part of the large Finch family, and happily turn to page 132 in Volume 7. The quest for knowledge would usually involve a bit of detective work—yet more valuable preparation for adulthood.*

The first volume of *Britannica Junior* carried a list of the many hundreds of authors "who have helped to make this encyclopaedia know a great deal." Many of them were not experienced at writing for children, so a specialist group of

* One American advertisement for what was also called *Britannica Junior* showed a mom and pop admiring their child from a distance: "Look! He's actually studying on his own—and loving it!"

editors in the *Britannica* office ensured that every article could be easily understood. The entries were also sent to be read by the pupils and teachers at a junior school, and if anything wasn't clear to them, more clarity was inserted. The authors then got the articles back, to ensure no errors had crept in during the clarification. The whole was then checked anew by an "educational adviser."

Unlike adult encyclopedias, each volume would end with a suggestion for hobbies and pastimes—how to act Shakespeare, how to draw animals—while the last volume included an alphabetical quiz to send you skittering back to previous volumes:

How did Androcles win the friendship of a lion?
What is meant by irrigation?
Of what metals does soft solder consist?

This was a publication aimed at the elementary years, although *Britannica* was keen to open up a market younger still. To this end, in 1954 it published a pamphlet called "Using *Britannica Junior* with your Preschool Child." (The cover illustration showed a smiling mother standing behind a smiling father in an armchair, with a boy of about four standing smiling at the side and a smiling girl sitting on her father's lap. They were all reading the same volume.) The foreword was written by Newton R. Calhoun, who was billed as a psychologist at Winnetka Public Schools in Winnetka, Illinois. "Has home seemed too confining for your child to discover new interests in it?" he asked. "It will take a great many different subjects to interest him from hour to hour and day to day."

The pamphlet explained that *Britannica* was the ideal way of dealing with a child's insatiable ("and, let's face it, sometimes overwhelming") curiosity. "Often a child asks the same question repeatedly because he remains confused or wants reassurance. It is important not to over-emphasise the giving of factual information if his question really refers to his feelings." *Britannica* chose an example one imagines that its committed editors had been asked by their own children: why do you drink so much coffee? "Sometimes actions are better answers than words," the adult should realize:

> He may want to know why it's right for you to drink but not for him. If this is his concern you will want to answer in a way that does not alarm him, and yet makes it clear that there is a good reason. Or the same question may mean that he wonders how you can like that stuff: it looks and smells quite unsavoury to him. If so, he will feel more satisfied by tasting coffee than by listening to words. You can give him some coffee diluted with milk and amply sweetened. He will be made to feel more secure because the gap between his and the adult word has been lessened.

He may then ask, "Where does it come from and what does it look like before it gets into the can?," and this is where having *Britannica* on hand really pays dividends. Coffee uses water, of course, and so a child will probably have other questions, such as where the water comes from, how does it get into the pipes, and where does it go after it goes down the drain. "The answers to these questions are given in simple form in the articles rain (Volume 13, Page 30, column a), water supply (15, 58, a) and sewage disposal (13, 292, b) . . . You can be sure of finding the answers in *Britannica Junior*."

The *Oxford Junior Encyclopaedia* (1948) reverted back to a thematic arrangement. The editors believed that it would be more "educationally beneficial" for its eleven-plus readership if each of the twelve volumes tackled a broader but more cohesive subject matter, with the alphabet only coming into play within each volume, a system that harked at least as far back as Samuel Taylor Coleridge. The subjects were humankind, natural history, the universe, communications, great lives, farming and fisheries, industry and commerce, engineering, recreations, law and society, home and health, and the arts.

The preface emphasized its serious intent: the work had been the subject of "authorizing" by the Delegates of the Oxford University Press. The editors hoped their encyclopedia would be an extended treatise on the value of reading as a whole. "To many children (and indeed to many adults) reading is not a natural activity; they do not turn to books for their own sake." They might be trained, however, to go to the *Oxford Junior* for a particular purpose, and thus "to form a habit which will be of lifelong value."

The set was primarily intended for school libraries, and in its preface the editors Laura E. Salt and Geoffrey Boumphrey explained their desire to provide a work of reference suitable for those who found standard encyclopedias too heavy and overly dense with technical information. They hoped that thousands of illustrations would lighten the load, as would their omission of "purely scientific" topics. Theirs was a humanistic outlook, more concerned with the modern world than the past, more practical than abstract. An encyclopedia, unlike a dictionary, "deals only with words and subjects about which there is something interesting to be said."

But what, for example, would the first volume of the *Oxford Junior* (Mankind) say about Americans? After a demographic and social breakdown—"people of the States are of very mixed origin—British, French, German, Scandinavian, Russian,

Finnish, people from the Balkans, Italians, Dutchmen, Greeks, Poles, Jews, even Chinese and Japanese"—we learn:

> The Americans are a people who are mentally very much alive. They have always stood for the great principles of liberty and democracy, although there are among them great variations of wealth and poverty and frequent bitter struggles between capital and labour. The spirit of free enterprise, still paramount in America, though it certainly stimulates initiative, may be leading to the development of an individualism which threatens the common good, and may lead Americans to put too high a value on financial and material success.

An entry titled British Peoples is illustrated by three photographs: haymaking in Suffolk, an aerial view of the pottery district of Staffordshire belching smoke from 100 chimneys, and Trafalgar Square, captioned "The Heart of the Empire." The English are characterized as having a fondness for understatement ("the expression 'not bad' is a typical example"), something that Americans find "most conspicuous, and put it down to false modesty." Elsewhere, Englishmen are noted for their "coldness," although they are "companionable" once one gets to know them.

England is also known abroad for what often appears as a willingness to combine expressions of high moral idealism with a very realistic ability to hold on to territory and business. The famous "White Man's Burden" as a slogan of empire has, for instance, always appeared to Britain's competitors as a piece of hypocrisy.

We should remind ourselves of the date of this writing: 1948, the year *Empire Windrush* unloaded its Jamaican passengers by the Thames, the year the British mandate ended in Palestine, the year George VI lost his title "Emperor of India." The young boys and girls reading those books will be in their eighties now, having run the country and influenced the course of the world for some fifty years.*

The critical response to the *Oxford Junior* was mixed. Because each of the volumes carried a different subject, they were reviewed primarily by specialist magazines. So the *Modern Law Review* of 1953 picked up Volume 10, Law and Order, and a certain J.A.G. Griffith found it diverse and excellently printed. He was less happy with the large number of errors: despite the statement to the contrary, Griffith observed, there was nothing to prevent a member of the National Coal Board standing for parliament; local authorities began to build housing estates long before the 1920s; and the explanation of the funding of the National Health Service was wrong. Apart from these mistakes and many others, the writer concluded, the volume was a "considerable achievement."

In 1950 *History* magazine found much to admire in the first three volumes, covering Mankind, Natural History and the Universe, but there was one black hole: a stark lack of History. "The history teacher has a fundamental grievance," wrote the history professor R.F. Treharne. "Thanks to the highly

* Arthur Mee's *The Children's Encyclopedia* no doubt had a similar impact in the decades before. An entry on the British Empire in South Africa praised "the part that has been played by our country in opening up the great African continent . . . it is not generally realized that the British Empire controls in Africa [in 1910] a larger area of the Earth's surface than it controls either in Canada or Australia." But we were slow to get going with our exploitation. "The reason for this was that only a small proportion of the continent had a climate in which white men could live healthily and work productively on white men's industries." Trade could still be conducted to some extent, because the continent had a large population, "mostly uncivilized, but capable of bringing to the coast things which civilized people desired, particularly gold dust and ivory."

arbitrary plan of the work, his subject seems to have been largely forgotten."

In its tortuously metaphorical analysis, the *Burlington Magazine* found the encyclopedia almost edible. Writing for the young is difficult, declared the author Wilfrid Blunt, brother of the art expert and spy Anthony Blunt. "The 'older young' may be persuaded to accept simple nourishment, but they will revolt against pap; the stomachs of the 'younger young,' on the other hand, cannot yet assimilate adult food." Irrespective of age and digestive systems, Blunt found that almost all readers would find the set admirable: "The pabulum there provided is easily digestible, yet not pre-digested; it is attractively served; it is eminently nourishing." Only occasionally was the editors' taste questionable, he felt. There should have been no entry on the Limerick, for one. And he disapproved of sullying the publication with even a passing mention of the blues, judging it "irritating" and "an ephemeral kind of music that is better forgotten." The prejudices of the reviewer sit uneasily upon the prejudices of the product. But as to accuracy—we'll see that this was anyone's guess.*

* The blues received only a few lines of coverage within a one-page entry on Jazz. And its very last words are questionable. It states that many blues songs are "deeply expressive of sadness, fear, even satire upon the lot of the black man at the expense of the white, but never of vindictiveness or hatred."

R

RULE BRITANNICA?

In the early 1960s, an American physicist named Harvey Einbinder took a break from his job advising defense contractors on missile projects to work on a series of television programs designed to explain great breakthroughs in science to a general audience. Consulting *Encyclopaedia Britannica* for his show on Galileo, he read that he had once disproven an ancient theory of gravity by dropping weights from the Leaning Tower of Pisa. Not true, alas. Even when a biography of Galileo highlighted the error in 1935, it remained in *Britannica* for another thirty years.

And so Harvey Einbinder began to wonder: did the encyclopedia contain many similar mistakes? Was it a catalogue of errors? He was alarmed by what he found. He brought his own knowledge to the entries on Heat, Vaporization and the Compton Effect, and discovered several flaws. Then he began a wider study, on the same principles as S.S. Van Dine's assault *Misinforming a Nation* from 1919, and his 390-page *The Myth of the Britannica* (1964) was his influential bestselling result. There were many erroneous comments passing as indisputable fact. Equally problematic was his finding that many articles had not been amended for more than fifty years; some had not been changed since 1875. Opinions were outdated, and bigotry was rife. On the whole, societal attitudes towards many topics—the role of women, racial issues, sexual politics, censorship—had changed and liberalized, but on a great many issues *Britannica* still had its feet planted in Victorian soil. When new historical evidence came to light it was often ignored, Einbinder found, and there was a particular reluctance to amend those articles written by famous contributors.

Dr. Einbinder chose for his survey the 1958 and 1963 printings, both updates of the fourteenth edition from 1929. If you had been one of the many purchasers of the 1963 printing in the United States (about 150,000 sets were sold annually in the early 1960s) you may have been convinced by the claims in its advertisements that it was "the most complete collection of facts and knowledge excitingly explained by leading authorities—learn about gardening, missiles, philosophy, science, just about any subject you've ever heard of and thousands you haven't." And you might have reason to feel both unsatisfied and misled if this turned out not to be the case.

Einbinder attacked his target with devilish pursuit. His study included a list of 666 articles, each occupying at least half a page in his two mid-century printings, that were unchanged from 1911 and in some cases 1889. Many were biographies—Hadrian, Henry Fielding, Goethe, Jonathan Swift, many King Henrys and Richards—and others considered major historical events without including any of the century's new discoveries or interpretations: the Gunpowder Plot, the French Revolutionary Wars, the Thirty Years' War, the Battle of Waterloo. A twelve-page essay on the

Renaissance by J.A. Symonds, grandiloquently composed, had lain virtually untouched for more than fifty years, even though modern scholarship had superseded many of its views.

Contemporary magazine advertisements from the 1960s considered the latest *Britannica* to be "the finest edition in 200 years," with 36 million words written by 10,300 "of the world's great authorities." It claimed that 17,900 articles had been revised, although in some cases this just amounted to spelling corrections. Dr. Einbinder found that some of these revisions inserted new errors, noting mistakes in a list of Beethoven's quartets and the biographical details of Abraham.*

The Myth of the Britannica had a lot of dastardly fun with animals, or what it called "fanciful zoology." Historically, encyclopedias have *always* had the biggest fun with animals, not least the mythical beasts to be found within Pliny's *Naturalis Historia* and Gervase of Tilbury's *Otia Imperialia*. But those are ancient classics; one might expect more from the middle of the twentieth century. But here is the camel, in which water is stored "chiefly in the hump" (it isn't—the hump is fatty tissue used as a source of food). The "voluntary suicide" and "blind impulse" that apparently causes hordes of lemmings to leap to their watery deaths is also a myth, still perpetuated: it is not blind impulse nor a death wish, it is rather overpopulation and

* I am grateful to Ray Ward (see footnote on page 195) for pointing out how many errors in *Britannica* and elsewhere were almost certainly the results of a writer mishearing a fact during research. Because of the amount of plagiarism from competing encyclopedias, these errors would exist for years in many editions, until someone with direct knowledge of the subject would spot the error and try to correct it. Ward points out that for many years the *Britannica* entry on Sheffield said one of the rivers of the region was the "Lordey." It should have been *Loxley*. Similarly, looking up the entry for Sheffield in the one-volume *Columbia Encyclopedia*, he found mention of "Hallain University" rather than Sheffield *Hallam* University, where Ward once worked. "It's often said that whenever one sees or hears anything in the media on which one has personal knowledge, it's always wrong!"

a search for food. Similarly, wolves do not generally hunt in large packs, as *Britannica* attests, and birds happily and annually migrate, despite *Britannica* remaining doubtful of this activity.

Social issues that may directly impact the reader were also in need of an overhaul. The article on birth control, for example, reflected both a very conservative and chauvinistic attitude, and clearly a callous and obdurate one. In 1963, *Britannica* was still reporting that "the poorest and least successful families, commonly handicapped in health and education as well as economic resources, produce and rear more than their proportion of children." In a contrastingly absurd vein, "It is the successful members of the more industrialised and supposedly advanced populations who seem headed for extinction for lack of fruitful breeding."

With regard to racial issues, discrimination was ever-present, often within subtle asides. In a not-so-subtle example, Dr. Einbinder quotes the article on Lynching from his 1958 set, an entry unchanged since it first appeared in 1910.

> After reconstruction, with the increase of Negro crimes, came an increase of lynchings, because of prejudice, the fact that for some time after reconstruction the governments were weak (especially in the districts where Negroes outnumbered whites), the fact that Negroes nearly always shielded criminals of their own race against whites, and because of the occurrence of the crime of rape by Negro men upon white women.

R

"This passage does not rest on facts," Einbinder notes, "but is merely an attempt to justify Southern mob violence." The entry was written by a dean of Vanderbilt University, then a largely white Southern school. "Although the article was revised within the last decade to include recent statistics on lynching, the only change made in this biased passage was to alter its punctuation and capitalise the word 'Negro.'"*

Harvey Einbinder's revelations of 1964 strengthened the demand for an entirely new edition, and he claimed this was his intention. He conducted his investigation more in love than in anger: he had always relied upon *Britannica* as a trustworthy source, he said, and he emphasized it was still a valuable enterprise with much rigorous text; he just wanted all of it to be better, more current. He almost apologizes for his scrutiny, suggesting it would be impossible for the editors of such an unwieldy institution to keep abreast of all the breakthroughs in the scientific journals or developments in natural history.

It would be another decade before the groundbreaking fifteenth edition was published with much fanfare in 1974, and we shall see how it endeavored to sweep away almost everything that had gone before. But in the meantime, there was an awful lot of old stock that needed to be sold.

R

* Three-quarters of the 3693 people lynched in the US between 1889 and 1929 were "Negroes." Of this number, 17 percent were accused of rape and an additional 7 percent of attempted rape. In many cases these charges were unfounded, and hence there is no basis for citing rape as a major cause of lynching.

Something for everyone: kitchen scales and first-aid kits seal the deal in the 1950s

S

SELLING

In October 1964, a seventeen-year-old Londoner named Peter Rosengard was attracted by a classified advertisement in the London *Evening Standard* that read, "International publishing company launching major new publication seeks young enthusiastic management trainees." His parents wanted him to become a dentist, but he had his eye on a sporty soft-top Sunbeam Alpine, and the management opportunity seemed to be the fastest way to get it. More than fifty years later, Rosengard recalls being interviewed by an American "in cowboy boots and ten-gallon hat" promising him the world. But it was clear early on that his job would be unlikely to include any management training at all.*

The American in the hat ran a franchise of Collier's, the New York publishing company that had been in the encyclopedia

* See *Talking to Strangers: The Adventures of a Life Insurance Salesman* (Coptic, 2013), which has a slightly different version of these events.

business since the 1880s. Its twenty-volume set was now being sold in Europe for the first time, and the company would use the same sales techniques it had perfected in the United States. Rosengard remembers the set costing £240, but being told that some recipients would be paying rather less.*

"We're doing an advance marketing campaign here in the UK to select a number of families to receive a free set," he was told at his interview. "They can tell everyone how good they are, so when we come to sell them we'll have a ready-primed market."

And there was something else too. "As well as the set of books, there is an annual information service and updated single volume to keep 'em abreast of new developments in the world. All we ask is that the selected families sign up for this service, which costs £12 a year for 20 years; but rather than have it round their necks for 20 years, like a mortgage, they can pay it over just 24 months at £10 a month. What do you think of that, Peter!?"

"Well that is really a fantastic offer. So they get the entire set of encyclopaedias absolutely free?"

"You've got it! Absolutely free, Peter!"

The next day he found he had joined a team of about fifty new recruits. "Every morning we had a pep talk which ended with us all standing on our chairs. 'OK, guys. What have you got?' 'Enthusiasm!' we shouted. 'What do you want?' 'Money!' we shouted. 'What are you going to do about it!?' 'Rock 'em!' 'OK, let's rock 'em!' Then we all ran down the small staircase

* *Collier's Cyclopedia*, published in 1882, promised "commercial and social information" and a "treasury of useful and entertaining knowledge on art, science, pastimes, belles-lettres, and many other subjects of interest in the American home circle." Some of the more enticing entries included "Hints for Stammerers," Various Forms of Invitations" and "Drowning."

out into the street, got into our group leader's car and roared off to Upminster or Slough, to whatever housing estate we were headed for."

He was invited into the first house he approached. "We had to learn a ten-page script, word for word. I was doing pretty well in the tiny living room of this young couple and just getting to the bit where I threw open my briefcase, took out the stuck-together concertinaed spines of the twenty volumes . . . when my mind went totally blank. I knew I was halfway down page six but I hadn't a clue what came next.

"'I'm terribly sorry, but it's my very first day and you are the first people I have done this to and actually, I have got a little stuck . . . but I have the script in my briefcase and if you don't mind, I can read the rest to you?'

"Amazingly, they were very understanding and so I got out the script and hurled the dead encyclopedia spines across their living room; it bounced off the wall. And they signed up. I had earned £16. By the end of the first week, I had signed up nine families and made £144. As the average income in 1964 was £15 a week, this was amazing. I got the top prize at the Friday morning meeting, a silver Dunhill lighter. It didn't matter I didn't smoke. I felt fantastic. And that's how I became a salesman."

Now in his seventies, Peter Rosengard has been a salesman his entire life, although for most of it his line has been life insurance (he sells the majority of his policies from his permanently reserved breakfast table at Claridge's). He has also enjoyed side-careers managing the eighties pop band Curiosity Killed the Cat and co-founding London's Comedy Store.

In 1964 it took him three months to realize he was selling anything at all. He writes, "I was angry; I felt I had been duped." But he was told, "You can't just knock on a door and say, 'Hello, I am an encyclopaedia salesman, would you like to buy one?' You have to make them feel they have been selected. Everyone wants to feel special. We selected you for this job, didn't we? Remember, you're saving their children from a life of ignorance, and therefore the yawning jaws of poverty."

The *Collier's Encyclopedia* of 1964 was an updated version of the 1962 edition, containing about 15,000 illustrations and 1,500 maps. The spines suggested an engagingly diverse range (Art Nouveau—Beetle, Heating—Infantry, Infinity—Katmandu), while its clear editorial tone was necessarily pitched below the brow of *Britannica*. Peter Rosengard had been selling it successfully for five months, making £250 a week, when he was called to a meeting at a hotel in Kensington.

"Guys, we have some big news!" he was told. "The reason not everyone is here today is because this is only for you, our very top guys. You are being selected to go on this exciting new journey. Guys, we are going to hit Germany!"

His employers explained that the consumer protection law in the UK allowed customers a seven-day cooling-off period, resulting in a large number of cancellations. Apparently, Germany had no such policy.

"On the ferry to Calais, I opened the briefcase we all had been given," Rosengard recalls. "Wait a minute! What's this? I had pulled out the sample encyclopaedia we showed the families we were selling to [but] I wasn't holding a *Collier's* encyclopaedia. The name in gold print on the cover said *Caxton Encyclopaedia*. I had never heard of the *Caxton Encyclopaedia*. What was it doing in my briefcase? I've never heard of them and I doubt anybody else has either, apart from the Caxton who invented the printing press, and I'm pretty sure he didn't do an encyclopaedia in his spare time."*

His boss replied, "Look, it's real simple, Pete. When you get to that page of the script when you say, 'Let me show you the new *Collier's* set of encyclopaedias . . .' all you do is say, 'Let me show you the new *Caxton* set of encyclopaedias!' Think you can manage that?"

In the United States, a more experienced salesman named James W. Murphy was also going door-to-door. In 1969, after several successful years as a typewriter salesman for IBM in North Florida, Murphy began selling the *World Book* encyclopedia, established in Chicago in 1917 as a more student friendly, less academic alternative to *Britannica*. He became one of the most successful members of a sales force of 50,000, and in his twenty-two years with the company he won many sales awards; he led a team in Kentucky that regularly achieved more than $5 million in annual revenue. In 2014, his son, James D. Murphy, noted that his father knew every angle of the script the company had perfected over many years. "He knew the objections, he knew the value propositions, and he could tell by the way you turned a book's pages whether you were ready for the close or not."

His father believed in his product: at home there were volumes everywhere, and he would frequently scamper away during mealtimes to find the particular book required to find a fact or settle an argument. He had a nice company briefcase containing the sample *A* volume, the thickest in the set, with the most science and the best illustrations—Animals, Art, Aviation.

---

* Rosengard was almost certainly selling the first edition of the *New Caxton Encyclopaedia*, the bound version of Purnell's *New English Encyclopaedia*, a 216-section part-work. Being a raconteur, and allowing for poetic license, I think he knew that Caxton didn't actually invent the printing press.

Murphy's father often spoke about his sales technique as "a true rip 'em and stick 'em mentality." He made ten house calls a day, usually on mothers while their husbands were at work and their children at school. If he found that the wives were hesitant to make a decision without consulting their husbands, he would leave behind the *A* volume for everyone to peruse in his absence, believing it would be working for him as his "silent salesman," giving the family something to think about besides the price. A complete set cost $500, but once the kids were looking at the pictures and using it for their homework, any parent would find it hard to give it back.

James Murphy Jr. also became a salesman for a while, but he knew he was never as good as his dad. "It was paint-by-numbers, sell-by-numbers. Every action had an equal and opposite reaction that got you closer to yes." The *World Book* sales script was encyclopedic in itself, covering all the ways to turn "I can't afford it" into a closed deal. "He made a sport out of it," his son says. "It was always fun. It was always a mental game."*

Murphy encouraged his father to write his memoirs, and in *Who Says You Can't Sell Ice to Eskimos?* Murphy Sr. revealed techniques that he hoped could apply to anyone selling anything. There was one constant: never enter a home saying you were selling encyclopedias. Instead, you were in the education business.†

Much of Murphy's advice sounded like a script by David Mamet:

* James Murphy Jr. sold Toshiba photocopiers before becoming a fighter pilot and then the founder and CEO of the consultancy firm Afterburner Inc.

† And this wasn't a disreputable claim in itself: *World Book* was then published by Field Enterprises Educational Corporation. *Who Says You Can't Sell Ice to Eskimos?* (CreateSpace Independent Publishing Platform, North Carolina, 2013). My thanks to James Murphy Jr. for quotation permissions.

"I did the first thing you got to do in selling: I sold myself."

"Once we've got the Influencer in front of the Wallet, we've married the end-user to the money."

"Parachute me in. I'm serious. You can give me a *World Book* sales book and an order pad, and parachute me anywhere in the English-speaking world, and I'll guarantee, in eight hours, I'll have a minimum of one order—and probably three. Guaranteed."

Murphy would never lie to a potential client; he was always smarter than that. One favorite trick was to agree with a prospective buyer that for all the benefits the *World Book* conferred on their schoolchildren—all the visuals of the human body to help with biology, all the little biographies of the presidents—the twenty-six-volume set was still a hefty buy at $500. Who could afford to pay that for books? But a lease agreement was surely within their range; paying $20 a month for two years, perhaps, or $10 a month for four.*

And if $10 a month seemed too much, how about three dimes a day? Murphy carried a money box in the shape of a

* Several friends I spoke to during my research recalled their own youthful experience of selling encyclopedias. As Peter Rosengard found, the job seemed like a lucrative stop-gap until something better came along. And like Rosengard, it wasn't initially evident they were selling anything at all. When the truth dawned, so did their conscience. The architect Robert Dye recalls answering an advert looking for adventurous salesmen in the mid-seventies. A training week taught him about getting his foot in the door and closing a deal, and he remembers setting off in a car with four others to an outer-London suburb. Having talked his way into a home, and convinced a family that the encyclopedias would be just the thing they needed (while aware they could barely afford it), he got a twinge of conscience just as the father was due to sign. He told the family he had reconsidered, left without the signed contract, and quit the next day. Another friend, the artist Naomi Frears, remembers selling to mining families in Nottinghamshire. Her sample volume contained the most impressive color illustrations from the whole set, including the layered see-through diagrams of the human body. "There was a technique to keep flicking through and pausing on good pages while talking. The goal was to get them to sign something there and then, and visits were timed in the hope that only wives would be in."

miniature book ("They'd always take it."). He would then drop in three dimes, clink, clink, clink. "Three dimes a day to put all the knowledge in the Western World at your child's fingertips," he would say. "He doesn't have to go to the library, doesn't have to stand in line to borrow these volumes kids want most. Don't have to bug your husband. I know he's the smartest man in the world . . . Could you put two dimes a day in there and let your husband put one dime in—for all this month?"

It was known as the Dime Bank Close. And it had a kicker. Murphy would say, "I sure don't want to take food off the table, or anything. But your husband eats lunch out every day, doesn't he? Well, I wonder what he tips the waitress if she's extra nice to him? And just let that settle in there a minute."

Did *Encyclopaedia Britannica* push as hard? Did it need to? Would its sterling reputation and elevated position shield it from the necessity of confronting its lower-grade competition?

There was now an epidemic of encyclopedias. *Grolier*, the *New Caxton*, *Compton's*, *Collier's*, *Encyclopedia Americana* were all different in pitch, but were all being enthusiastically sold in the territorially assigned living rooms of the United States and Europe. Because of its higher price, and the higher cost of production, *Britannica*'s advertising and highly trained sales force now had to fight harder to assert its dominance and maintain market share.

Which explained why, in the early 1960s, it was becoming difficult to turn a page of the *Saturday Evening Post*, *Good Housekeeping* or the *New York Times* without seeing one of *Britannica*'s advertisements. While Vietnam occupied the news, here was a fresh battle for hearts and minds: "The greatest treasury of knowledge ever published . . . thousands of subjects that you and your family will refer to in the course of your normal day-today affairs . . . you pay later on convenient budget terms . . . the most readable, interesting and easy to use in our entire history . . . equivalent to a library of 1,000 books . . . think of it!"*

And one aspect of the advertisements had changed fundamentally. In the late 1950s, the campaigns altered their course. Once marketed exclusively to mature adults ("No professional home should be regarded as complete without one . . . its articles are not mere outline sketches, always so unsatisfactory to the information seeker"), the focus moved in the late 1950s to younger parents and their children. The obligation of educating one's offspring—and the guilt that would descend if you didn't—had always been a part of the marketing kit, but now this approach moved center stage.

"How can you express the inexpressible love you feel for your child?" asked an American advert in 1961 adorned with a proud mother looking at her pre-teen boy. You guessed right: education. A certain Dr. D. Alan Walter advised that only through education could a child achieve "a full measure of success and happiness." And because you wanted your child to be happy, "Children who are taught to 'look it up in *Britannica*' are taught to inquire, to seek, to learn, to think. Could you give the child you love a more priceless heritage?"†

But these carried a fundamental misdirection. The detailed style of *Britannica*'s articles—written by all those world authorities, most of whom were experts often writing for their

* Although it rarely revealed the price of a set in its adverts, the cost of its 1963 edition ranged from $397 to $597 according to the binding, at least $100 more than any of its smaller rivals. In the same year, the thirty-volume *Encyclopedia Americana* cost between $299 and $499, while in 1961 you could buy the nineteen-volume *World Book* in its "President Red" covers for $129.

† Likewise, an advertisement for *Compton's Pictured Encyclopedia* in the 1960s was illustrated with a boy looking forlorn behind metal bars. "Is your child's mind being imprisoned?" the copy read.

peers, and not necessarily educators—was solely directed at adults. As Harvey Einbinder explained in 1964, "the fact that the *Britannica* is not intended for children—and cannot be used by children because of its scholarly and technical content—is immaterial as far as copywriters are concerned. Their mission is to increase sales, and the truth of their copy is secondary."*

A priceless heritage: you're not in the encyclopedia business, you're in the education business

---

* *Britannica* was not alone in this approach. In 1958, an advert for *Encyclopedia Americana* featured a befuddled-looking boy ringed by the latest thirty-volume set and the tagline "Knowledge Makes Dreams Come True." The text explained, "Every ambitious youngster dreams of becoming a success. But success doesn't come from just dreaming." Another advert for the same publication, this time touting the quality of its writing rather than its value to a child, contained the immortal lines: "Then there's our biography of Poe. It reads like a novel. It ought to. It was written by the celebrated author-critic Joseph Wood Krutch." A year before, an advertisement featured a boy and a girl climbing a staircase made from volumes of the *World Book*. A similar *World Book* ad explained "it cost over $2,000,000 to bring you and your children" the latest edition, as a teenager is pictured examining a volume and exclaiming, "Gosh, it's got everything!" But this was indeed a more child-centered publication, and its success may have been one of the reasons *Britannica* adopted a similar approach when selling its standard adult editions.

SELLING DECEPTIVELY

Beyond the highly competitive market in which they operated, there was another reason these print advertisements had to work so hard in the 1960s: the door-to-door rep was having a hard time with the authorities. The Federal Trade Commission (FTC), the governmental body established in 1914 to protect and promote consumers' rights, was frequently bringing the encyclopedia companies to account. If there was a rule to be broken, a successful sales team was breaking it; indeed, this would have been one of the prime reasons for its success.

In 1960, the FTC found that *Britannica* salesmen were misrepresenting the true price to the buyer. A sales brochure would be deliberately "padded" to reflect a higher total so that when a buyer was offered a discount it would seem like a bargain. The *New York Times*, reporting on the findings, noted that the company stated a sales offer "was available at a reduced price for a limited time only when actually it was regularly available at the same prices and terms." Britannica was partially successful in appealing this complaint, the FTC conceding that the padding was not $120, as it had originally found, but only $49.50 (the basic price of a set in the "Royal Red" binding was just under $400). At the same time, the magazine *Sales Management* carried an interview with a G. Clay Cole, a senior vice president at Britannica, who described his company's sales presentation as "politely aggressive." His encyclopedia was "a product for which a feeling of immediate need must be created," he said. Which was perhaps another way of saying that his ultimate book of learning, with famous contributions from more than 1000 famous world authorities, was being sold just like any other can of beans in a competitive marketplace.

Britannica was far from alone, of course. *Encyclopedia Americana* and the *New Standard Encyclopedia* were reprimanded for the classic tricks: claiming the price was a limited-time deal; saying that the prospective purchasers had been exclusively selected for a very special offer; or explaining that the volumes were free if only the buyer subscribed to an exclusive phone line information service.

In 1971, the *Poughkeepsie Journal* revealed further sleights. Its reporter George Bernstein had been an encyclopedia salesman in the 1960s, and not a terribly good one: "After all, it is pretty hard to sell people something they really don't need, especially when the family could use some bread and butter." Among the techniques he failed to master: get the client to say yes as much as possible, "so they get in a 'Yes' frame of mind"; this could be as simple as asking, "Aren't these colour photographs beautiful?" He learned never to refer to the product as "books," as most clients would find this "a psychological turn-off." A line that occasionally seemed to work: "A house without an encyclopedia is just a house—not a home. Definitely not a home." Bernstein found there was little point trying to close a deal with just one half of a married couple present, as "the spouse that didn't hear the pitch probably will cancel the contract." (He didn't name the encyclopedia brand he was selling.) And he was told to wear a wedding ring himself, as this would make him seem more honest and reliable.*

A year earlier, in the *Democrat and Chronicle* of Rochester,

* "Remembrances of Things as an Encyclopedia Salesman," *Poughkeepsie Journal*, 29 July 1971, p. 4.

New York, the investigative reporter A.F. Ehrbar went undercover as a trainee with an experienced salesman from the Grolier Society, Inc. (who remained in the dark about the sting until it was too late). They called at the house of a newly married young couple. One of the rep's colleagues would later tell the reporter, "Never try to pitch to rich people. They're too smart and won't fall for it."

When one of the newlyweds opened the door, the salesman told them: "I'm with the publicity department of Grolier. I bet you wonder why I'm here. Well, don't worry. I'm not a salesman, and I'm not going to sell you anything."

The couple were intrigued, if a little suspicious. The Grolier man explained that he wished to use the couple as a "sponsor family" in a new campaign, and in return they would get some wonderful books. Except he didn't call them "books."*

"In return, we ask only three helps from you," the rep explained. He wanted to use their name in Grolier's advertising. He wanted them to write a letter "telling us what you think of the product once a year for ten years." And they needed to give him the names of five families who might want to buy the encyclopedias (they might even make them a little jealous, given that they were getting their set for free).

At this point the reporter, who was posing as a trainee, was sent out to the car to collect the display case. "Never take the case in with you or they'll think you're a salesman," said the salesman afterwards. He laid out three-foot-long reprints along the young couple's floor. They were still thinking the set of *Grolier* encyclopedias (and various other books including a *Popular Science Library* and a *Child's Guidance Program*) would be

* "The Encyclopedia Pitchmen," *Democrat and Chronicle* (Rochester, New York), 6 July 1970.

theirs for free. In fact, by the end of the forty-five-minute visit, they would end up agreeing to pay $554.50.

The salesman told the couple that unfortunately his company wasn't able to write off the total cost as an advertising expense, and they would have to pay for paper and binding. This would be $49.95 for ten years. To keep up to date they could also opt to buy the yearbooks, which they could have for almost half the price (down from $12 annually to $6.95). And if they wanted to stop getting the yearbooks, they would simply have to write in. The salesman would get $88 in commission for each set sold in this way. The reporter from the *Democrat and Chronicle* noted that he closed his pitch with a clever admonition: "Don't tell your friends to expect the same deal."

For a while, *Britannica* salesmen operated in much the same way, also suggesting the buyers would be taking part in an advertising promotion; the main difference was, they only had to supply the names of four neighboring friends, rather than five. The difference for the salesmen (and a very few saleswomen) was that they didn't work solely on commission. They received a $700-a-month salary, but on certain conditions. They had to complete full pitches at three homes every night (sixty a month), with the prospective buyer required to sign a document that they had been pitched to, whether or not this resulted in a sale. The salesperson would have to buy their "leads"—i.e., target names and addresses—for $3 each, deducted from their salary.

There was a happy ending, of sorts: the following day the young couple in Rochester changed their mind and declined to complete the contract; they even refused when another salesman called and offered them the same books for $100 less.

In the corporate world of the 1970s, the Federal Trade Commission was widely regarded as toothless; the greater the profits to be made, the more a successful company found the fines and other reprimands—usually a cease-and-desist order—a price worth paying. In an entry in its last printed edition, *Britannica* itself appeared to endorse this view in its own entry on the FTC. In reference to a judgment against Campbell's Soup Company for false promotion (it used glass marbles to make a photo of its vegetables appear more abundant than they were), it stated, "The FTC, however, had not been given the legal instruments or the staff necessary to effectively administer and monitor advertising. Moreover, in many cases, the FTC relied heavily upon making deals with companies, in the form of consent orders, to halt misleading or false advertising."

In 1971, the New York Department of Consumer Affairs reported that deceptive encyclopedia salesmen were "still on the scene." It had received around 500 individual complaints. Accordingly, it had persuaded Encyclopaedia Britannica, Inc. to sign a ten-point "assurance of discontinuance," by which it agreed that its salesmen would not "instil fear and anxiety" during their pitches in the home, nor to suggest to a parent that their child could underachieve unless they bought the encyclopedia. They also agreed not to offer a "special deal" wherein a set would be sold at a cheaper price than originally stated, the reduction merely reflecting the same set in a cheaper binding. In its defense, Britannica, Inc. said it was happy to sign the assurance, but admitted no wrongdoing apart from "isolated cases." This was at the peak of its doorstepping: in 1970, Britannica had about 2000 traveling salespeople.*

The department also found that Field Educational

* The figure stood at about 1000 in 1996, the year before Google.com registered as a domain. Two years later, Britannica laid off the last of its sales team.

Enterprises, the publishers of *World Book*, frequently failed to leave purchasers with a post-paid reply card that enabled them to cancel their orders during the three-day cooling-off period. Grolier fought back, claiming the attacks were unwarranted. "We're the favorite whipping boy," said William J. Murphy, the company's president. "This is the day to be against business, against everything."*

A year later the FTC found that *Britannica* representatives were still failing to reveal the true purpose of their visit when they entered a person's home, often claiming they were engaged in "advertising research." Further, the company was charged with deceiving its own prospective salespeople in its recruitment adverts. Britannica unsuccessfully took the case to the US Court of Appeals, and were instructed to remedy its deceptive practices by fully disclosing the nature of any domestic visit. In 1979, in a similar case, the FTC ordered the publishers of the *Grolier Encyclopedia* "to cease misrepresenting, failing to make relevant disclosures, or using any other unfair or deceptive method to recruit door-to-door sales personnel, sell merchandise and services, and collect delinquent accounts."†

Perhaps the greatest shame about these stories is that the product they were selling was generally a good one. Encyclopedia companies, through their marketing wheezes

* *New York Times*, 26 September 1971, p. 1.

† In 1974, at the launch of the fifteenth edition, Britannica's director of Educational Planning, Dr. Mortimer Adler, was asked about "switch selling," where a rep entered a home on the pretext they were running an educational poll. His reply, on the British television show *Nationwide*, was a little flustered, but he reassured viewers that "I think that's ten years ago in the past. I'm delighted to say that the selling methods have been reformed before this new encyclopedia came out. This will be purchasable in bookstores, and no representative will ring doorbells—they'll only come at your invitation if you want to see one. What in the United States we call 'high pressure' selling has been a thing of the past."

and sales representatives, had somehow managed to give their entire industry—this vast educational resource—a bad name. This was the truly dastardly irony: they were selling a valuable trove of well-intentioned and trustworthy information in a mean-spirited and duplicitous way. The industry was unable to shake off this reputation to the very end.

SEXUALITY (a diversion . . .)

To paraphrase Philip Larkin, homosexuality began in 1929. This was rather too late for *Britannica*'s eleventh edition (1910–11), which made no mention of it between Homonym and Homs, and also the supplementary volumes of the twelfth (1922), where there was nothing between the German theologian Heinrich Julius Holtzman and Honduras, nor the thirteenth (1926), an omission between the British painter Sir Charles Holroyd and the American zoologist William Temple Hornaday.

The fourteenth edition made a little headway. Homosexuality was afforded a single page, whereas Home Equipment (water softeners and electrically heated utensils) was allocated six, and Homer got fourteen. Alas, what did appear from 1929 to 1973 was disparaging, hysterical and malicious.

The subject was referred to as "Sexual Inversion." The entry began by studying animals, notably apes; the suggestion was clear. The article explained that among the Greeks and certain ancient "pre-literate" societies, homosexuality was regarded as a normal practice, but in modern societies it existed even when repressed: "The death penalty itself has failed to stamp it out."

The article then looks for a cause, suggesting homosexuality is disproven as both "a genetic aberration" and an endocrine disorder, and it dismissed the theory that it was the cause of the collapse of the Roman Empire ("It is now thought that any deterioration in the Romans that cannot be explained by political or economic causes is better attributed to malaria than to perversion"). The modern "social aspects" are regarded by the encyclopedia as the most troubling. Homosexual prostitutes are frequent blackmailers, which "explains the fact that homosexuals sometimes sink down the social scale." On the other hand, "not all male homosexuals are outwardly effeminate, and some can be dangerously violent." Some homosexuals "have made valuable contributions to society, notably in the arts, though it is improbable that it is the sole or even the main cause of genius."

It wasn't until the fifteenth edition (1974) that a more modern, dispassionate view appeared, although this too sanctioned a level of disapproval. Homosexuality was a "sexual interest in and attraction to members of one's own sex. This attraction usually but not always leads to physical contact culminating in orgasm."

The entry mentioned lesbianism, and how the term "gay" had become an acceptable substitute for both men and women. Historically, *Britannica* notes, and in different cultures, homosexuality was either approved of, treated or banned. Modern Western attitudes were said to be "in flux." "Until the early 1970s the US psychiatric establishment classified homosexuality as a mental illness, but that designation was dropped amid increased political activity and efforts by homosexuals to be seen as individuals exercising a different sexual preference rather than as aberrant personalities." Possible causes are examined (Freudian; physiological events in fetal development), and not dismissed.

The Kinsey surveys get a look-in, noting the dubious finding that only about half as many women as men are homosexual, and "a large population of bisexuals" are mentioned for the first time.

> The concepts that all male homosexuals are effeminate or that all lesbians are masculine and aggressive, widespread in the West as recently as the 1950s and early 1960s, have largely been discarded. Similarly, the notion that homosexuals are "sick" individuals who need only to meet the right person of the opposite sex to be "cured" has largely given way, particularly in areas with large homosexual populations, to some degree of tolerance or acceptance.*

As one might expect, the classification of homosexuality in religion-based encyclopedias ranges from dismissive to intolerant. The *New Catholic Encyclopedia* found that

> usually, temporary homosexuality is due to specific environmental conditions, such as those found in prisons, army camps, and boarding schools, or to passing emotionalism (crushes) or adolescent curiosity. Some men are homosexual for a time because nothing else is available; and some adolescents are curious and have no other outlets. The vast majority of boys who engage in homosexual activity, even for several years during their adolescence, grow out of it. Permanent homosexuality, on the other hand, is found in the true sexual invert.†

* The first Kinsey study of 1948 had been completely ignored by earlier printings, despite (or probably because of) its findings that a third of its male respondents had had some kind of homosexual experience.

† Produced in nineteen volumes by the Catholic University of America in Washington, DC, and published by McGraw Hill in 1967.

The publication went on to examine this inversion in some depth, analyzing incidence, causes and morality, before considering Pastoral Guidance. This again divided the topic between adolescence and adulthood, and between the "apparent" and "real" homosexual. "The priest must re-educate the homosexual youth on the nature of love," it advised. "All true love is a going-out of oneself, a self-giving; but, all unconsciously, homosexual love is bent back upon the self in a closed circle, a sterile love of self, disguised in apparent love for another." With regard to adults,

> It should be stressed that a homosexual is just as pleasing to God as a heterosexual, as long as he makes a sincere effort to control his deviate bent with the help of grace . . . God must become the driving motive in the life of the homosexual who, otherwise, will grow lonely for the kind of fellowship found in homosexual haunts—in which he had been formerly enslaved, to which he is still attracted, and in place of which a stronger love must be found.

The sixteen-volume *Encyclopaedia Judaica*, published in Jerusalem in 1972, pursues a similar line. According to the Torah, homosexuality is a "sexual perversion" punishable by capital punishment; Talmudic law commutes the punishment to flagellation, and extends it to lesbianism. Historically these "abhorrent practices" are linked to the Egyptians and Canaanites. The prohibition of homosexuality is omitted from Joseph Caro's *Shulhan Arukh* (the sixteenth-century code of Jewish law); the *Encyclopaedia Judaica* explains that "This omission reflects the virtual absence of homosexuality among Jews rather than any difference of views on the criminality of these acts," while noting that Rabbi Caro felt obliged to add,

"Nevertheless, in our times, when lewdness is rampant, one should abstain from being alone with another male."*

Homosexuality was judged illegal for three reasons. It might lead to the male abandoning his wife; it might debase the dignity of man; it will almost certainly lead to "spilling the seed in vain." The practice should be confined to "the abominations of the sinful city of Sodom." The *Judaica* concludes, "Whereas the more liberal attitude found in some Christian circles is possibly due to the exaggerated importance Christians have traditionally accorded to the term 'love,' Jewish law holds that no hedonistic ethic, even if called 'love,' can justify the morality of homosexuality any more than it can legitimise adultery, incest or polygamy, however genuinely such acts may be performed out of love and by mutual consent."

Why are these entries worthy of our consideration today? Why should they not be dismissed as the predictable reactionary objections of organized groups threatened by the subject in hand? Because they question the very concept of the encyclopedia. These multi-volume publications are necessarily conceived as a physical compression of definitive knowledge. Far from the historical equivalent of the rant on social media, they are instead the tablets from the mountain. The influence they impart is immense, and these particular entries (which I have predominantly culled from the open shelves of the London Library) have the power to transform lives. As the *New Catholic Encyclopedia* makes clear, "it is not unknown for adolescents who were told that they were homosexual to commit suicide." (The original publication date of 1967 is no

* Likewise, the thirteen-volume *Encyclopaedia of Islam* (published by Koninklijke, Netherlands, latest update 2004), omits homosexuality as a feature of either historical or current Islamic life.

sad apologia; when the set was updated for the fourth time in 1996, the text remained untouched.)

Such entries should serve as a check on the contents of all encyclopedias, an invitation to question authorship and intentions. The notion of opinion masquerading as fact is something we've become increasingly aware of in the digital age, not least with the emergence of open editorial access. But it is something we should question with regard to even the most revered print editions, and something we may wonder about historically. Encyclopedias are a mirror of contemporary knowledge, a spotlight on current learning, and we may legitimately question what sort of opinions we have formed from our consultations with apparently irrefutable text at an impressionable age. How has the monolithic reference slab—be it in our homes or in the school or local library—shaped us as individuals? Marginally, I would argue, but not entirely academically.

With regard to *Britannica*, the early omissions and persistent damnation were consistent with the encyclopedia's prudishness regarding all matters deemed potentially upsetting to adults (and necessarily intriguing to children). Biographies of the famous obscured any incidence of sexual matters that differed from either morally good or "normal" behavior. Oscar Wilde, for example, was imprisoned in Reading Gaol for offenses "under the Criminal Law Amendment Act," a statute most widely known for protecting underage girls. In earlier years at Oxford, Wilde "adopted what to undergraduates appeared the effeminate pose of casting scorn on manly sports, wearing his hair long, decorating his room with peacock's feathers, lilies, sunflowers."

In addition to his survey of factual errors, Harvey Einbinder uncovered numerous incidences of clumsy euphemism. Paul Verlaine's personal life was disturbed when "the strange young poet Jean Arthur Rimbaud came somewhat troublingly into his life"; a later reference described their relationship as "extravagant." Of the naturalist Alexander von Humboldt we learn how, "in his later years the sway of an old and faithful servant held him in more than matrimonial bondage." And Tchaikovsky's marriage to Antonina Ivanovna Milyukova was described as "an impossible one through no fault of hers but simply through his own abnormality of temperament."

"The Victorian desire to make artists and poets respectable members of society is sometimes carried to amusing extremes," Einbinder writes, quoting the entry on Robert Browning: "He frequented literary and artistic circles, and was passionately fond of the theatre; but he was entirely free of a coarse Bohemianism, and never went to bed, we are told, without kissing his mother." The entry on Dickens from the 1930s is similarly shy of a full biography when it came to the turbulent details of his relationship with Ellen Ternan. "The little that needs saying has already been said," wrote G.K. Chesterton, an oddly terse comment in an otherwise comprehensive account (and more to the point, it hasn't been said in this great encyclopedia of record). Einbinder concludes that "Chesterton grew up under the influence of Victorian ideals which demanded moral perfection from its heroes," an influence that also shielded the personal life of William Thackeray.

Britannica's influence was far greater than a regular biography, and its impact reverberated globally for decades. "Prudery is like a rare disease that strikes infrequently but leaves serious consequences in its wake," Einbinder concludes. Effectively, the encyclopedia's frailty when confronted with a true life lived, "seals off important areas of human experience from mature examination and perpetuates taboos which are no longer accepted by educated readers."

In 1974, the fifteenth edition did modify these matters. Tchaikovsky is now definitely homosexual, as is his younger brother Modest. His marriage was hastily conceived to conceal this, and a letter to his other brother Anatoly from 1878 is quoted: "Only now . . . have I finally begun to understand that there is nothing more fruitless than not wanting to be that which I am by nature."

The trials of Oscar Wilde and his imprisonment are also now explained, although there is still a disapproving reference to his "reckless pursuit of pleasure." Elsewhere, a certain studied suggestiveness presides. Alexander von Humboldt is a "gregarious" figure appearing "regularly in the salons of Parisian society." He was "always willing and anxious to assist young scientists at the beginning of their careers."

The fact that encyclopedias—our irrefutable bastions of uniformity and correctness—should view homosexuality as distasteful (at best) and abhorrent (at worst), should come as little surprise. More remarkable, perhaps, is the fact that, as the twentieth century advanced, it should devote so much of its energy to this disapproval and disavowal, evidently enthralled. One may only wonder at the true sexual tendencies of some of its editors, and the fervid atmosphere within its largely male offices.

T

THE SINGLE VOLUME

In the early 1930s, Columbia University decided it would expand its teaching facility into a new area. It would capitalize on its reputation by publishing its own encyclopedia, and it would stand out from the crowd by cramming everything between one set of covers. The full title was *The Columbia Encyclopedia in One Volume,* and when it launched in 1935 the first topic to look up was Hernia. The surface area of a breadboard, the thickness of a mattress, here was an organ that had burst its regular boundaries. It had 1949 pages, and consulting it was fraught with bad possibilities, including ruptured intestines, broken limbs, and (if you dropped it on someone's head) murder. In later years it became known as the *Columbia Desk Encyclopedia,* not only because it was often to be found on the issuing desk of a library, but also because moving it was like moving a bureau.

What was the big idea? This wasn't a junior encyclopedia (there were no illustrations), and it obviously wasn't a condensed one (it contained 52,000 articles compared to 45,000 in the full *Britannica*). Its preface explains that not long ago, an encyclopedia would contain "substantially all the book learning of the minister, the physician, the lawyer, the teacher, the businessman, the scientist and the historian. Specialization has made any such achievement now quite hopeless . . . First aid is all that a general encyclopedia can now give successfully."

There were no treatises; the articles were unsigned; no maps or illustrations; no expert was allowed to present their interpretation of a subject without it being inspected and amended by others (an article about a Roman Catholic topic, for example, would be read and revised by either a Protestant or a Jew). Its chief editor Clarke F. Ansley explained that a reference work as authoritative as this one hoped to be could never succeed if its accuracy was compromised by original opinion. If this made for a rather dull but reliable read (and it generally did), then that was an acceptable compromise. And it steered away from anything that might cause controversy or offense, so here too there was no mention of homosexuality, or indeed any sexuality, and "Sex" was limited to the reproductive organs of animals. Sexpartite Vault, on the other hand, was awarded thirty lines, the first of which began, "Developed in medieval masonry construction, from the difficulty of vaulting an oblong space with ribs of exclusively semicircular form, since the diagonal ribs, being longer, would unavoidably rise to a higher crown than the transverse ones."*

* But by the time the third edition appeared in the 1960s, popular opinion and competition from its rivals forced a change of hand: forty-two pages of illustrations were added, and twenty maps, "without compromising what was known and loved of this admired work," a claim which necessitated an additional 200 pages and the continued inclusion of a biography of every name in the Bible and a mention of every community in the United States with a population exceeding 1000, and almost everywhere else in the world with a population exceeding 10,000 (so just after Hernia there was Herning, a city with a population of 10,866 east of Ringkjöbing, Jutland, Denmark, a railway and trading center).

The *New York Times* judged the *Columbia* an essential tool in a fast-moving world, and praised both its simplicity and intelligibility. It was stronger on science than literature, however, particularly when it came to biography; the articles on Ralph Waldo Emerson and Nathaniel Hawthorne were mere skeletons of a life. The length of entries was unpredictable: Julius Caesar received 2800 words, but Napoleon only 1350; Mussolini got 850. But overall its 5 million words were a welcome addition to the reference shelf, and it was very well bound.*

The *Columbia* set a trend. Exacting, precise, manageable—it was once again the world in a book, but now it really was one book. To have the world explained between single covers, without multi-volume cross-referencing, was a God-like achievement.

How far could the shrinking go? It could go a lot smaller. There is something quietly absurd about the very notion of the *pocket* encyclopedia, as if the world itself was suddenly considered more containable than before. Or perhaps it was an admission of defeat: the world's knowledge was just too vast, too complex, to include in a multi-volume encyclopedia suitable for home consumption, so instead here's something for your backpack.

The variety of pocket editions was almost as diverse as the full-sized versions. The *Wordsworth* ("An up-to-date guide to the changing world") was arranged thematically (Society, The Arts, Science & Technology), and was aimed at an adult readership: the entry on the United Nations

* The finely stitched binding and durable paper was indeed a major key to its success. Almost ninety years on, and what I imagine to have been considerable use in a Wisconsin library, the volume I now own has held up remarkably well, with no loose or torn pages.

included individual sections on the General Assembly, the Security Council, the Economic and Social Council, the Trusteeship Council and three others; NATO was given a similar breakdown.

The *Hutchinson Pocket Encyclopedia* was derived from its larger-scale single volume first published in 1948. It handled almost every entry at between six and twelve lines. It was hard to ascertain the relative importance of a subject when Camus was only a few lines shorter than the entire entry on Canada, and Chaos Theory received six lines next to Charlie Chaplin's ten. When first published in 1995, everything was as important as everything else: from Aristotle to Zen, from Black Holes to Smart Weapons, from DNA to MS-DOS. One wonders what the Nobel Prize winners, listed at the back, would have thought of it all.

Richard P. Feynman, who won the Nobel Prize for Physics in 1965, formulated his own logical conclusion to the shrinkage of knowledge: he offered a cash prize to anyone who could shrink it even more. In December 1959 he delivered a lecture to the annual meeting of the American Physical Society at the California Institute of Technology entitled "There's Plenty of Room at the Bottom." He reasoned it was now possible to take almost any usefully bulky object and make it smaller, and perhaps more useful. He wasn't talking specifically about microchips, although he acknowledged that computers that were no longer the size of a room might one day prove beneficial. For the moment, he had an exacting challenge for his audience: to reduce a page of a book to 1/25,000 of its regular size, and then be able to read it on an electron microscope. Anyone who could do this (he used the phrase "any *guy*") would win $1000.*

---

* He issued another challenge at the same time: to make a micro-motor. For the full text visit: http://calteches.library.caltech.edu/47/2/1960Bottom.pdf. Professor Feynman's love went way back: "We had the *Encyclopaedia Britannica*

Feynman actually had more than one page in mind for his miniaturization, and more than one book. "Why cannot we write the entire twenty-four volumes of the *Encyclopaedia Britannica* on the head of a pin?" he asked. He then examined what might be involved, beginning with the head of a pin measuring one-sixteenth of an inch across. He reasoned that all one had to do was reduce all the writing in an encyclopedia by 25,000 times. Then he figured how it would be inscribed on to the pin. And then he concluded, "I don't know why this hasn't been done yet!"*

But of course one could go the other way with encyclopedias. One could practically begin again, completely rethinking what a modern edition should look like. Perhaps the way forward was not shorter but longer, and more elaborate, an encyclopedia sold on the premise that it would last forever.

at home," he told the BBC *Horizon* program in 1981. "Even when I was a small boy [my father] used to sit me on his lap and read to me . . . We would read, say, about dinosaurs, and maybe it would be talking about the brontosaurus or the tyrannosaurus rex. It would say something like, this thing is 25 feet high and the head is six feet across. And he'd stop always, and say, 'Let's see what that means. That would mean that if he stood in our front yard he would be high enough to put his head through the window. But not quite, as the head is a little bit too wide—it would break the window as it came by.' Everything we'd read would be translated as best we could into some reality. So I'd learn to do that: everything I read I'd try to figure out what it really means, what it's really saying."

* Feynman then calculated that it would require about a million pinheads to reproduce all the books in the world, which, if laid on their side, would occupy an area of about three square yards. The $1000 prize money for the single page wasn't claimed for twenty-five years, until a Stanford graduate named Thomas H. Newman spent a month in 1984 shrinking the first page of Dickens's *A Tale of Two Cities*. In my book *In Miniature* I had speculated it was the best of Times New Roman, it was the worst of Times New Roman.

U

UNPRECEDENTED

At the peak of his fame, the broadcaster Michael Aspel turned his hand to many things. He was "suave" and "silver-tongued," and for a while British television couldn't get enough of him. He began his career as a newsreader, and would soon be one of the most popular, respected and reliably bland personalities on air, presenting *Ask Aspel, Antiques Roadshow* and long-running radio shows on London's Capital Radio and BBC Radio 2.

In 1973 I was in the audience at the Golders Green Hippodrome when he presented the children's comedy/ challenge show *Crackerjack*. That was also the year he was asked by *Encyclopaedia Britannica* to promote its latest edition.

Aspel appeared in magazine adverts in a grey flannel suit leaning against a shiny bookcase displaying twenty-four slabs bound in crimson. The wraparound text explained the usual stuff: 10,000 and more leading world authorities, 28,000 pages, 22,000 pictures, illustrations and maps. The text also explained that if you wanted yet more of Aspel he would come to your home free of charge, and with absolutely no obligation, in the form of a flexi disc, a 7-inch record made from very thin plastic that spun at 33 revolutions per minute. I sent off for the disc, and it was good to hear Michael's voice.

"This is Michael Aspel," he began, as familiar music played in the background. "No doubt you'll recognize this bit of Beethoven," he said. "This great composer is described in *Encyclopaedia Britannica* as having 'a musical imagination that was constantly alive.' Do *you* enjoy meeting people who have minds that are constantly alive?"

Imagine answering "no" to that.

Children have lively minds, Aspel continues, and they want answers. "Lively minds shouldn't be starved," he reasons. "That leads to apathy, frustration, waste." There was, of course, an easy way to feed these minds: *Britannica* was "a powerhouse of knowledge."

Then there was a forty-five-second audio clip of an Apollo launch, and an assurance from Aspel that the *Britannica* was right up to date; he said there was even an article about color television. And the *Britannica* had many uses beyond just helping the children—you could also widen your social contacts and further your business career. "Whatever the reason, I hope you will extend the courtesy you have shown in listening to me to the *Encyclopaedia Britannica* representative when he calls." (It was understood that because you had requested this record, a salesman now had your address and would be appearing on your doorstep soon.) Aspel closed by suggesting that by listening this far in the record you have already displayed a lively mind, and you would probably enjoy the quiz on the other side.

The quiz, which was read by someone other than Aspel, had twelve questions. Where did the camel come from? What has campanology to do with? How did the saxophone get its name? Alas, the record supplied no answers. For those you would have to wait until the *Britannica* representative paid you a little visit.

But then, a year later, Aspel's sales pitch—all that dapper effort—was useful no more. The edition he was plugging, and the one the representative had subsequently tried hard to sell you—the fourteenth, which, since its first publication in 1929, had been revised in 1930, 1932, 1933, 1936, 1937, and every year to 1973—had now been declared redundant. Harvey Einbinder's time had come: the publication would soon receive a complete overhaul, including the information about the camel, campanology and the saxophone. Aspel would be all right—he would go on to advertise no-calorie Sweetex and host *This Is Your Life*—but the *Britannica* would never be the same again.

Lively minds shouldn't be starved: Michael Aspel sells *Britannica* in the 1970s

The fifteenth edition of 1974 was unlike any encyclopedia that preceded it, and its editors hoped there would never be a need for another. It was a vast and complicated endeavor, thirteen years in the making, and it arrived with the sort of operating instructions that might have floored Steve Wozniak. Gone were the days when *Britannica* came with a statement of intent and an explanation of cross-referencing. Taking possession of the new thirty-volume edition now involved a personal handover, and its instructions came with pie charts.*

The intention was both forward-looking and retrograde. The preface referred to a "Circle of Learning," a concept that rooted it in the traditions of the ancient Greeks. The new edition aimed to give the reader access to its contents by both alphabetical order and topical subject matter. This time a reader didn't get one encyclopedia but three (indeed, rather than the fifteenth edition, it was sometimes called *Britannica 3*). There was the one-volume "Propaedia," described as "a kind of preamble or antechamber to the world of learning that the rest of the encyclopedia aims to encompass." This encompassing was to be found in the ten-volume "Micropaedia" ("ready reference" volumes containing short information on 102,000 topics) and the nineteen-volume "Macropaedia" (containing knowledge in greater depth on 4200 topics). There was also the promise of annual yearbooks, the latter designed to keep the reader up to speed with world events at about the same pace as the information they'd already purchased in thirty volumes hastened towards obsolescence. No one gets to launch a monument like this without the stats: 33,141 pages, 43 million words, 25,000 illustrations. There were

* The Fifteenth was the edition I picked up from Cambridge in the Introduction.

4000 contributing authors from more than 100 countries. In June 1974 the advertisements heralded "the first new idea in encyclopaedias for 200 years . . . the encyclopaedia that will wear out from use, not from time."

The price was at least £249, or about $500, and considerably more if you wanted the full morocco. The editorial creation of the work cost $32 million exclusive of printing costs: the *Britannica* justifiably claimed that this made it the largest single private investment in publishing history.*

Explaining the concept in a BBC interview at the time of its launch, Mortimer J. Adler, the chairman of the Board of Editors, said:

> Let's take Napoleon for a moment . . . You're doing some research, and you want to find out very quickly the date that Napoleon crowned himself Holy Roman Emperor. If you went to the old *Britannica* you'd find a ten-page article, twenty columns on Napoleon, and somewhere in that the date would be buried—you couldn't find it quickly, you might thumb through it but you wouldn't find it. Here you'd turn to the Micropaedia first and you'd get 700 words on Napoleon, with all the facts. And then if you wanted to read more we give you index references to the long article. We've separated the long background pieces from the short information pieces because they have two separate functions.†

* By the time the fifteenth edition was launched, *Britannica* had been an American publication for about sixty years. For decades it had been owned by Sears, Roebuck and Co., the mail order company based in Chicago, and then by a private charitable trust, the William Benton Foundation, which endowed the University of Chicago with *Britannica*'s proceeds.

† BBC *Nationwide*, 16 January 1974, interview by Christopher Rainbow.

This sounded easy enough, but the preface of the Propaedia showed how the presentation of the world's knowledge in the world's most famous encyclopedia was now much more complicated than a bit of thumbing-through.

> Each section number [in the Propaedia's seven-page Contents section] incorporates the numbers of the part and division to which it belongs. For example, Section 725 is the fifth section in Part Seven, Division II; Section 96/10 is the Tenth Section in Part Nine, Division VI. In each sectional outline the major subjects are indicated by capital letters ("A," "B" etc). There are always at least two major subjects, but there may be many more in a given section. When it is necessary to subdivide a major subject, up to three additional levels may appear in the outline; the first is indicated by Arabic numerals, the second by lowercase letters, and the third by Roman numerals.

There were then five pie charts relating to ten subject matters (from Life on Earth to The History of Mankind), each subject rotating to occupy a different piece of pie in the circle depending on which subject was at the center, and therefore at the heart of a reader's initial inquiry. And these were followed by some detailed examples designed to make finding information (about biology, say) a little easier.

> Section 10.34 in Division III of Part Ten examines the nature, methods, problems and history of the biological sciences; but the knowledge of life that the biological sciences afford is outlined in Part Three. Or, to take another example, Section 10/41 in Division IV of Part Ten examines historiography and the study of history; but the actual history of mankind is outlined in Part Nine.

Not everyone found this classification edifying (or knew what the hell was going on). It is worth noting that this was not some elaborate and very expensive joke; it was a genuine and clearly overthought attempt to redefine how the communication of knowledge was absorbed in the last quarter of the twentieth century. Alas, this fabulously complex system may have already come too late: 1974 marked at least one other milestone in communication—the first mobile phone call. In the *New Yorker,* Hans Koning reasoned that the very form in which the fifteenth edition was published "showed that knowledge now came in a shattered, scattered avalanche of data, to which no category such as 'purpose' was attached."

According to an essay by Geoffrey Wolff in the *Atlantic* in 1974, the editors of the fifteenth edition "worried copy mercilessly." Every article was rigorously outlined before the contributor got to work, and the writer "was warned that to add to the material in his outline would be to duplicate material appearing elsewhere in the set, while to ignore something included in the outline would be to leave it out of the set." Wolff quotes one of *Britannica*'s executive editors: "We really shoved it down their throats."

This may explain why this edition sometimes reads as if it's written by a committee, and a committee devoid of character or warmth. Geoffrey Wolff reasoned convincingly that one shouldn't expect to have much fun with it, for it lacked eccentricity, elegance and surprise, "the singular qualities that make learning an inviting transaction." He singled out the article on Gout. In the eleventh edition this ran to two and a half pages (gout provoked "a remarkable tendency to gnashing of the teeth," and the parts affected "cannot bear the weight of the bedclothes"). There was also a fascinating if questionable moral aspect (gout was less common in countries where its citizens had fewer "errors in living"). "That's the kind of stuff a gouty reader can take some pleasure from," Wolff declared. The shorter methodical entry in the fifteenth edition observes how "the elevation of uric acid appears to be transmitted by an autosomal gene."*

That said, it still does what any encyclopedia should. It carries tens of thousands of authoritative, interesting and useful articles. That's in the general Macropaedia, the sort of encyclopedia one has grown accustomed to over the years. But upon opening the highly exacting world of the Micropaedia we enter a very different and strange universe. One tries to apply some logic to it—by examining, for example, the fifty-six-page article on "Logic, The History and Kinds of," all 70,000-plus words and equations of it—and one is left exhausted. This was not general learning, this was extreme obsession, and it was not an exception. There are hundreds of columns on such far-reaching and rather hard-to-grapple topics such as Cities (ten pages), Climate and Weather (eighty-six pages), and Continental Landforms (fifty-five pages). After Climate and Weather there are six pages on Cnidarians.†

As always, this exhaustive enterprise could be paid for in monthly installments, the precise amount dependent on the quality of leather slapped around it. But the fifteenth edition also came with the revival of something *Britannica* hadn't

---

* "*Britannica 3*, History Of" by Geoffrey Wolff, the *Atlantic*, June 1974. Wolff's essay also revealed how carefully the Britannica board kept their plans for the new edition secret not only from its competitors but also from much of its own sales force; it was important they continued to sell the fourteenth edition just a few weeks before it was superseded. Of course, present-day computer and mobile phone companies do much the same thing.

† I had to read the entry to find out: cnidarians are a particular type of aquatic animal comprising polyp and medusa, the latter commonly known as jellyfish. The more one wrote, the more one got paid, of course. The usual rate was 10 cents per word, and major contributors also received a complete edition when published.

offered for decades—a "personal knowledge assistant." If the volumes in your possession didn't already answer everything under the sun, or didn't provide answers in enough depth, and if the world was moving just too fast for its pages, you were entitled to call on Britannica's Library Research Service. This had been created in 1936, and its department of "Answer Girls" featured heavily in its promotions. Having fallen from favor in the 1960s, it was now being revived with vigor.*

Every purchaser received 100 coupons to be redeemed for one of two products. The first was an "instant response system" by which the coupon-holder could select from 10,000 written reports that didn't make it into either the Micropaedia or Macropaedia. The extensive catalogue included: R-201—"The Value and Utilization of Poultry Manure and Deep Litter as Fertilizer and Stock Feed"; 3R-53—"The Hazards of Wind Shear and Microbursts"; 3R-148—"Establishing a Pecan Grove"; R-140—"Zea Diploperennis and the Possibility of Breeding Perennial Corn"; and R-5662—"Influences of Oriental Mysticism upon Ralph Waldo Emerson" (to sample just the Agriculture, Aeronautics and American Literature sections).

The second research product was up to you. For ten years from the date of purchase, a *Britannica* owner could ask up to 100 questions "on matters of fact," as many as ten questions per year. The answers to these questions would then arrive in the post, varying in length from a few lines to a few pages. It was a sort of Alexa/Siri service before its time, although it did take up to a month for any questions to be answered, and the

* At its peak the Library Research Service employed more than 100 women producing about 100,000 reports. The attendant publicity material described a glamorous life, with many employees traveling from city to city by train in the interests of research, picking up a special Britannica typewriter left by a previous researcher at a railway station locker.

service would be suspended in the event of a user slipping into arrears on their installment plan, and no questions could be answered regarding personal medical or legal matters, and no research would be conducted relating to public competitions with a cash prize.

In the same interview in which he'd explained the diminution and aggrandizement of Napoleon, Dr. Mortimer Adler was asked about the possibility of mistakes in his thirty-two volumes.

"We have a vast staff of data verifiers or fact checkers," he said. "And even so, of course, errors do creep in. I would guess there may be 2000 or 3000 small errors, typographical errors, little errors of fact that we have to correct within the next printing and the printing after that. It's impossible not to. Every encyclopedia has errors, and it's a constant vigilance to keep finding them and correcting them."

"So when will the information that a cricket pitch is ten-foot long [rather than the correct 66 feet] be corrected?" asked the man from the BBC.

"In the next printing! In 1975!"

The BBC man also wondered how long it would be before the new edition went out of date.

"We think we have produced an encyclopedia that is so flexible, and so capacious in its structure that it will accommodate any changes in knowledge in the next fifty years at least."*

If we still have the *Encyclopaedia Britannica* in our homes, the fifteenth edition is probably the one we have. True to Dr. Adler's

* That would take us to 2024. But in 1974, when Dr. Adler was speaking, something else had just been born: the first node of the Internet.

word, annual revisions continued into the late 1990s, and the set received a major overhaul in 1985. Articles were redesigned, reorganized and amalgamated, and the set expanded to thirty-two volumes, including a two-volume index that readers had suggested would have been useful when trying to negotiate the original version. The price was now about £1000 or $1500.

Perhaps—out of curiosity, or because we felt sorry for it just lying there—we might even consult the monolith from time to time. What we would never do, unless we were crazy, is read it in its entirety.

Step forward the enthusiastic A.J. Jacobs. In 2003, much to the amusement and then consternation of his wife, he undertook to tackle the literary equivalent of the north face of the Eiger, reading the fifteenth edition complete and unabridged in a year. Jacobs, a writer on *Esquire*, hoped to achieve two goals: reduce his television consumption, and in the process "become the smartest person in the world." He then achieved a third goal: writing an amusing book about his challenge. He revels in the joys of learning, although often plays the clown:

"I'm completely ignorant of this man," he writes of Petrarch, "but he sounds like someone I should know about." He concludes that Petrarch's devotion to his chaste love Laura would today be called stalking and result in a restraining order. He throws in a large amount of pop-culture gags and interjections from family and friends. He reads the entry on Plato on a train journey with his wife, Julie, to see her brother Doug in Philadelphia. If that isn't too much information in a book about information, we also learn that his wife's rash has cleared up. This is clearly a running gag, but there is no cross-referencing.*

A.J. Jacobs was not the first to attempt a complete read.

* *The Know-It-All* by A.J. Jacobs (William Heinemann, 2005).

George Bernard Shaw claimed he had studied most of *Britannica*'s ninth in the British Museum reading room, although he admitted to glossing over some of the science articles. The son of the novelist C.S. Forester remembers his father reading *Britannica* in bed, a physical as well as a literary achievement; in fact, he may have read the whole thing three times. A man called George Forman Goodyear, a lawyer in Buffalo, New York, took twenty-two years to read the complete fourteenth edition; the pioneering heart surgeon Michael DeBakey read the whole of the eleventh in his teens; Aldous Huxley apparently read the whole of the fourteenth, but randomly. He focused on a particular volume, and would then amuse a party crowd by his knowledge of things beginning with the letter *N* or *P*. And in 1934 the *New Yorker* reported on a man called A. Urban Shirk. Shirk was the advertising and sales manager of the International Products Corporation, which apparently isn't a made-up name, and in his spare time on lonely business trips, Shirk liked nothing more than reading the fourteenth. He spent two to six months on each volume, and was currently up to Volume 4 (Brai to Cast). If some of the entries seemed familiar to him it was because he had already spent four and a half years reading the whole of the twenty-nine-volume eleventh edition.

UPMANSHIP (a diversion . . .)

For those unfamiliar with what people with greying hair like to call "the golden age of British television," *The Two Ronnies* were Ronnie Barker (rotund, bumbling, professorial) and Ronnie Corbett (petite, pernickety, anecdotal). As comedians they were peak-time and family friendly, and they loved lexicography, spoonerisms and good puns. When, in 1975, a year after the latest *Britannica,* they pilloried the dreaded encyclopedia salesman, they chose not to target the hapless soul himself, for he was just spreading knowledge and making ends meet, but instead something broader, and something all British viewers would understand: the class system. And like Python before them, they succeeded in undercutting all expectations.

The scene is a clichéd depiction of a northern working-class front room. A wife called Elsie is at the ironing board in curlers, a husband in a vest called Arthur is pumping the tires on his upturned bike; all that's missing is a whippet. A knock on the door reveals a hatted, raincoated salesman with a chirpy greeting. He is the middle-class invasion, probably from the south.

Ronnie Corbett (as the salesman): "Good morning, Sonny! Is your mummy in?"

Arthur is played by Ronnie Barker. It's safe to assume that no one has called him "Sonny" for at least forty years.

"It's another one of them sales, m'love," he calls to his wife in the front room.

The salesman enters and wonders whether he can interest them in a nice set of encyclopedias. Each volume is full of very interesting information. For example, did they know that Siberian Lake Balkhash has an area of no less than 7050 square miles?

"Yes." Arthur says as he returns to his bicycle.

Well how about the fact that the Yangtze Kiang is some 3400 miles long?

Yes, he knew that too.

Fine, but did he know that the highest mountain in South America was Mount Illampu at 3012 feet?

"I think you're wrong there, lad," Arthur says. "The highest mountain in South America is surely Mount Aconcagua, isn't it? Which is over 69 feet higher than the Illampu, isn't that right, our Elsie?"

Our Elsie disagrees—she thinks it's Mount Cotopaxi. Luckily, their daughter Lily has just entered the room to settle the matter.

"Oh, you're not on that one again, are you?" she asks as she settles in the easy chair to file her nails. "It's Mount Chimborazo."

This goes on for a while. The salesman has various other items to tease them with. Who said "Many a good hanging prevents a bad marriage?" How does the diameter of Neptune compare with that of Earth? Name the dwarf monkey that lives in the Amazonian mountains and feeds on small flowers, roots and small birds. The window cleaner outside the parlor window, for some reason on a ladder on the ground floor, chips in with the answer: it's the white-eared marmoset.

There is also mention of a neighbor named Mrs. Butterworth, who recently "proved the existence of a fourth dimension." The salesman, increasingly infuriated, begins ripping up pages from the book in his hands. He says he hasn't sold one all week.

But then there's a twist. Arthur says he'll buy a set.

And then another twist: the salesman says the cost is £2 a week for five weeks, but Arthur, Elsie and Lily can't agree what that will be in total. It may be £10, but it may also be £7.

V

VALEDICTORY

In 1994 Kenneth F. Kister, a reference book enthusiast in Tampa, Florida, published the second edition of *Kister's Best Encyclopedias.* It was, almost inevitably, a 500-page single-volume encyclopedia itself, and covered the big general encyclopedias alongside medium-sized encyclopedias and small encyclopedias, as well as children's encyclopedias and specialist encyclopedias on the decorative arts, engineering and childcare. There was even a small section on the leading encyclopedias in China, Japan, Korea, Spain and Russia. (In Russia there was only one, *Bol'shavia Sovetskaia Entsiklopediia*, or *Great Soviet Encyclopaedia*, not entirely the work of the Central Committee, but certainly a publication with a Marxist-Leninist bias, with, for example, the American Declaration of Independence derided as the product of a disastrous bourgeois revolution.)

Among Japanese sets, Kenneth F. Kister singles out the "serviceable" single-volume *Daijiten Desuku* (Tokyo, 1983) and the "well-edited, handsomely illustrated" twenty-three-volume

Dai-Nixon Hakka Jitendra (Tokyo, 1973). Among Korean-language volumes, Kister notes that when a translated *Britannica* appeared with added Korean-interest articles in 1992, its publishers in Seoul had an optimistic message. They had taken "great pains to cover North Korean topics in a realistic manner. In this way the editors have made their own contribution to realising a unified Korea." Nothing if not ambitious.

Kister's exhaustive survey was timely in a way he couldn't have known when he began. The mid-1990s marked a long slow funeral for the print encyclopedias that occupied nine-tenths of his report. The CD-ROM was taking over, and not long after that most people would have some sort of dial-up online service provider, and his guide swiftly came to resemble the passenger list on the *Titanic*.*

But what a list, and what a story was winding down. He mentions many briefly popular volumes from the 1950s and '60s, the heyday of small-scale editions produced by established publishing houses eager for a slice. The *Macmillan Family Encyclopedia, Webster's Family Encyclopedia, Barnes & Noble Encyclopedia, Random House Encyclopedia,* many of them with student or children's versions.

Kister's tone is as generous as his analysis is bland. "Information in *Funk & Wagnalls* is normally reliable and presented in an impartial manner," he declares. The *Grolier Encyclopedia of Knowledge,* a slightly reduced version of the standard *Grolier Academic American* produced primarily for sale in supermarkets, was praised for its "broad and carefully balanced coverage, accurate and impartial presentation of material, sound organization and effective access to specific topics and facts, first-rate illustrations, impeccable authority."

* See encyclopedia-titanica.org.

In other words, like the vast majority of publications under consideration, it was a *good* encyclopedia, or, at the very worst, good for its intended market.

What made *Kister's* interesting were his comparison tables, in which he rated one publication next to another in terms of number of words, pages and illustrations, and then cross-references, index entries and price. Each encyclopedia was then assigned a grade, with A being "excellent" and D "below average." In the fourteen medium-sized adult encyclopedias under consideration, eleven were either A or B, with one C and two Ds. Prospective purchasers were encouraged not to base their judgment purely on the grades, "which are necessarily arbitrary."

Equally arbitrary were the "report cards" he assigned according to the treatment of various topics. For the medium-sized publications he took a list of ten subjects, including Computers, Halloween, Magic Johnson, Measles, Nuclear Energy and Sex Education, and gave each a grade for Coverage, Accuracy, Clarity and "Recency." In *Compton's*, almost every topic got an A in every category, although Computers and Nuclear Energy only got a C for Clarity. For the large adult comparison between *Britannica*, *Americana* and *Collier's*, Kister reshuffled his subject list, now selecting topics including Philip Glass and the Shroud of Turin. The best overall performance was judged to be *Collier's* with As across the board, followed by *Americana* with only a little slippage when it came to Galileo, and lastly there was *Britannica*, which let itself down with poor Recency when it came to both Circumcision and Heart Disease.

Who was Mr. Kister to conduct such a guide? He billed himself as "North America's best known reviewer of information materials," although this in itself must have been hard to quantify. As well as encyclopedias, he had written comprehensive guides to atlases and dictionaries, and he held a master's in library science from the Simmons College Graduate School of Library and Information Science in Boston.

Kister was also the new Laurance Hart. Beginning in 1929, and for the next thirty-five years, Hart had published his "Comparison of Encyclopedias," known universally as The Hart Chart. This was a sheet measuring 17 by 11 inches sent every six months from his home in New Jersey at a cost of 35 cents for the first sheet and then 15 cents thereafter. Each sheet contained eleven tables, some of them primitive in their appraisal: he measured both "price per 100 pages" and "price per million words," thus penalizing elegant typography and good editing. His obituaries in at least two library journals praised the role his work played in raising standards in reference works and simplifying the work of acquisition.

A few years later, librarians would be faced with other, less familiar, choices. In June 1998, at the Annual Conference of the American Library Association in Washington, DC, one of the topics concerned the future of digital encyclopedias. Specifically, members were concerned with how confusing this new world could be, and how fast this landscape was changing. They wanted to know where to invest their energies and budget.

James Rettig, a librarian at the University of Richmond, Virginia, presented a conference paper marking this radical transformation over the last fifteen years. It started, he said, with the "simple porting over of imageless ASCII text to pre-Web online systems," but then things got complicated.

> Then we had text-only CD-ROM encyclopedias, followed by text and-still-image encyclopedias, followed by text-still-image sound-and-video CD-ROM encyclopedias, followed by text-

still image-sound-and-video CD-ROM encyclopedias including simulations and animations, followed by text-still image-sound-and-video CD-ROM encyclopedias including simulations and animations and links to Web sites, followed, of course, by online interactive encyclopedias combining all of the above.

The field now resembled a forest of wires at the back of an early computer. Amid the confusion, mistakes could be costly: early CD-ROMs cost hundreds of dollars. Library users would all want the latest and most exciting versions, but when would the technology reach its zenith? The answer, of course was "never," but at some stage a decision had to be made. The confusion and mistakes could, of course, prove costlier still to the encyclopedia makers themselves.

In June 1983, the big digital questions descended upon the offices of *Encyclopaedia Britannica*. The sales promotion department met to consider precisely how much of a threat to its business was the computer. A memo documenting the main discussion points of that meeting was issued to its sales teams (as ammunition against potential customers wanting a digital version), and years later it was published on the website of Robert McHenry, for several years *Britannica*'s editor-in-chief.

"One of the questions we are most frequently asked, by both our own people and outsiders, is 'When will *Britannica* be available on a computer?,'" the memo began. "The answer we give is, 'Not for a long time.'"

The memo then outlines several reasons for this decision.

1. None of the popular models of home computer had enough memory to store *Britannica*. The company calculated how many floppy disks would be required just to store the index, and it came to a vague figure of 100–200.

2. The option of putting the encyclopedia on a large mainframe computer and allowing a user to access it via their home computer and a telephone was deemed unwieldy and expensive. It was difficult to find your way around and it was easy to lose your place. On a screen one could read only a few words at a time. "A book is a lot easier to use and is more cost effective at this time."
3. A computer makes searching fast, but it is not an intelligent way of negotiating an encyclopedia. The memo gave the example of "orange," which would offer the possibilities of the fruit, the colour, Orange County, or William of Orange. In the print version *Britannica* indexers had already done that sifting for the reader, eliminating trivial or random references.

"Until new ways are developed," the memo concluded, "we can provide a better, easier-to-use encyclopedia in printed form than in any computerized version. We will not change our delivery method from the printed page to the electronic form until we are sure that it is the most efficient way for our readers to receive it."

Within a decade, *Britannica* would be all but overrun by the forward-thinking, distinctly glamorous, multimedia and easily searchable CD-ROMs marketed by Compton's, Grolier and Microsoft. Tradition—even one stretching back to the eighteenth century—would be afforded little respect as it crashed head-on into a digital future.

V

VANQUISHED!

If the sport was boxing, the pre-match betting would have evened out nicely. In one corner stood the behemoth, a champion of such towering intellectual prowess and competitive experience that it was surely able to outsmart anyone. And in the other stood the sprightly upstart with fanciful ideas backed by new money. In late 1985, with *Britannica*'s sales flourishing and Microsoft Windows still at its launch pad, only the foolhardy or visionary would feel secure about the outcome. But then the rules seemed to change mid-fight, and the sport was suddenly being marketed to a new and younger audience watching it on reflective screens, and all the hard-won expertise acquired in the traditional training camp seemed suddenly irrelevant. Rather than fight to the end, as it had done in all its other contests, the hardened behemoth collapsed, tragic in its shocking fall.

A tortuous analogy, admittedly, and quite lacking the redemptive Hollywood ending (it wasn't *Rocky*). But it could all have turned out rather differently. In the mid-1980s, a fledgling Microsoft had tried to entice Encyclopaedia Britannica, Inc. into a digital partnership. The software company knew that a CD-ROM encyclopedia would encourage people to adopt its Windows operating system, and it tried to persuade Britannica that a partnership would keep it relevant in the twenty-first century—a searchable database of the world's knowledge available on home computers at a fraction of the cost of the original, with minimal delivery complications and no shelving issues. Britannica said no, partly out of pride, one imagines, and certainly because it feared a diminution of profits. The deal seemed far too one-sided in Microsoft's favor. Only with hindsight, as the project Microsoft had codenamed "Gandalf" turned into *Encarta,* does this seem like a calamitous decision.

In 2016, Shane Greenstein, a professor at the Technology Operations and Management Unit at Harvard Business School,

published a paper called "The Reference Wars," a forensic account of *Britannica*'s failure to embrace digital technology. It was really a story of the decline of all standard encyclopedias, and the old-model notions of how an encyclopedia should be bought and read. There was an obvious moral too. This was a story of how the personal computer "could visit major trauma" on an old institution, and how no enterprise could afford to consider itself too revered or intellectually superior to take on the challenge.*

Professor Greenstein suggests that Britannica executives were thoroughly aware of the threats of new technology to their business, but were too tied into the old model—the old sales methods, the reliable profits from book sales that had sustained the company for 220 years—to even *want* to move fast enough in the digital world. "In Britannica's case . . . even the best outcome in the new market would have been a decline in sales and profitability," he notes. "As executives begin to manage this uncomfortable situation, the situation goes from bad to worse in the old market. The demand for the old falls at almost the same time that Britannica fails to succeed in the new." It was like an addict helplessly acting against their own best interests. "When no rational manager could maintain an illusion about the prospects for growth in the old market, management still chose to not favor the new market."

It was all the more perplexing because Britannica, Inc. had an early toehold in this new world. It had owned *Compton's Encyclopaedia* since 1961, and had launched *Compton's MultiMedia Encyclopedia* in 1989, the first such product on the market.

The *Compton's* operating manual reminds us just how unfamiliar the system must have appeared. "To scroll through an article select

* "The Reference Wars: *Encyclopaedia Britannica*'s Decline and *Encarta*'s Emergence," April 2016.

Play using button 1. Pushing button 1 several times allows you to scroll faster. To page through an article select Play using button 2. Some short articles may be complete in themselves, but in most cases the article will contain one or more cross-references to major articles in Compton's. These are indicated by Jump icons. To go to a reference select the Jump Arrow."

But there were also imaginative attempts to make the information (30,000 short articles) enticing. Icons indicated sound and video clips, and links to maps. For some entries, *Star Trek*'s Patrick Stewart guided users through a Time Machine, a tour through specific historical periods and major events: "First, select Enter Machine then select Past (Rewind). Eras are indicated by drawings in the window, with dates above the window. To go toward the future select Future (Play)."

If operating it was clunky, selling it was half-hearted. The *Compton's* CD-ROM came bundled "for free" to anyone who bought a full print set of *Britannica* (at between $1500–$2000), but it was vastly overpriced at $895 when bought on its own. At the beginning of the 1990s, Britannica's 2000-strong sales force still sold most of their sets through solicited house calls. They had no idea how to use a compact disc, let alone market one. Shane Greenstein quotes a Britannica employee who recalls, "I conducted over a year of training with the sales force and taught them step by step how to use the demo on it; they didn't know how to operate the computers in the potential buyers' homes."*

Four years later, having fumbled its early chance to dominate the market, Britannica, Inc. sold its interest in *Compton's* to the Chicago-based Tribune media group. By the

* They could be forgiven for underestimating the speed at which home ownership of personal computers would increase. About 8 percent of US households had a PC in 1984. Five years later it was 15 percent. When *Encarta* became successful in 1993 the figure was 23 percent.

time Britannica tried again, and released its own expensive and unexciting *Britannica* CD-ROM in 1994, it had already lost out to Microsoft's much cheaper all-bells-and-whistles *Encarta* by a year. And it was no consolation for the Britannica executives to tell themselves that *Encarta* was an inferior product. In fact, it was only inferior when judged by the reverentially high standards of print; judged by the clickable criteria of the new world, it would change the game.

Encyclopedias behind them, the future ahead: Bill and Melinda Gates like what they see

The development of *Encarta* wasn't smooth, but its main champion—Bill Gates himself—was persistent. After Britannica had rejected its overtures, Microsoft pursued its encyclopedic content one rung down, to the popular and successful *World Book*. But *World Book* also turned down a Microsoft partnership, as did *Collier's*. Like Britannica, the publishers feared a big dent in print sales, and *World Book* was hatching plans to launch its own disc version in 1990. Microsoft's frustration increased when it learned that Grolier would soon be partnering with Apple, making its content more easily accessible with a point-and-click mouse than it was in the PC MS-DOS version.*

In 1989, Gates finally found a match in Funk & Wagnalls, the company that reasoned that if it wanted to sell its low-budget encyclopedias to a mass market, the best place to do that might be in supermarkets.†

Once a licensing deal was agreed upon, Microsoft set about enhancing the text for its digital offering. The *Grolier* had been criticized for including only grainy images in its disc, and so Microsoft employed the great media buzzword of the time—synergy—to use its recently created Corbis photo and video library to bring *Encarta* alive. Faced with storage limitations (at a time before MP3s and efficient image compression), *Encarta* editors added clips that would grab most attention at its presentations—the Apollo moon shots, a recording of Einstein, spuming whales. It also included more entries on popular culture and business affairs, and it reflected as many

* The *Grolier* Multimedia CD-ROM would come bundled with the Mac II, and although Apple still only had a relatively small market share in the early 1990s, it was making steady inroads into desktop publishing, appealing in particular to the less office-orientated, more creative side of the market. For a thorough analysis of the contents of the main players in the early days see Henry Jay Becker, "Encyclopedias on CD-ROM: Two Orders of Magnitude More Than Any Other Educational Software Has Ever Delivered Before" (*Educational Technology*, vol. 31, no. 2, February 1991).

† They really did sell it like bargain crackers. An advertisement for the A&P chain from this time offered the "Eldorado Deluxe" edition of its Standard Reference set—gilded page tops—for half the regular price if purchased in-store. "Only 49 cents for Volume No 1 and $1.49 each for the other volumes of the set with money-saving coupons. Make it a habit to pick up an additional volume every time you shop." An entire encyclopedia for about $30: not much more than British subscribers were paying in the 1780s.

recent events as it could. Meanwhile, in the world of ink and tree-felling, Britannica kept on pushing its exhaustive and leaden yearbooks.

The initial launch of *Encarta* towards the end of 1992 was not a success. Its marketing team missed the holiday season, and it was deemed much too costly at $295. But the following year it tried again. It now cost only $99, and was faster and more exciting than its rivals (it included a video clip of the Israel–Arab Oslo peace accord that occurred only a few weeks before its release). It received solid but not rave reviews, yet the sales were phenomenal.

Encarta sold 120,000 copies in the 1993 holiday period alone, and production couldn't keep up with demand. In its first year 350,000 copies were ordered, and 1 million the year after. Clearly, no encyclopedia had ever sold like this.

Initially, users didn't seem to mind that they were reading a less-than-great series of articles; the fact they were accessing such a fast reference tool on a screen, without a visit to the library or an outdated print volume, was appealing enough, and the audiovisual buzzes were fun too. A modern encyclopedia may even have appealed to the modern child the way it was supposed to in the adverts, although most of their time with *Encarta* was probably spent clicking on the videos. Over the next few years, Microsoft did much to increase the quality of its product, meeting an educational responsibility it had never expected to bear.

"We consciously invested in the contextual value," wrote Tom Corddry, Encarta's former team leader, on the *New York Times* website in 2009. "In expanding the core content, in creating the world's first truly global encyclopedia, and in an efficient update cycle. We had enough 'multimedia' in the original product to keep the reviewers happy, but focused on the overall usefulness of the whole product much more than on the relative handful of video clips."

Corddry disputes the idea that *Funk & Wagnalls'* original text was low quality compared to *Britannica*. For *Encarta*'s needs it was almost ideal: its "structured data" ensured a consistency of text from one article to the next, easing the construction of a highly efficient set of links and navigational tools across the entire content.

"*Britannica*, by contrast, was a bloated mishmash," Corddry maintained, "a consequence of its long tradition of having articles written by many different celebrity authors . . . I'd argue that within its first five years, *Encarta* became the best encyclopedia in history: it had tremendously consistent quality and usefulness across a very broad range of topics, and added a great deal of value by the relationships it illuminated between topics."

All of this has since been rendered a bit quaint, the *Encarta* chief conceded, but in its day it did more than unsettle the traditional print encyclopedia—"it pretty much destroyed it."

In 1990, the last year it saw a profit, Britannica made $40 million on a sales revenue of $650 million. That year it sold 117,000 printed sets, but by the time revenue dropped to $453 million in 1994 it was selling only 51,000, and a large proportion of its sales force (2000-plus in 1990) was being laid off.

"We need capital and are confident we can secure it," said Peter B. Norton, the company's president, in a statement in April 1995. But Britannica, Inc. took more than a year to find a buyer, and when it did, the Swiss investor Jacob Safra paid only $130 million, a fraction of its value in the 1980s. By 1996, revenue had fallen to $325 million, sales were just a few thousand sets each year, and losses were mounting. At the time of the sale, computers were in more than a third of American homes. The exciting writing was on the screen.

But there was another way of looking at this. Perhaps *Britannica* and other traditional encyclopedias had simply misjudged the competition: the boxer it thought it was fighting was actually someone else.

In 2000, *Britannica*'s fall had been studied by two senior vice presidents of the Boston Consulting Group. In the opening pages of *Blown to Bits,* their account of what they call "the new economics of information," Philip Evans and Thomas S. Wurster considered that the company simply underestimated the challenge. "Judging from their inaction, Britannica executives at first seemed to have viewed the CD-ROM encyclopedia as an irrelevance: a child's toy, one step above video games. This perception was entirely reasonable."*

One reason for this was a predicament they shared with almost every other traditional business: old incumbents were saddled with "legacy assets"—bricks and mortar, sales and distribution teams, mainframe systems. It was just hard to destroy these things. "Instead, blame comes into play, and last-ditch financial calculations hit a wall of internal political debates and personal self-protection."

Then there were the psychological elements. Evans and Wurster argue that the key decision makers at Britannica were blinded by their own history and myths, making them unable to appreciate something that didn't fit into their collective mental framework. Worse, they failed to see how one of their oldest and most reliable sales principles—parents wanting to do something valuable for their children's education and feeling bad if they

* *Blown to Bits: How the New Economics of Information Transforms Strategy,* by Philip Evans and Thomas S. Wurster (Harvard Business Review Press, 1999). The reference to video games is perhaps doubly unfortunate, given that this industry now generates billions of dollars in worldwide sales (in 2018 one estimate put this figure at $135 billion).

didn't—had been subconsciously transferred to a new medium. "If the fundamental value proposition is assuaging parental guilt, then the fundamental competitor is not Encarta, it is the PC." Writing twenty years ago, Evans and Wurster state:

> Today, when parents are anxious about their children's performance in school, when they feel guilty about not doing enough to help, they buy a computer. The new PC may never be used for anything other than chat rooms and video games, but parental guilt has again been duly salved. It just so happens that the computer costs about the same amount as *Britannica*. And along with that computer comes a CD-ROM drive. And along with the CD-ROM drive come several free CD-ROMS, one of which is a promotional copy of *Encarta*.

Certainly *Encarta* did its job. It sold millions of copies, and Microsoft reaped rewards both from the disc and its operating system. That it couldn't continue being successful forever would have been clear to all those who worked on it, not least to the person who wrote *Encarta*'s entry on the irrepressible growth of the Internet.

In March 2009 *Encarta* announced its "shuttering," the phrase suggestive of a shop pulling down its grille as a new supermarket destroys its livelihood. It was indeed stuck in the past, a victim of the speed of technological advance that had once crowned it king. It was almost tragicomic: only twenty years before, it was conceived as the indomitable future. In its last year it dropped its price to $22.95, the clearest indication that almost all of its knowledge was already available elsewhere.

Encarta did try to keep its brand alive online, but it had entered the arena far too late. According to the Internet ratings service Hitwise, two months before it closed, *Encarta* had just 1.27 percent of all US Internet traffic to encyclopedia sites. "The category of traditional encyclopedias and reference material has changed," Microsoft announced, a rare understatement in a world of hyperbole. "People today seek and consume information in considerably different ways than in years past. As part of Microsoft's goal to deliver the most effective and engaging resources for today's consumer, it has made the decision to exit the *Encarta* business."

This was a huge admission of defeat (from such a huge corporation). It had been beaten by its inability to keep pace—with popular demand, with the spread of information itself. What *Encarta* achieved above all was expectation: as computer users engaged in information retrieval, we came to anticipate constant progress and increasing value; our insatiable desire for all the knowledge in the world would not content itself with a noisily whirring disc of coated plastic.

VIETNAM (a diversion . . .)

Joey Tribbiani is removing the chewing gum from the underside of a small metal patio table in his New York apartment when he hears a knock at the door. There is a big man waiting there, and he has a big question:

"Good afternoon. Are you the decision maker of the house?" This is the salesman's classic opener: even a child might find it hard to answer "no" to this one. But Joey hesitates. He looks around his apartment. He is alone, but still he pauses. He opens his mouth, still pondering. All he can offer is "Er . . . ," so the salesman intervenes.

"Do you currently own a set of encyclopedias?"

This one Joey can answer. "No," he says, "but try the classifieds—people sell everything in there."

The salesman says he's not buying, but selling, and he offers his hand as he asks him another question. Do Joey's friends ever have the sort of conversations during which he just nods along, not quite sure what they're talking about? Cue the flashback of Joey nodding along as his friends sit around talking about something "unconstitutional"; and then one in which they refer to something as "the Algonquin's kids' table." Joey is clueless, but he laughs along heartily with his buddies nonetheless.

The salesman notes that Joey has been silently flashing back for about two and a half minutes. He wonders, "Are you *at all* interested?" "Sure," Joey says, "come on in." The salesman already has a volume in his hand, the one with the letter *V*. They sit down at the patio furniture and the salesman wonders what Joey knows about Van Gogh. Not much, apart from the fact that he cut off his ear "because he sucked." Selecting another page brings another question: where does the pope live? In the woods, Joey says. The next flick-through brings up Vulcanized Rubber. After an ad break the volume has moved from the salesman's hands to Joey's, and he realizes there's a lot he didn't know about Vomit.

The whole set can be his for $1200, or $50 per book. Joey is astonished that the salesman thinks he may have that much to spend. Asked how much he can actually afford, he offers "Zero down, and zero a month for a long, long time." He starts to empty out his pockets: a baby Tootsie Roll, a movie stub, keys, a Kleenex, a rock, but as the salesman turns to go he finds a $50 note, and he thinks for a moment that he must be wearing his friend's jeans. This $50 buys him one book, and rather than take the *A* volume, Joey decides to stick with the *V*.

The pay-off comes at Central Perk. As Joey's friends talk of relationships, he mentions how one particular girlfriend could blow up "like that Vesuvius." When his friends question why they're suddenly talking about volcanoes, Joey says he's happy to talk about something else. Vivisection? The vas deferens? The Vietnam War? But when Monica asks whether anyone else saw that documentary about the *Korean* War, Joey is once again all knitted brows and confusion.

That was in October 1997, from *Friends'* fourth season, "The One with the Cuffs," with Matt LeBlanc as Joey, Penn Jillette as the salesman. To this day, Jillette says, whenever he does a magic show anywhere in the world, someone always comes up to him afterwards and asks about his *Friends* appearance. Selling is all about vocation, Jillette tells them. And about volume.

W

WIKIMANIA

Each summer, the staff of Wikipedia get together with their most fanatical contributors for a five-day conference called Wikimania, a sort of WrestleMania for the brainy and pedantic. There is soul searching, navel gazing, pulse taking and crystal balling, not forgetting punch pulling and verbal flame throwing. Popular issues for discussion include inclusion, deletion, citation, representation, notability, harassment of editors, empowerment of users, and the open-source software operating system called Ubuntu. Astonishingly, perhaps, the event sells out fast. In 2014 the venue was London, in 2018 Cape Town, in 2019 Stockholm.

Like the textual behemoth that inspired it, Wikimania goes high and low. You turn up from all corners of the globe, get the bright yellow T-shirt, and within minutes you're embedded in a break-out group called "Wiki Loves Butterfly," or "Serbia Loves Wikipedians in Residence," or "Let's Completely Change How Templates Work!" The conference also holds board meetings,

and pledges to do better next year on issues of gender and racial diversity. It even announces its Wikimedian of the Year, a title awarded in 2020 to Emna Mizouni, a Tunisian human rights activist praised for organizing the conference WikiArabia and contributing to the photographic project Wiki Loves Monuments.

And then, as the sky darkens, and should you have the stomach for such things, you may join the gatekeepers of the world's knowledge as they knock back tequila-based wikishots and indulge in their "passion projects." You would be surprised if these didn't include making snow globes, real-life Quidditch, "being awesome" and jail-friendly power yoga, at the very least.

Wikipedia is a universe unto itself, its ambition unequalled and its scale unprecedented. Its staff are fond of a single phrase: "Thank God our enterprise works in practice, because it could never work in theory." In theory, Wikipedia should be a disaster. The work of world experts and world amateurs, creators and vandals, anarchists and trainspotters, super-grammarians and super-creeps, many hundreds of thousands of each from all the world's nations, every one vaguely suspicious of everyone else, some using Google Translate in hilarious ways, all battling for some sort of supremacy in a multiverse of ultimate truth—that doesn't bode well. And yet that's what Wikipedia is—an errant community of career-long academics and lone-wolf information crackpots that continues to create something of brilliance with almost every keystroke.

In 2021, Wikimania was scheduled for Bangkok, and the focus was on Wikipedia's twentieth birthday, but the party was derailed by Covid-19. In all other respects, Wikipedia flourished under the pandemic, tracking the first weeks in a masterful way, and like nothing else. It was on the ground everywhere, in 100 languages, keyboarded up. Many thousands of people contributed their knowledge of the virus and its impact on their lives and local area (as always, for no financial reward). Sometimes it seemed as if the virus itself was contributing, such was the speed of the spread. The number of words grew from a few hundred in mid-January 2020 to a few hundred thousand by mid-March; many hundreds of useful links brought the reader to current medical journals, historical accounts of pandemics, and an early discussion on the efficacy of masks. Conspiracy theorists were given very little credibility, and deliberately malicious information was removed within minutes.

Between December 2019 and April 2020 Wikipedia pages relating to the pandemic received on average 163 edits per hour. By 23 April 2020 there were about 4500 pandemic-related Wikipedia pages across all languages.*

All of this led the writer Noam Cohen of *Wired* magazine to suggest that Wikipedia had "developed a conscience," which, with the exception of Diderot's *Encyclopédie,* was not something regularly attributed to an encyclopedia, and would not always be considered a compliment. But it stayed free of hysteria, and as free as it could from propaganda. It was, ultimately, instantly useful.

Since its creation in January 2001, Wikipedia has grown into the world's largest online reference work, attracting more than 500 million page views per day and 1 billion unique visitors each month (who make 5.6 billion monthly visits in total and hang around for an average of four minutes). It offers a total of more than 54 million articles in about 270 languages,

* Daily interactions may include pages accessed multiple times by the same person. Wikipedia's own statistics are as fascinating as any article. The data provides a glimpse into use around the world, its changing size month on month, and the number of pages and edits, among many other things. Begin here: https://stats.wikimedia.org.

including—at 11.25 GMT on Saturday 9 October 2021—6,390,565 articles in English that have been subject to 1,044,294,099 edits since 2001 (with 19.21 edits per page). That makes it 93.11 times the size of *Encyclopaedia Britannica*, and the equivalent of 2979.7 *Britannica* volumes.

According to the analytics company SimilarWeb, Wikipedia is the world's seventh most visited site, sitting behind Google, YouTube, Facebook, Twitter, Instagram and the Chinese search engine Baidu. (Wikipedia is actually seventh-equal with Czech-based X Videos, and only just ahead of Cyprus-based Pornhub.) In the UK, Wikipedia stands ninth in the charts, overtaken by eBay and the BBC. (Since you're wondering, the highest ranked porn site in the UK is Pornhub at number thirteen, which is just one place above the *Daily Mail*.)

More than any other float in this parade, Wikipedia settles arguments and ignites debate. It sends you down rabbit holes so fathomless that you emerge gasping, astonished at what other people know and consider important, dismayed at where the time has gone. Its offshoots help you with your degree (Wikiversity), your wedding speeches (Wikiquote), your journals and presentations (Wikimedia Commons), your online sightseeing and travel adventures (Wikivoyage) and your spelling (Wiktionary). The rest of it just helps you with your life, and the placing of it within contexts both modern and historical. It combines every highbrow piece of technicality with every lowbrow piece of junkery. It has the track length of the fourth song on the third album by a band you've never heard of and never will, a list of the seventy-four churches preserved by the Churches Conservation Trust in the English Midlands, the complete text of Darwin's treatise *The Various Contrivances by which Orchids are Fertilised by Insects*, and a biography of the mathematics teacher Riyaz Ahmad Naikoo (also known as Zubair), one of the top ten most wanted rebels in the disputed territory of Jammu and Kashmir.*

But obscurity never overwhelms relevance. I watched in awe as its Covid-19 pages expanded in number, depth and sober analysis from the first cases at the end of 2019 to its global peak seven months later, as it diligently modified facts, trends and theories as they emerged. There was nowhere else with such a calm and comprehensive global approach, and nowhere else where the common reader could go for a comparative overview of every other deadly virus in our richly plague-ridden past.

You could make a strong case for suggesting that Wikipedia is the most valuable single site online, and the most eloquent and enduring representative of the Internet as a force for good. It has indeed completely changed how templates work. It strives for democracy in its performance and neutrality in its effect. It is ad-free, pop-up free, cookie-free and free. It confounds human venality and appeals to our better nature.

It certainly confounds its co-founder Jimmy Wales. Wales set up Wikipedia to supplement an earlier online open-source encyclopedia he had founded with Larry Sanger the year before, named Nupedia. The problem with Nupedia was its concept: its articles were written by experts and peer-reviewed, which rendered it much too slow for mass appeal in the digital world. Wiki means "quick" in Hawaiian, and Wikipedia joined the growing number of online communal wikis already available that could be compiled and edited swiftly by anyone with a basic knowledge of digital etiquette. Everyone who contributed to Wikipedia was a volunteer, and from the start the site was governed by its contributors.

"Although I have often described myself as a 'pathological

* @depthsofwiki is a great Twitter feed. It may suck up all your spare time.

optimist,'" Jimmy Wales told me via email for an *Esquire* story I was writing in May 2020, "I don't think I really understood the depth of the impact that we would have. I certainly didn't foresee how some very early decisions against collecting, sharing, and selling data would end up setting us fundamentally apart from the sector of the Internet that people are increasingly uneasy with."

The techlash against Facebook and Twitter has left Wikipedia largely unscathed. Or rather, Wikipedia is saddled with many of the same sorts of criticisms and shortcomings it has always had. Wales calls these "difficult questions about behaviour."

"We are humans, and people do get into arguments, and people who 'aren't here to build an encyclopedia' show up to push an agenda, or to troll or harass. And dealing with those cases requires a great deal of calm and sensible judgment. It requires building robust institutions and mechanisms. If we were to deal with some problems in the community by allowing the Wikimedia Foundation to become like other Internet institutions (Twitter comes to mind), where policing the site for bad behaviour is taken out of the hands of the community, we'd end up like Twitter—unscalable, out of control, a cesspool."

I asked Wales what he thought of his own Wikipedia entry, which includes his nickname (Jimbo), his background in the financial sector, and his involvement in an online portal that specialized in adult content.

"It's as right as the media about me is right," he replied. "I don't think it mentions that I'm a passionate chef, which is a pity. But I think that's because it's never been covered in the press. You can mention it—that'll set the world to rights."*

* The mention of cookery in the *Esquire* article had its desired effect. A few days after the story appeared, the following line was added to his Wikipedia entry: "According to Wales, he is a passionate chef."

Wales is now chair emeritus of the Wikimedia Foundation. When I asked him to describe his present role in the empire, he made an unusual comparison. "I think UK audiences will understand this better than other audiences. I view my role as being very much like the modern monarch of the UK: no real power, but the right to be consulted, the right to encourage, and the right to warn."

I wondered whether he regretted not being a billionaire like all the other pioneers on that top ten chart: did he never regret not monetizing Wikipedia in some way? ("Just a bit of advertising," I suggested facetiously. "Think of what good all that money could do . . .")

He replied, "No, I'm content with where we are. In 500 years Wikipedia will be remembered and (if we do our job well in setting things up with a long-term perspective for safety) still be informing the public. I doubt many of our commercial colleagues will even be remembered, much less still here."*

Writing in the *New York Review of Books* in 2008, Nicholson Baker conjured a cute image of Wikipedia's early methodology.

> It was like a giant community leaf-raking project in which everyone was called a groundskeeper. Some brought very fancy professional metal rakes, or even back-mounted leaf-

* In December 2021, Wales auctioned his first personal Wikipedia entry—"Hello, World!"—as a non-fungible token (NFT). Christie's listed the item as a "digital sculpture," and it was a living thing: in a nice twist, Wales enabled his entry to be edited, while also setting a digital timer that would reset the page to its original state. "The idea is not just to have an NFT of this moment in time," he explained, "but to have an NFT which recreates the emotional experience of the moment: here it is, Wikipedia, ready to edit. What will you make of it? What will it become? Will it succeed? Can it really change the world?"

It sold for $750,000, while the strawberry-colored iMac on which Wales composed the words went for $187,500.

blowing systems, and some were just kids thrashing away with the sides of their feet or stuffing handfuls in the pockets of their sweatshirts, but all the leaves they brought to the pile were appreciated. And the pile grew and everyone jumped up and down in it having a wonderful time.

But there was a problem. Not long into adolescence, "self-promoted leaf-pile guards appeared, doubters and deprecators who would look askance at your proffered handful and shake their heads, saying that your leaves were too crumpled or too slimy or too common, throwing them to the side." What is and isn't valued knowledge, and how best to present it, has been the recurring headache of every encyclopedia editor in history. Add in the digital world's perfectionists, elitists, sticklers and bullies, and you have a recipe for chaos. So certain policies and guidelines evolved to keep the leaf pile both useful and valuable.

While its freeform open-access ethos still holds (anyone can contribute new articles and edit old ones), the appearance of new material on the site is subject to approval from the rest of the editing community. You cannot, for example, just go in and write that your teacher or boss is a feeble-minded moron, however accurate that may be, and expect it to be hyperlinked to the site's many other feeble-minded morons, or the history of feeble-mindedness, or the Ancient Greek derivation of the word "moron." If you have some sort of published evidence, though, that's a different matter; very early on, Wikipedia decided that it would not publish original unsourced material on its site, relying instead on information published elsewhere.

The funny thing is, Wikipedia used to be considered a joke. When, around 2005, an editor emailed to say that he was putting together an entry on my work and would I be prepared to supply some additional information, I let the email pass. I wasn't sure it was genuine. And even if it had been, Wikipedia was unreliable and prone to so much misinformation that I didn't think much of being a part of it.

Although many early elements were sound, large portions resembled a six-year-old's birthday party. Some entries have become famous for their uncompromising subjectivity; among the most elegant was an early article on the poodle, which remained on the site for some time and stated simply, "A dog by which all others are measured." Nicholson Baker found incisive early entries on the Pop-Tart: "Pop-Tarts is German for Little Iced Pastry O'Germany . . . George Washington invented them . . . Popular flavours included 'frosted strawberry, frosted brown sugar cinnamon, and semen.'"

Although most large errors are corrected by a system of flags and checks (many Wikipedians enjoy nothing more than controlling bad new entries like minesweepers on a beach), a large number of new small errors are inserted every day, either mischievously or inadvertently, and some persist for a long time. Often, the closer one is connected to the truth of a topic, the harder it can be. One is not allowed to edit anything with which one may have a personal connection (and therefore insider knowledge). One cannot edit one's own biography, for instance, or ask anyone associated with you to do it. Case in point: the entry on the bestselling chronicler of the human condition Yuval Noah Harari. On 28 October 2020 he appeared on the podcast *The Tim Ferriss Show,* and Wikipedia came up at the very beginning:

Yuval Noah Harari: It's good to be here. Thank you for inviting me.

Tim Ferriss: We're going to start in an unusual place,

perhaps. And that is with correcting my pronunciation on a word, M-O-S-H-A-V. How do you pronounce that, and what does it mean?

Harari: M-O-S-H-A-V. Oh, that's actually a mistake on Wikipedia. It's a moshav. It somehow got around that I live on a moshav, which is some kind of socialist, collective community, less radical than the kibbutz, but one of the experiments of socialists in Israel like decades ago. And it's just not true. I live in a kind of middle-class suburb of Tel Aviv.

Ferriss: So this is an example, for those listening, of something that some people call the Wikipedia echo effect because I actually—

Harari: Yes. I tried to correct it so many times, and it's just, I gave up. It's stronger than me. [Wikipedia stated that Harari lived at the moshav with his husband.]

Ferriss: Right. So, at some point, it got into Wikipedia, then it ended up in the *Guardian*. Then, other people cite the *Guardian*, and it just will not go away. So, it just keeps coming back.

Wikipedia has thousands, and probably tens of thousands of these kinds of mistakes, and it would be strange if it didn't; given that it is the largest store of global information ever assembled, and given that it is written by humans, it would be *untrustworthy* if it didn't. It would also be untrustworthy if these kinds of errors weren't corrected, and at 08.54 on 1 November 2020, three days after the podcast with Harari was released, Paco2718 removed the line stating "The couple lives in a moshav (a type of cooperative agricultural community of individual farms) in Mesilat Zion, near Jerusalem." Paco2718 also removed three references in which this statement appeared in *Haaretz*, the *Sunday Times* and the *Financial Times*. In the six months before this correction, Paco2718 had made small amendments to entries on Socrates, the Barack Obama "Hope" poster and the Big Bang. In the six months after, he made small changes to Brontë Family, Republican senator Ted Cruz and Mount Everest. His brief biographical entry on his Wikipedia user page reads "Hi! I am Amir. I don't understand how everything works here but I am doing the best I can."

My own entry is basic and bland, and predominantly accurate. There is one very small mistake in it, the name of the publisher of my last book. As I am not permitted to correct this myself, or nominate anyone I know to do it, I shall await the time until a stranger spots it (or reads this book and quotes it as a reliable source).*

These kinds of errors, however, are only one of Wikipedia's dilemmas. More involved issues, and the attempts to solve them, were acknowledged in a company progress report in 2017: "Toxic behaviors and harassment have had a negative impact on participation in our projects. Our success has generated an overwhelming amount of maintenance and monitoring, and we have addressed these challenges with tools and practices that have turned good-faith community members away . . . the structures of our movement are often opaque or centralized, with high barriers to entry."

The fact that Wikipedia is a non-profit organization that doesn't track its readers (and thus doesn't sell on a reader's information) must necessarily raise the question of how it keeps going: it has a lot of servers and cyber security to maintain, as well as about 550 staff and contractors, and its headquarters in San Francisco, and it has a legacy-maintaining charitable foundation to run.

---

* Shortly after I had fact-checked this section with a regular contributor, the error was corrected.

Part of the answer lies in an email I received recently from Katherine Maher, Wikimedia Foundation's executive director. The subject was "Simon—this is a little awkward," and the message, which came with a photograph of the smiling sender, was an appeal for a donation.

Two years earlier I had responded to another appeal. Wikipedia received the occasional large donation (in 2018, Amazon gave it $1 million, not least, one suspects, because Alexa mines it for information), but most of its $100 million-plus annual income comes from small personal donations from users. In 2017 I donated the huge sum of £2 to carry on its sterling work, but the foundation was insatiable—it wanted yet more.

Maher wrote in her email: "98% of our readers don't give. They simply look the other way. And without more one-time donors, we need to turn to you, our past donors, in the hope that you'll show up again for Wikipedia, as you so generously have in the past." If I didn't give again, she feared, Wikipedia's integrity was at stake. "You're the reason we exist. The fate of Wikipedia rests in your hands and we wouldn't have it any other way."

"You're the reason we exist": Katherine Maher and friends at WikiConference India in 2016

I ignored it. But a month later Katherine Maher wrote to me again. There was a new photo of her, still smiling, but she had a darker message: the email was titled "We've had enough." It explained how every year Wikipedia has had to resist the pressure of accepting advertising or selling on information or establishing a paywall, and every year they've been proud to resist. But "we're not salespeople," Maher wrote. "We're librarians, archivists, and information junkies. We rely on our readers to become our donors, and it's worked for 18 years." Katherine Maher now wanted another £2, although there were also click-buttons to give £20, £35 or £50.

Obviously these weren't personal emails—hundreds of thousands of others received the same messages—but I thought I'd make it personal by going to see her. As with Wikimania, the virus scuppered our plans, so we met on Zoom, which meant I got to watch her eat breakfast eggs on her partner's sourdough at her home in San Francisco.

She told me she was in her late thirties and that her surname rhymes with car. She says she began editing Wikipedia as a university student in 2004, an article about the Middle East which she doesn't think survived on the site for very long. She joined the Wikimedia Foundation in 2014 as chief communications officer after a career in communications technology at UNICEF and a digital rights company. Soon after becoming executive director in 2016, she encountered a problem about herself: the freshly created Wikipedia page detailing her appointment and early career was marked for deletion. "I wasn't notable enough," she told me. "The thinking was, 'just because she runs the foundation doesn't mean that she's actually done anything of great note in the world.'" She says she loved this utterly compliant nature of the beast she was now running, although she wondered whether the

proposed deletion also had a gendered element to it. The article stayed.

Our chat necessarily led to a discussion of what, after four years in the job, she would now regard as the most notable achievements of her tenure. She spoke in terms of an ongoing battle. "While Wikipedia is not a site on the Internet that has really obvious issues of harassment . . . it is not an environment that is particularly welcoming to new people. It is not an environment that is particularly welcoming to women. It is not particularly welcoming to minorities or marginalized communities."

She says the aggressive approach she's taken towards those editors she sees as destructive has occasionally "blown up in my face," not least her decision last year to ban an editor she saw as "prolific, but not productive . . . somebody who was driving other editors away through their behavior." She has upset others by her insistence that the world in which Wikipedia will operate in the future will demand large additional and alternative sources of revenue. Machine learning and artificial intelligence will require new tools that are computationally expensive. The site, though efficient, may need a complete aesthetic rethink (it does look increasingly twentieth century). And the expansion into emerging communities in Africa and elsewhere will also require new resources.

When we spoke again a few weeks later, our conversation turned philosophical. "I don't think Wikipedia represents truth," she began. "I think it represents what we know or can agree on at any point in time. This doesn't mean that it's inaccurate, it just means that the concept of truth has sort of a different resonance. When I think about what knowledge is . . . what Wikipedia offers is context. And that's what differentiates it from similar data or original research, not that that isn't vital to us."

Original research is what news organizations push out every single day. Maher mentions a YouGov poll from 2014 that found Wikipedia to be more trusted in the UK than the BBC. "I think for a lot of companies, they would say, 'That's wonderful, we beat our competitors.' My response was, first, the BBC is not a competitor. And second, that's not wonderful at all. If there's a trust deficit with the sources that we rely on then ultimately that deficit will catch up with us as well. We require that the ecosystem be trusted."

Maher calls herself an inclusionist, arguing against those who wish to keep Wikipedia on a high intellectual footing, reasoning that anything that involves a learning journey is beneficial. "If we don't have your Bollywood star, or pop singer, then you'll come to us and you'll bounce right off, because you don't see anything that's relevant to your life."

She says the people who are most excited to meet her are the ones who use Wikipedia every day, but the ones who give her frosty looks are those who have the highest public profile. She recalls sitting next to two distinguished female scientists at a recent conference. "I introduced myself, and very often in a context like that it's 'Oh, another woman who's going to be a speaker and that's fantastic.' So I say I run the foundation that runs Wikipedia. And the first thing I heard was, 'We don't like our articles.' One of the things they reflected on was, 'Look, my body of work has changed dramatically since the article was first written, and it hasn't kept up to date with my newest thinking in the area.' And that's a very legitimate concern."

But at least they had an entry, which was not the case with Canadian scientist Donna Strickland. On 2 October 2018, Strickland was awarded the Nobel Prize in Physics for her work on chirped pulse amplification, something that may have a direct bearing on the future of eye surgery and other medical laser

applications. But good luck trying to find more information on her on Wikipedia the day after the announcement. Her absence became a cause célèbre. There had been an entry prepared about her, but it was rejected on the grounds of insufficient references from secondary sources. That is to say, because she was only famous in the world of physics, and had not previously been written about in the popular media, she then couldn't be written about in the world's most popular encyclopedia.

No one was keener to point out the anomaly than Maher. Soon after Strickland's entry finally appeared, Maher blogged that as of the beginning of October 2019, only 17.82 percent of Wikipedia's biographies were about women. She is proud that women gather frequently for day-long "editathons" to improve this figure, and flags up the site's recent focus on improving and expanding articles concerning women's health and the history of the black diaspora. This is not merely a worthy ambition, it is regarded as crucial to Wikipedia's global standing. Maher has a neat phrase for another cultural imbalance: "Too many articles on battleships, not enough on poetry."

Conversely, Maher says there is a "whole industry" based upon changing existing Wikipedia profiles from people who don't like what's written about them. It's considered "black hat editing," and the community really gets upset by it. "We encourage people not to do it, because usually you'll get caught, and when you do get caught white-washing your own Wikipedia page it's not a good look. We always tell elected officials this."

Even Boris Johnson seemed to grasp the difficulty. In June 2020, referring to the destruction of statues of dishonored men, he columnized thus: "If we start purging the record and removing the images of all but those whose attitudes conform to our own, we are engaged in a great lie, a distortion of our history, like some public figure furtively trying to make themselves look better by editing their own Wikipedia entry." Was I the only one to think he was writing from experience?

Between our two chats, Maher had attended a Zoom board meeting that sounded like every other board meeting: performance reviews, financial shortfalls, expansion or the lack of it. But then there were more specific issues: how to celebrate Wikipedia's twentieth anniversary in January, and continuing discussions about the impact of small screens on people's ability to absorb content and make edits. Does this inevitably mean less deep reading, or does it vastly increase accessibility? Both. Between March and May 2020, 43 percent of users accessed Wikipedia on a computer, and 57 percent on a phone.

Wikipedia's mobile app is a fascinating thing in itself, not least its article randomizer. This is an addictive lucky dip through millions of its pages: you click on a dice symbol and you get a nice way to spend a minute or a day. On one occasion it threw up the following, in the following order: Peters's wrinkle-lipped bat; Roads in Northern Ireland; Eddie Izzard *Live at the Ambassadors*; Proper palmar digital nerves of median nerve [nerves in the palm of your hand]; Vincenz Fettmilch [early seventeenth-century gingerbread maker]; Herman Myhrberg [Swedish footballer who played in the 1912 Olympics]; List of Guangzhou Metro stations; *Hand Cut* [1983 album by Bucks Fizz]; Methyl isothiocyanate [chemical compound responsible for tears]; and Lusty Lady [defunct peep show establishment in Seattle, which once boasted a marquee wishing passersby "Happy Spanksgiving"].

The thing that set Wikipedia apart from everything else that had fired the digital world over the past three decades—

Google and other search engines, Facebook and other social media—was that Wikipedia's code wasn't new; all the software and hardware already existed and was being made use of elsewhere.

What distinguished Wikipedia was—as sappy as it sounds—a belief in humanity and the triumph of good behavior over bad. There were other things too, including a commitment to information sharing, a celebration of specialization and exactitude, and a deep and fundamental acknowledgment of the value of accumulated learning.

The very first home page, composed at 19.27 GMT on 15 January 2001, stated:

> This is the new WikiPedia!

Its creator, Office.bomis.com, made the first edit twenty-three minutes later, adding a list of subjects WikiPedia should contain. "Foundational disciplines" included Philosophy and Logic, Mathematics and Statistics. Natural Sciences included Physics, Chemistry, Astronomy, Earth Sciences, Biology, Botany and Zoology. There were also to be sections on Social Sciences, Applied Arts, Urban Planning, Aerospace Technology, Classics, Performing Arts, Religion and Recreation, the last category including Sports, Games, Hobbies and Tourism.

The following day at 19.00, Office.bomis.com created a mission statement:

> This is the new WikiPedia! The idea here is to write a complete encyclopedia from scratch, without peer review process, etc. Some people think that this may be a hopeless endeavor, that the result will necessarily suck. We aren't so sure. So, let's get to work!

Just over an hour later, the page received its first edit from an external contributor, Eiffel.demon.co.uk, who made a few small changes to the priority and presentation of the subject list, and added the topics Air Transport, Rail Transport, Road Transport and Sea Transport.

And the day after that, just after midnight on 17 January 2001, user Dhcp058.246.lvcm.com, who was evidently connected to the project, elaborated on the mission statement, added some links, and rallied the troops:

> This is the new WikiPedia! The idea here is to write a complete encyclopedia from scratch, collaboratively. Add a page, come back tomorrow, look what others have added, and then add some more. We think this might be fun . . .

The links included

WhatIsaWiki?
WhatsaWikiFor?
WhyOnEarthWouldIWantToContributeToaWiki?

The new entry ended with a forceful announcement.

> This wiki is an experiment. But, for those who might be confused about this point, it is not Nupedia. Nupedia is a serious encyclopedia project found at http://www.nupedia.com. This wiki is a proposed “fun” supplement to Nupedia!

Its founders Jimmy Wales and Larry Sanger would subsequently fall out over several issues, not least factors surrounding the protocols of the reliability of entries. Sanger departed in 2002, and four years later formed his own

knowledge website Citizendium, designed as a more rigorously fact-checked and peer-reviewed site than Wikipedia. Although launched with much publicity, and an initial burst of activity, the project soon lost momentum.*

By the end of its first year, Wikipedia had approximately 20,000 articles, including many entries on the original subject list, and many that would not have been included in more traditional encyclopedias. Some of the earliest articles took for their subject matter the American philosopher William Alston, the singer Fiona Apple, the slapstick silent film director Mack Sennett, the civil rights activist Rosa Parks, a list of the amendments in the US Constitution, a full list of the characters and locations in the novel *Atlas Shrugged* by Ayn Rand, details about the number of people in the Algerian military, a definition of oligopoly, a description of duopoly, the French actress Leslie Caron, and a list of female tennis players. Because its creators were also its readers, from the outset it reflected a world as varied as the interests of its inhabitants. In the first few weeks there were also articles on the meaning of the word "Machiavellian," the postage stamp, a track listing of the album *Horses* by Patti Smith, a description of uric acid and a brief biography of the Soviet cosmonaut Yuri Gagarin. The randomness reflected the joy of the blank page: "We're tiny and new, so Just Write anything!" Twenty years later it has become very difficult to find anything that doesn't have an entry.

And then Wikipedia got bigger. By the end of 2003,

---

* According to Citizendium's own statistics, quoted by Wikipedia, by 27 October 2011 the site had fewer than 100 active members, and Sanger had relinquished his post as editor-in-chief. As of 24 September 2020, it had 17,103 articles, of which 166 had achieved editorial approval, and sixteen contributors who had performed an action in the previous thirty days. Sanger left Citizendium entirely in 2020, announcing he would be forever cheering it on from the sidelines.

Wikipedia had more than 100,000 articles in English, and in 2005 the figure exceeded 750,000. By 2008, the figure topped 2 million, and by October 2021 the figure was 6.39 million. The total number of words on the site (not including discussion and other behind-the-scenes entries) has increased from 4.8 million at the beginning of 2002 to 1.8 billion in 2010 to 3.98 billion by 20 October 2021. The number of people who had used Wikipedia up to that date came to 42,410,237.*

The first mention of global warming—an eighty-word article noting an increase in surface temperature over the last 150 years and stating "whether this increase is significant or not is open to debate"—appeared in October 2001. By 23 October 2021, a week before the global climate summit in Glasgow, the name of the entry had become Climate Change and stood at almost 8640 words. It had received 25,396 edits at an average rate of 4.4 per day. There were 14,252 links directing readers to the article from other pages, and 924 directions to external links. There were 347 references, and hyperlinks to more than 200 peer-reviewed sources. Over the previous year the entry had been viewed 1,911,705 times.

The entry titled Climate Change, like a great many other articles on topics deemed important, was "semi-protected": it meant there were restrictions on new edits that could be made at any point. Anyone wishing to make a change would have had to be a "confirmed" user, which meant having a registered account for at least four days and making at least ten other edits

* Those were the English language stats. Towards the end of 2021 the number of articles in all the different language editions stood at 57.5 million. German Wikipedia has 2.6 million, French Wikipedia has 2.36m, Dutch 2.06m, Russian 1.76m, Spanish and Italian both about 1.72m. There are two greater figures—the Cebuano language edition with 6 million articles and the Swedish edition with 2.9 million—but these have been largely automatically generated by bots. The Cebuano edition has only 164 active users.

in that time. An edit would then be moderated, and possibly challenged or removed for a stated reason, often due to a lack of a recognized source.*

Long after it was shown to work, and once it had become hugely popular, the executives at Wikipedia found themselves skilled at coming up with retrospective summations of desire. "When we talk about Wikipedia being a free encyclopedia," one said, "what we're really talking about is not the price that it takes to access it, but rather the freedom that you have to take it and adapt it and use it however you like." Someone else had another thought: "We make the Internet not suck."

Wikipedia has an obvious and magnificent advantage over the print stores it supplanted: incredible speed. *Britannica* in particular had the habit of being published in the same month as calamitous events. (A new printing of the fourteenth edition arrived from the printers just three weeks before Germany invaded Poland; a new printing on thin Indian onion paper in July 1945 narrowly managed to miss the dropping of the first atomic bomb.) These days, when someone notable dies, the cause of death is on Wikipedia before the funeral.

Similarly, the prevalence of what may best be described as dubiousness in print might have a pernicious effect for decades, much to our amusement today. How best to treat tuberculosis, for example? "The most sovereign remedy," *Britannica*'s first

* By contrast, on Britannica.com the article entitled Climate Change is longer, at 12,126 words, and has been principally written by one person, Stephen T. Jackson, Professor Emeritus of Botany at the University of Wyoming. Revisions have been made by five named editors as well as the unnamed "Editors of *Encyclopaedia Britannica*." There are only eighteen major edits listed from 2008—four in 2021 and five between 2013 and 2020. There is an extensive list of Further Reading, but a small fraction of the links and sources available on Wikipedia. Apart from 100 words, the article is all behind a subscriber paywall.

edition assured, "is to get on horseback everyday." Childhood teething could, the encyclopedia assured, be treated by the placing of leeches beneath the ears (in those days leeches cured *everything*). The ninth edition, published volume by volume between 1875 and 1889, advised its readers on how to become a vampire (get a cat to jump over your corpse), while thirty years later the eleventh found werewolves "in leopard form" among "the people of Banana (Congo)."

I looked up "People of Banana" on Wikipedia and found this: "The page 'People of Banana' does not exist. You can ask for it to be created, but consider checking the search results below to see whether the topic is already covered." The search results included Banana, Banana republic, Banana leaf, Banana Fish, Banana ketchup, Speech banana, Banana Yoshimoto and everyone's favorite, Banana sundae.

So I asked for "People of Banana" to be created. I prepared my entry: "The 'People of Banana' is said to be one location where you may find werewolves." I cited "Entry on Werewolves, Encyclopaedia Britannica, 11th Edition (1910–11), as referenced in Britannica's special 250th anniversary collector's edition, 2018."

I didn't hold out much hope. My submission joined 2160 other pending submissions, 114 of which had been waiting five weeks for a Wikipedia administrator to approve or dismiss it (other recent submissions included items whose titles I didn't understand: "Dog Puller," "IBTS Greenhouse" and "Bug Music").

My administrator would probably dismiss my Banana entry on the grounds that it did not pass muster. "There is a very good chance that the topic is not notable and will never be accepted as an article," the guidelines informed me. Other reasons why my entry could be rejected were divided into thirty-four subcategories, including "declined as a non-notable film," "declined as jokes," "declined as not written in a neutral

point of view" and—the ultimate—"declined as not suitable for Wikipedia."

I had a vague twenty-first-century fear that something—anything—connecting banana with Africa might be rejected on the basis of racial assumption. But then, with almost all hopes dashed, I found that I had mis-searched, and a place called Banana in the Democratic Republic of Congo did indeed have its own entry, albeit a tiny one. There was no mention of the people of Banana specifically, and none of werewolves, but I learned that Banana was a very small seaport situated in Banana Creek, an inlet about 1km wide on the north bank of the Congo River's mouth, separated from the ocean by a spit of land 3km long and 100 to 400m wide.

The article, like all articles on Wikipedia, was accompanied by its own "History" page, a behind-the-scenes catalogue of the edits that had made the page accurate and compliant, and attuned to house style. Often, these "making of" comments are more fascinating than the article they scrutinize. In this case, a Danish contributor called Morten Blaabjerg—one of relatively few to use a real name (other editors on this Banana page plumped for Warofdreams, Prince Hubris and Tabletop)—added the "Henry" to "Henry Morton Stanley" (Stanley used Banana as a starting-off point for an expedition in 1879).

That edit was made in July 2005. The page had received relatively few edits since its inception the year before, although for a short while in 2007 there was a nice little hoo-ha over whether Banana was a seaport or a township. As far as contributor Morten Blaabjerg goes, we learn that he now lives in Odense, but was born in 1973 in the small southern Danish town of Strib, near Middelfart.

WUB

On Thursday, 7 May 2020, at five to seven in the evening, a man calling himself "the wub" added the following sentence to the article Exploding Animal: "The *Los Angeles Herald* in 1910 reported a duck which exploded after consuming yeast."

A simple statement and possibly a true one. Since he began contributing to Wikipedia on 24 March 2005, the wub has made thousands of similar entries. In fact, by the beginning of October 2021 he had made 85,788 edits to 64,283 pages at an average rate of 14.2 edits a day. He had created a great many original entries on subjects as diverse as Fitzrovia Chapel in London, the British rower Mark Aldred, the former Lord Mayor of London Ian Luder, the history and significance of the hotel rating, and the centuries-old concept of putting a message in a bottle. He has also made hundreds of contributions to Wikipedia's Talk pages, a behind-the-scenes forum in which fellow Wikipedians discuss whether someone is notable enough to merit their own article and how best to deal with people who enjoy deleting paragraphs at random and adding "I am the King!" in their place.

On some mornings the wub will make twenty small corrections an hour. Some of his longer edits reflect the diversity of Wikipedia as a whole: the 2019 North Korea–United States Hanoi summit, the M12 motorway, the British politician Claudia Webbe, the Worshipful Company of Pewterers. To accompany his sentence on the exploding duck, the wub included a link to the archive of the newspaper in which the fate of the animal was originally recorded. One clicks on the link and finds that on 31 January 1910, a reporter from Des Moines, Iowa, even managed to get the poor duck's name:

Rhadamanthus, a prize-winning duck at the recent poultry show, is no more, having exploded into several hundred bits, one of which struck Silas Perkins in the eye, destroying the sight. The cause of the explosion was the eating of yeast, which was placed in a pan upon the back porch, and tempted his duckship, which was taking a morning stroll.

Upon returning from church Mr. Perkins discovered his prize duck in a somewhat loggy condition. Telltale marks around the pan of yeast gave him his clew. He was about to pick up the bird when the latter quacked and exploded with a loud report and Mr. Perkins ran into the house holding both hands over one eye. A surgeon was called, who found that the eyeball had been penetrated by a fragment of flying duck and gave no hope of saving the optic.

The wub is a big reader, as one might expect, sometimes managing a book a week, and his tastes are as wide-ranging as his edits: Oliver Sacks, John Steinbeck, Neil Gaiman, George Orwell, Ursula K. Le Guin and Sue Townsend. He's read plenty of Philip K. Dick too, and that's where he found his Wikipedia name, in the short story "Beyond Lies the Wub." If you look up "Beyond Lies the Wub" on Wikipedia you'll discover that the story first appeared in the pulp magazine *Planet Stories* in July 1952, and has since appeared in more than a dozen anthologies. The story received its own Wikipedia entry on 6 February 2004, an article in which user 68.86.220.131 explained the fantastical plot, noting that the Wub is a large and intelligent pig-like creature capable of polite conversation and telepathy. More than a year later, on 15 July 2005, an editor called The Anome added that Philip K. Dick liked his creation so much that "he revisted The Wub in his short story 'Not By Its Cover.'" The article then lay untouched and little read for three months, until, at 16.01 GMT on 14 October 2005, the wub changed the spelling of revisted to revisited.

The wub's bookshelves also include *A Short History of Nearly Everything* by Bill Bryson and the E.H. Gombrich classic *A Little History of the World*. One would be forgiven for thinking that both of those would have been of great use to him in his role as a Wikipedia editor, but most of his Wiki work—which began as an occasional glancing pastime and has since blossomed into what seems like a full-on obsession—is concerned not with great historical events but with minutiae.

Many of his amendments go unnoticed by the general reader. Commas, the addition of capital letters, correcting bad links, other things that add uniformity to the millions of articles. His first contribution in March 2005 involved the removal of a contentious comment in the biography of the motoring journalist and television presenter Jeremy Clarkson. (Another editor had written that Clarkson "is known for continually rubbishing MG-Rover, Britain's last remaining volume car manufacturer, threatening thousands of jobs in the UK Car Industry." The wub removed "threatening thousands of jobs in the UK Car Industry.") Three minutes later, the wub edited an article about the television series *Grumpy Old Men*, changing the word "was" to "were." Six days after that he italicized the film *Vincent* in the biography of the film director Tim Burton, and a day after that he contributed to Wikipedia's April Fool's Day hoax about the takeover of Wikipedia by *Encyclopaedia Britannica*.

Clearly, none of these items change the world. But with the exception of the last, they illuminate Wikipedia's daily grind: the grand ambition, if it ever existed, has long been replaced by process. This is one of the few things it shares

with every encyclopedia that preceded it. There are a few necessary egomaniacs in the creation of every enterprise like this, but most of the work—and most of the things that make it work—are created by the largely unthanked, traddling away.

As well as being a Wikipedia editor, the wub is also an administrator, a janitorial role which allows him to block other users, protect pages from editing and delete pages when required. Because he is an experienced Wikipedian, he has also been granted certain privileges not available to a novice, such as the ability to change the biographies of very famous people, which are often the subject of vandalism: things like "Mozart wrote the symphonies of Beethoven and vice-versa."

The wub receives no payment for his edits. In 2011, a survey into what motivates its users to contribute found that the key reasons were: people enjoyed giving their time to share and improve available information; they believed information should be freely available; they enjoyed sharing their areas of expertise; it was fun; they appreciated Wikipedia's policy of openness; they enjoyed finding and correcting mistakes—it was a quest, a challenge and a puzzle; they wanted to gain a reputation as an accurate and productive editor. But they didn't like: being patronized by more experienced editors; having their edits deleted or reverted without explanation; heated arguments with other editors on discussion pages; seeing articles they were working on being spoiled by inaccurate or offensive information.

The number of the wub's edits, while impressive, is not enough to get him into the Top 500 list of the most prolific Wikipedians. His 85,788 edits only puts him at number 880, just behind Tony Sidaway, Animalparty, Anythingyouwant, Rsrikanth05 and RogDel. Those who have made more than 90,000 edits include SuperJew, SNAAAAKE!!, Bryan Derksen, Summer PhD and Edward. Edward must have got in really early to snag a username like that.

The first person to have made one million edits was a man calling himself Koavf, who got there, amid some fanfare, on 19 April 2012. The following day, Wikipedia declared 20 April should henceforth be known as Justin Knapp day, in honor of Koavf's achievement and real name. Knapp, who was twenty-nine, was taking a nursing degree at Indiana University. He said he found his Wikipedia work both relaxing and rewarding; his proudest achievement on the site was his contribution to the entry on George Orwell, which he estimated took about 100 hours. But he didn't stop there. As I write he's made 2,098,059 edits. But wait—Koavf is online at this very moment, and the number has jumped to 2,098,061. He's just added some details to the page concerned with the Bruce Springsteen song "Letter to You," and the German technical pen company Rotring.

But dark news has recently cast a shadow over Koavf's door. Today he is only number two in the charts. He's been dramatically eclipsed by Ser Amantio di Nicolao, who's made 3,756,703 edits. By the time you read this it is likely that Ser's total will have exceeded 4 million. Even the world's most prolific authors do not come close to writing 4 million words in their lifetime. But *4 million edits*?

By now you may be thinking: Who are these people? How do they find the time? What qualifies them to do this? And why should they want to, given that they often receive vituperation for their work (and no money)? What complex combination of altruism, oneupmanship, ego,

deep learning and extreme pedantry would make people like Rich Farmborough (1.7 million edits and counting) and BrownHairedGirl (2.04 million edits) stay up until 2.37 a.m. to make an encyclopedia and the world it informs a slightly more accurate place?

The wub's real name is Peter Coombe. He began editing Wikipedia on his gap year before university and describes his first contributions as "essentially vandalism," messing around with deletions and stupid additions. He found the site increasingly interesting when he saw how quickly his comments were corrected. It was as if he was being looked after.

Coombe was born in 1987 and looks like an aging cherub, his light-brown fringe and beard framing a gentle round face. His Zoom background shows rolling hills and the bluest sky, but I think that's wishful thinking: most of his waking hours are spent with screens and software. He says he was a quiet child, finding books and computers faithful companions. He was entranced by his *Encarta* CD-ROM before his teens, not least the videos and interactive features. "We only got the Internet quite late in our house, so that was the encyclopaedia I grew up with. I loved it, and I still feel really bad that Wikipedia killed it."*

At Cambridge he studied natural sciences, and met other people who shared his enthusiasm for Wikipedia as a concept: the reliability and depth of the articles were beginning to improve, but the greatest delight was still to be had in the practical elements and the open-source

* His screen background is called Bliss. Unsurprisingly, Bliss has its own page on Wikipedia, which explains that the photo was taken by Charles O'Rear in January 1996, and that Microsoft bought the rights for its Windows operating system in 2000. Its ubiquity may make it the most viewed picture in history.

idealism, the fact that a community could indeed create its own encyclopedia from scratch, the fact that a twenty-one-year-old could sit in his bedroom and write useful additions to one's online knowledge of Zürich's Hauptbahnhof, and useful deletions to mischievous entries on obscure railway stations in Australia.

"I looked behind it and saw that there were all these systems," Coombe says, delighting in the site's machinery as much as the content, the ability for certain software programs to detect possible vandalism and refer it for discussion. These tools have become more sophisticated over the years, but are still far from foolproof. In October 2020, for example, Coombe spent much of his month making hundreds of edits made by the benign invasion of a rogue bit of software that could only be corrected manually. The Bloomberg.com news agency had erected a wall on its website preventing automated programs being able to link directly to its site; a human user had to complete a CAPTCHA test to prove they weren't a bot. And so the wub spent many days correcting hyperlinks to articles on Eduardo Bolsonaro, Justin Trudeau and the 2020 floods in Jakarta—more than 600 edits in all—on each occasion removing more than 600 insertions of the line "Are you a robot?" "It's a pretty simple, mindless task and I can do it while I'm listening to a podcast."

Many established editors on Wikipedia have their own User page, a biographical diversion in which to reveal as much personal information as they feel comfortable with. At the foot of the wub's page is a list of "Barnstars," accolades awarded for various achievements, each accompanied by a different badge, illustration and description. He has fourteen in all, ranging from the simple ("Excellent new help pages, well done!") to the historical ("The true mark of great character is defending someone when there is no possible benefit to such actions—your comments on the

ANI [Administrators noticeboard/Incidents] today were brave and selfless") to the cryptic ("Your assistance was Eaten By A Bear [from Karmafist]"). The wub's page also contains a display of wind-blown flags of all the countries he's visited: Sweden, Iceland, Hong Kong, the United States and many others.

There was one other reward. Coombe was now a "Looshpah Laureate of the Encyclopedia," which meant he was able to display a photograph of the battered cover of *The Complete Compendium of Universal Knowledge* from 1891. This volume, printed in Philadelphia by the Franklin Square Bible House, and running to 833 pages, was fully titled: *The Complete Compendium of Human Knowledge, containing All You Want To Know of Language, History, Government, Business and Social Forms, And a Thousand and One Other Useful Subjects.**

At 19.58 GMT on 31 July 2020, fifteen years after mistyping "revisted" in his line about Philip K. Dick, The Anome created a brief article called "Thank you NHS," describing a heart-warming collective act in the early bewildering weeks of Covid-19. The Anome wrote:

> "Thank you NHS" was a social phenomenon in the United Kingdom in 2020, in which people and organizations posted messages of support for the National Health Service for its efforts in the COVID-19 epidemic in the United Kingdom.

---

* Within its pages: the Capacity of Famous Churches, the Area of Oceans, the World's Earliest Newspapers, and How to Get Rich. Not forgetting How to Get a Passport, the Light from Candles and the Age of Electricity, the Barometer and What it is, How to Take Out a Patent, a List of Pretenders to the House of Bonaparte, the Solar System, and the Speed of Railroads. The light of the Sun was "equal to that of 5,563 wax candles held at a distance of one foot from the eye." How far was the Sun from the Earth? "It would take an express train travelling at the rate of 30 miles an hour, day and night, 352 years to reach its destination."

Organizations supporting the campaign include the British Labour Party and Hull City Council.

That was the entirety of the entry, fewer than 100 words. The Anome actually entered his text much as one would write an email, in a simple text format that enabled those quite unfamiliar with programming to make their own additions. The format placed it in line with all other Wikipedia entries, and enabled links to other Wikipedia pages and external sources. But behind the curtain there was:

> ““Thank you NHS”” was a social phenomenon in the United Kingdom in 2020, in which people and organizations posted messages of support for the [[National Health Service]] for its efforts in the [[COVID-19 epidemic in the United Kingdom]].
>
> Organizations supporting the campaign include the British [[Labour Party]]<ref>{{Cite web|title=On the 72nd birthday of the NHS we say thank you.|url=https://action.labour.org.uk/page/content/thank-you-nhs|access-date=2020-07-31|website=action.labour.org.uk|language=en}}</ref> and [[Hull City Council]].<ref>{{Cite web|date=2020-04-24|title=City's thank you message to NHS staff|url=https://www.hey.nhs.uk/news/2020/04/24/citys-thank-you-message-to-nhs-staff/|access-date=2020-07-31|website=Hull University Teaching Hospitals NHS Trust|language=en-GB}}</ref>

One minute later, The Anome made a revision, replacing the word “epidemic” with “pandemic.”

And a few seconds after that he changed the title of the page from “Thank you NHS” to “Thank You NHS.”

Eight minutes later, also in simple text code, he added: “Other sponsors included sports teams such as the Hibernians.”

Less than a minute later he added: "Large number of private individuals placed home-made signs in their windows to thank the NHS workers." He also added a "See also" link to the article "Clap for carers" that had been created four months before by Philipwhiuk, a user who had earned the respect of his peers fourteen years earlier by reinstating hundreds of words of text about Bletchley Park that had been deleted by an anonymous user and replaced with the two words "Miss Grimley."

Three minutes after that The Anome extended this to: "Large numbers of private individuals placed home-made signs in their windows and outrside their homes to thank the NHS workers."

Two minutes later he changed "the Hibernians" to "Hibernian F.C."

Fifteen minutes later, at 20.27, he made two additions: "The handmade posters frequently featured drawings of rainbows," followed by: "Some media outlets released poster artwork for people to print and display."

At 23.17, in what would be his last contribution to his new page that day, The Anome added a photograph showing the words "Thank You NHS" displayed on an electronic billboard in Leeds. And then he went to bed; his creation had been logged on Wikipedia's hard drive as Page ID 64695292.

The following morning, at 10.23, he corrected the typo "outrside their homes" to "outside their homes."

Other editors made additional changes over the coming days, including a destructive move by someone assigned the user number 95.149.192.174. This user added the phrase "Complete bollocks" to the introduction. It took less than a minute for a bot patrolling Wikipedia to remove it, and to bring it to the attention of human administrators. The bot—a software "robot" programmed to perform repetitive tasks that would be too tedious to perform manually—was called ClueBot NG and was created specifically to root out vandalism and to aid Operation Enduring Encyclopedia, one of the site's many mission statements. According to the bot's own page on Wikipedia it makes "Over 9,000" such edits per minute, most of them correcting the work of malicious bots intent on spoiling. Although "over 9,000" is not, by Wikipedia's standards, a usefully accurate figure—the amount is more of a phrase than a number, denoting something unfeasibly large—one thing was clear: in the quest for truth and learning, Wikipedia faced a newly destructive dilemma: bot versus bot. This was a problem *Encyclopaedia Britannica* never had to face. Open access lays bare a wide and varied community: like the NHS, it is free at the point of entry.

Over the next six weeks, The Anome added several pictures to "Thank You NHS" and continued to tweak it as the real-life story developed. And then he moved on, shifting his gaze to other topics, including the intricate explanation of "Turingery," the manual code-breaking method devised by Alan Turing at Bletchley Park during the Second World War, to which he made more than twenty small changes.

Among the many behavioral guidelines circulated to experienced editors on Wikipedia is a gentle reminder to "Please do not bite the newcomers." The text is accompanied by a photo of a large dog with a cat in its mouth.

"Nothing scares potentially valuable contributors away faster than hostility," the message begins. "It is very unlikely for a newcomer to be completely familiar with Wikipedia's markup language and its myriad of policies, guidelines, and community standards when they start editing."

The message reminds editors that many of their first

contributions were probably "unencyclopedic" in their nature, and yet slowly they learned how to write according to house style. "Communicating with newcomers patiently and thoroughly is integral to ensure they stay on Wikipedia and ultimately contribute in a constructive manner."

World experts and world amateurs: Wikimania in London in 2014

Newcomers to Wikipedia are its lifeblood. A study in 2006 suggested that the majority of substantive edits—new articles and lasting content—were contributed by those who weren't long-term users and often weren't registered on the site at all: they knew something that others didn't, or at least hadn't thought to add, and then often they went away. More established users were more responsible for tweaking, reverting and rearranging content. Experienced editors were reminded that newly registered users were encouraged to be bold in their actions, and not to be thwarted by too many regulations and guidelines. "A newcomer brings a wealth of ideas, creativity and experience from other areas that, current rules and standards aside, have the potential to better our community and Wikipedia as a whole."

Wikipedia's suggestions carried the tone of the benign schoolteacher welcoming a child to a new class. "If a newcomer seems to have made a small mistake, e.g. forgot to put a book title in italics, correct it yourself but do not slam the newcomer. A gentle note on their user page explaining the Wikipedia standard and how to achieve it in the future may prove helpful, as they may be unfamiliar with the norm or merely how to achieve it . . . If you use bad manners or curse at newcomers, they may decide not to contribute again."

Elsewhere the benevolent parent comes to mind. "If you feel that you must say something to a newcomer about a mistake, please do so in a constructive and respectful manner. Begin by introducing yourself with a greeting on the user's talk page to let them know that they are welcomed here, and present your corrections calmly and as a peer. If possible, point out something they've done correctly or especially well. Do not call newcomers disparaging names such as 'sockpuppet' or 'meatpuppet.'"

"We inevitably deal with a few difficult people," Wikipedia administrators tell their newest editors. "Some editors are only here to cause trouble, either by making destructive edits, by pushing an agenda, or by stirring up controversy. Others may believe so strongly that they are right that they are unable to edit collaboratively." Such people may be blocked or banned by higher powers on the site, but it is inadvisable to take matters into your own hands. Calling a spade a spade "can be a very bad idea," editors are told, as such conflict often leads to escalation.

The key is to correct or dispute the edits, not the editor.

This advice is accompanied by a clever illusion, a drawing that sometimes looks like a duck and sometimes like a rabbit. It recalls the aphorism "If it looks like a duck, swims like a duck and quacks like a duck, it's probably a duck." But ducks don't know they are ducks. "A humane way to communicate with an anatid that you believe to be a duck would be to calmly inform it of its duck-like behaviour. Shouting 'IT'S A DUCK' is likely to excite the duck, and it may quack at you, and when you're in a shouting match with a duck, no one really wins." This note to editors contained underlined hypertext links for both "anatid" and "quack." Clicking on "quack" takes you directly to the Wikipedia article entitled Anger.

Wikipedia is a very live thing. That is its beauty and occasional failing; it is humanity in all its forms. The project will not be finished until we are all finished, or until something destroys Wikipedia's servers in Virginia, Texas, Amsterdam, San Francisco and Singapore, and all its mirror sites globally, and then possibly the entire Internet and our ability to rebuild it.

The people concerned with Wikipedia's security take their roles reassuringly seriously, for they realize how much is at stake if they do not. When it began in 2001, its existence could not possibly have seemed so important. Its custodians are also rightly concerned with its future, and the future of how we obtain and comprehend information as we evolve.

When I Zoomed with Janeen Uzzell, Wikimedia's chief operating officer, we predominantly discussed Wikimedia 2030, the strategic plan concerned with broadening access to the company's resources. "Information and access to information has always been in the hands of the privileged," she said, while the plan talks of Wikimedia as a "social movement" that will focus on dismantling the barriers preventing people from accessing and contributing to free knowledge. "Our current communities don't represent the diversity of the human population," the document notes. That is to say, there are many other forms of knowledge beyond the printable page.

Katherine Maher told me that these days she seldom thinks of Wikipedia as an encyclopedia at all. It is rather an "information ecosystem" that will ideally link to many others (she mentions the Library of Congress and movie studios). She talks of "the integration of structured information with unstructured knowledge," which will allow us to enter a newly concentrated world of learning open to all. Its 53 million articles will just be a jumping-off point.

Intriguingly, some of this ambition comes very close to the nineteenth-century liberal thinking of the poet Matthew Arnold and his supporters, who proposed an integrated "thoroughness of thought" from "knowing ourselves and the world," through a shared culture of science and literature. Arnold was largely thinking of the high-minded ivory tower, of course, while the Wikimedia Foundation aims to make this a universal global reality in the rather more complex digital sphere. It's an impossibly noble project. And it inevitably made me glance back at Wikipedia's home page from the end of its first year. "We already have 19,000 articles," it stated. "We want to make over 100,000, so let's get to work."

"You know, with Wikipedia, it's merely a protocol," Katherine Maher told me. "It's a reference point, a place that people know has been doing this work already. How do you expand that outwards so that others can join in, getting all that knowledge together around the globe? So there's just always going to be more to do."

She wouldn't do it herself. At the beginning of 2022 she

was replaced as CEO by Maryana Iskander, an Egyptian lawyer with degrees from Yale and Oxford. She told the Associated Press that her principal objective was to continue expanding the diversity of Wikipedia's writers and editors, and by extension its content; the "global south" should have as much presence as the "global north." And beyond this lay the exacting and continual maintenance of one rudimentary principle, the universal right to wisdom. These days, Iskander reasoned, "The idea that anything belongs to all of us is really quite revolutionary."

X

EXTINCTION

According to Wikipedia, *Funk & Wagnalls Standard Encyclopedia* began life as twenty-five volumes in 1912. In 1931 it was renamed *Funk & Wagnalls New Standard Encyclopedia*, and by 1945 it was known variously as *New Funk & Wagnalls Encyclopedia, Universal Standard Encyclopedia, Funk & Wagnalls Standard Reference Encyclopedia*, and *Funk & Wagnalls New Encyclopedia*. Like Ben & Jerry's, its founders Isaac Kaufmann Funk and Adam Willis Wagnalls: a) established a reliable brand based on their name and b) found that their product really took flight when it became available in supermarkets. We have seen how its metamorphosis into Microsoft *Encarta* helped to destroy the very sector in which it once played a significant role.

What Wikipedia cannot help us with, is what the funk to do with the old print sets when they're, yes, defunct. "The adult reader will find the encyclopedia an indispensable companion throughout his life," wrote the renowned Notre Dame University educator George N. Shuster in the preface to an edition from the 1960s. "I am sure that this *Funk & Wagnalls New Encyclopedia* will, as did its predecessors, long hold an honoured place and a well-deserved reputation among English-speaking people everywhere." Apparently not. Not if one believes the discussion boards on the homemaker community site thriftyfun.com.

"Are Funk & Wagnalls encyclopedias from 1959 worth anything?" asks a forum member named Diana in August 2011.

"Unfortunately these old encyclopedias do not sell at any price," replies Kathie K. "Most thrift stores will not even accept them as a donated item."

"You will never find anyone to take them so just put them out for the trash," adds Lilac. "Sorry."

"Maybe you can use them as a 'safe' of sorts," suggests Stacy. "Just hollow out a portion of the pages to make a 'well' and glue the pages' edges together (but not the front cover or you won't be able to get in it!)."

"Libraries won't take them," Lilac adds to her last message. "I know because I tried to get rid of my parents' set. If you live in an area where this is allowed, put them in a box marked 'free' and set them on your curb. If they are not gone in three days put them in the trash."

The following year, the philosopher and writer Julian Baggini posted a video on YouTube with a different solution: he had decided to burn his set of *Britannica*. His film follows him from his garden, where we see the thirty-two-volume fifteenth edition gathering mold and seepage in leaky plastic storage tubs, to a big bonfire in a field. It's a spectacular burn and a spectacular gesture.

A few months later, Baggini weighed the magnitude of his actions in the online magazine *Aeon*. He quoted Heinrich Heine: "Wherever they burn books they will also, in the end, burn human beings," the German poet and playwright wrote in

1821. The most egregiously insulted were "all the parents who, like mine, sacrificed so much for the benefit of their children's education," Baggini continued. "Most families who signed up to the 'book a month payment plan' were really buying a promise of a better life for their children." This was often advertised as The Britannica Advantage, a position of privilege available to those already advantaged, and of course that advantage had long since been eroded by the Internet. "Encyclopedias belong to a time when knowledge was owned by a handful of established authorities, who decided not only what was true but what deserved to be ennobled by its inclusion. Their feel of leather-bound permanence encouraged us to forget the dynamic nature of scientific knowledge."

In the end Baggini believed the books were already dead, slain not only by pixels and bytes but the erosion of our belief in experts.

Forest of knowledge: *Britannica* grows anew in "Branches Unbound" by Wendy Wahl (2011)

Before the incineration, Baggini had considered making his *Britannica* into an art project. He thought about transforming each volume by shredding it in public and using the paper ribbons to make papier-mâché facsimiles. These would then be auctioned online, with proceeds possibly going to buy books or computers for Africa. He concluded that "as with other conceptual art projects, perhaps as much is achieved by describing it as by actually creating it."

Online, there are many other exciting uses for a dead encyclopedia: lampshades, footstools, dolls' houses. Many volumes have never been so useful. One of the strangest repurposings involves a man named Peter Yearsley, a veteran of audio books (perhaps you've heard him read *Alice's Adventures in Wonderland* or Kafka's *In the Penal Colony*; his technique is solid rather than involving, more BBC News than Stephen Fry).

For our purposes his biggest hit is a fifty-two-minute video on YouTube entitled "Soft Spoken Man Reads Encyclopedia." The additional title is "A really boring video to help you sleep now." Yearsley reads entries beginning with C from *Britannica*'s classic eleventh edition. The visuals are easygoing—a bankside view of the Pacific Ocean gently lapping up on Bowen Island, British Columbia, with the leaves of a book obscuring the bottom right of the picture. This may then have been judged too stimulating, as the screen turns entirely black at 15.50. Audio highlights include:

Cookery (Lat. coquus, a cook): the art of preparing and dressing food of all sorts for human consumption, of converting the raw materials, by the application of heat or otherwise, into a digestible and pleasing condition, and generally ministering to the satisfaction of the appetite and the delight of the palate.

We may take it that some form of cookery has existed from the earliest times, and its progress has been from the simple to the elaborate, dominated partly by the foods accessible to man, partly by the stage of civilization he has attained, and partly by the appliances at his command for the purpose either of treating the food, or of consuming it when served.

If you're still awake at this point you will be entertained by the history of cooking, with things warming up when the story reaches France. In dulcet tones, we learn, for example, that "The French Revolution was temporarily a blow to Parisian cookery, as to everything else of the *Ancien Régime*."

And if you're still lively after this I suggest you scroll back an entry or two to

Convolvulaceae: a botanical natural order belonging to the series Tubiflorae of the sympetalous group of Dicotyledons. It contains about forty genera with more than 1000 species, and is found in all parts of the world except the coldest, but is especially well developed in tropical Asia and tropical America. The most characteristic members of the order are twining plants with generally smooth heart-shaped leaves and large showy white or purple flowers, as, for instance, the greater bindweed of English hedges, Calystegia sepium, and many species of the genus Ipomaea, the largest of the order, including the "convolvulus major" of gardens.

And so it goes on, until you are well entwined, if not in the arms of Morpheus, at least by the alluring roots of the efficient tropical sand-binder Ipomaea Pes-Caprae. I did find it mildly soporific, and perhaps only the task of typing it out kept me awake. Mostly I found Yearsley's rendition annoying. But the comments below the video are appreciative. "Is it weird that I actually find this really interesting? Especially the section about cookery." "I just slept with this on and now I'm Albert Einstein." "Used this the night before my final flight test. Got a great night sleep and now I'm a commercial airline pilot."

YouTube, of course, will not let you go at that. Dead encyclopedias continue to entertain almost as much as they did in rude health. In September 2021 a short clip emerged of the England footballer Jack Grealish being interviewed about his footballing knowledge. A few weeks before, Grealish had signed to Manchester City for £100 million, a new British transfer record.

Interviewer: Dean Smith also says you're an encyclopaedia of football. Where does that come from?

Grealish: A what?

Interviewer: An encyclopaedia of football.

Grealish: I don't know what that means.

Interviewer: Well, you know what an encyclopaedia is . . . an encyclopaedia is a book that has descriptions of every word and thing and everything else in it, and in terms of football you have an encyclopaedic knowledge.

Grealish: Oh. Erm, yeah.

But these old books were already an unexpectedly novel proposition to young people in 2015, when the YouTube channel React posted the video "Teens React to Encyclopedias." It's a rather sweet eight-minute watch, very sharply edited, with eleven kids between fourteen and nineteen displaying a range of spontaneous emotions as they're presented with the complete *World Book* from 2005. There's astonishment, intrigue, annoyance, delight, eye-rolling, face-covering, gesticulating. There's a lot of "Wait—*what*?"

As the books pile up in front of them, a sample:

"I don't got to read all these do I?"

"They're encyclopedias!"

"Can I look at them? [Opens one.] Yup, boring already."

"In ancient areas of our library they have dusty books that look exactly like this."

[Host:] "What *is* an encyclopedia?"

"It tells you about stuff."

"It's like a dictionary for different stuff."

"A collection of books of knowledge."

"It's the Internet in books."

"It was Google way back in the day. It was the worst of times!"

[Host:] "So go ahead and find the chapter on Reading."

"Oh . . . R!"

"Okay . . . wait."

[Flipping through:] "Dang. This is so, so much."

"Come on. It takes forever. This is why I don't use these."

"R-E-A . . . Oh, I'm getting close!"

"Ah, Reading. I found it!"

[Host:] "Now let's test the encyclopedia. Come up with anything that you can think of."

"Are there people in encyclopedias? Let's look up Tycho Brahe. Tycho Brahe was an astronomer who was most famous for having his nose cut off in a battle and it was replaced with a metal nose. Here's Braiding. Here's Bracks. Brahe, Tycho! Heyyyy!"

[Host:] "Can you imagine relying just on these books for information compared to the information that's at your fingertips today?"

"In theory I could."

"I would hate it, I would hate it, I would hate it."

"Five whole minutes of my life is gone! When I could have found it in .000098 seconds with Google."

[Host:] Are there any advantages to a physical encyclopedia compared to the Internet or Wikipedia?"

"I'm pretty sure there is, but no."

The video has been watched more than 4 million times. It left me with the intended reaction, a very clear sense of how something so much a part of my life for so long can suddenly seem so absurd to a younger generation. *World Book* isn't like the vinyl LP; it shows no sign of making a comeback. It's more like the horse and cart; you can understand it, and you can understand how eager we were to grasp its brilliant if problematic replacement.

Y

YESTERDAY

Throughout their editing work on Wikipedia, the wub and The Anome were aware of many principles—ground rules, foundational ethics, stylistic recommendations—that guided their contributions, and chief among them was the concept of neutrality. For the encyclopedia to reflect knowledge rather than opinion, and to limit the time its writers and users spent in endless argument, Wikipedia strove for impartiality and objectivity. The Anome was thus discouraged from writing about "Thank You NHS" as "heart-warming," no matter how universally true this was considered to be.

All of Wikipedia's hundreds of thousands of other active registered editors are expected to abide by two further policy cornerstones: verifiability and the notion of No Original Research. All material and quotation open to challenge must be attributed to a reliable, published source. The familiar "citation needed" tag is a note from one editor to another that a linked source is absent and should be supplied, or in time the material will be removed. Wikipedia has several paragraphs devoted to what may or may not be regarded as a reliable source: published books, recognized journals, trusted newspapers and other media channels are generally acceptable, while social media and personal blogs are usually frowned upon.*

The concept of an encyclopedia with No Original Research is something that many first-time editors and many first-time readers find hard to grasp. The rule insists that no facts, ideas or allegations may appear on Wikipedia's main pages for which no reliable published sources exist. A source should exist for all material, even for statements that are unlikely to be challenged. So whenever The Anome or the wub created a new article or amended an old one, let's say on Noah's Ark or the ozone layer, they could only do so if they were based on writing or thinking that already existed. It was a distinct type of creativity, one rewarding affirmation more than pioneering or inceptive thought. It was the world as it was, rather than how it could be, which one might also assume might make it less of a venue for controversy or dispute.

But a problem remained. "I always advise people to check the sources," Peter Coombe (the wub) told me. It was not enough to have citations, because these too could be unreliable, or even fabricated. The fact checkers had to fact-check the fact checks. Which would naturally make the general reader wonder: how could one know what one knew?

* In February 2021, I found the warning note amended to a page on George Orwell's *The Road to Wigan Pier* particularly arresting, although it was typical: "This section possibly contains original research. Please improve it by verifying the claims made and adding inline citations. Statements consisting only of original research should be removed."

On 15 October 1968, the guests sat down to velouté of Cornish crab, fillet of Dover sole in Cheshire sauce, quail in port wine aspic, a mint sorbet palate cleanser followed by noisette of Southdown lamb, and pears in Madeira. *Encyclopaedia Britannica* was 200 years old, and damned if there wasn't going to be a party.

The 500 guests at the Guildhall in the City of London included Prime Minister Harold Wilson, the editor of *The Times*, the director of the British Museum, the Lord Mayor, the Lord High Commissioner, a great many masters and vice chancellors of universities, representatives of forty press and broadcasting outlets, the directors of the Wallace Collection and the Victoria and Albert Museum, controllers of BBC radio, deans of several cathedrals, high-ups at W.H. Smith, W. & G. Foyle and W. Heffer, poet Stephen Spender, novelist Anthony Powell, the chairman of Weidenfeld & Nicolson, and two great-great-granddaughters and one great-great-grandson of *Britannica*'s first editor William Smellie.

The Queen sent a telegram with warmest congratulations and thanked the board of editors for her special anniversary edition (full morocco). Britannica's chairman Senator William Benton gave a speech, as did its newly appointed editor-in-chief Sir William Haley. Everyone thanked everyone. There had been some rocky periods, everyone said, not least during wars and depressions, but the encyclopedia pulled through and would always pull through. It was, as Dr. Robert M. Hutchins, chairman of the board of editors, proclaimed, "the common expression, the common possession, and the common contribution of the English-speaking peoples. This institution, and this one alone, symbolises the joint effort of those peoples to engage on a world scale in the highest of all human activities, learning and teaching."*

Everyone looked forward to their grandchildren and great-grandchildren celebrating *Britannica*'s 300th anniversary in 2068. The champagne was Charles Heidsieck 1959.

Six months earlier, an exhibition celebrating the same anniversary opened at the Newberry Library in Chicago. The items on display included many early editions of *Britannica*, and copies of its forerunners, including *Historia naturalis* (Pliny the Elder), *Etymologiae* (Isidore of Seville), *Speculum historiale* (Vincent de Beauvais), Francis Bacon's classification of knowledge expounded in *Instauratio magna*, and Ephraim Chambers's *Cyclopaedia*.

The show also displayed the typescript, with additions, of Leon Trotsky's biography of Lenin for the thirteenth edition, written in 1925. Trotsky was paid $106, which he pocketed just before fleeing Moscow. "The article," an exhibition card explains, "is reasonably accurate and surprisingly dispassionate." Of particular interest elsewhere is a collection of letters from the archives, predominantly noteworthy for their narrow range of subject matter. Most are complaints from contributors about either the space allotted to them or the rate of pay. A few request a deadline extension to allow for the inclusion of an upcoming statute or conference. One reflects an editor's desire for accuracy: having asked Nikola Tesla to confirm whether he was born on 9 or 10 July 1856, the inventor replied that he was born at midnight between the two.

No one in 1968 would have dared suggest that the exhibition

* All details from the commemorative booklet published by Britannica Encyclopaedia International, Ltd., and sent to all attendees a few weeks after the event.

would one day come to resemble a shrine. The meteorite in the sky wasn't yet visible; *Britannica*'s entry on Economic Forecasting was too interested in existing markets to worry about the shrinking of computers or their inter-networking. And when the *New York Times* reviewed John Updike's *In the Beauty of the Lilies* in 1996, and saw in it a reassessment of the American Dream, surely no one at Britannica's headquarters in Chicago who might have read the novel would have agreed with Clarence Wilmot's assessment that all the information within an encyclopedia "breaks your heart at the end, because it leaves you as alone and bewildered as you were not knowing anything."

The very structure of the traditional encyclopedia dooms itself. It can never know it all or show enough of what it knows. It can't hope to keep up with important developments in the world, nor take back what it said about Hitler or slavery. And it can never answer the most searching questions about its own existence: are the people who read it from *A-Z* better able to understand the world than those who only read the preface? Does the present lowly cost of a fine set of *Britannica* or *World Book* or *Brockhaus* from 2005—ten pounds or ten dollars or ten euros on eBay—mean that we no longer value things we held dear when the century was young? Is the information we receive today more or less reliable than the information we received in our childhood?

Knowledge is not general; it is specific, and only specifically useful at certain points and intervals. The hope of the ancients to capture everything between covers now seems as futile as counting the number of stars in the universe. Or, with hindsight, as futile as *Britannica*'s attempts in its twilight years to find a viable future: the 2011 Seiko ER8100 folding electronic "Britannica Concise" with keyboard and grey-green screen, perhaps, or the 2012 Britannica Ultimate Reference Suite DVD (with 82,000+ articles and Biography Bonus: Great Minds and Heroes & Villains).

Encyclopaedia Britannica is now just Britannica.com, and it's not a bad place to hang out for a while. There is a lot of information one doesn't need to pay for, and a neat home page displayed as a sort of historical newspaper, with stories on the Cuban Missile Crisis and the Cold War, a good array of quizzes and crosswords, and an "On This Day . . ." column (featuring, on the day I last visited, an anniversary marking the date Dr. Crippen murdered his wife). It is more democratic than its print version (in so far as it doesn't distinguish between ownership in full morocco or half morocco), and when you get to the page for your annual premium subscription ($74.95 inclusive of what appears to be a permanent 30 percent discount), you are reminded of the immense detail within and the 110 Nobel Prize winners and fifty Notable Sport Figures who contributed in the golden age. Importantly, the site emphasizes its credentials regarding truth: "Facts matter more than ever, but they are becoming increasingly hard to find. Every Britannica article has been written by *experts* [and] vetted by *fact-checkers.*" It didn't actually say, "suck on that, Wikipedia," but it didn't have to.

Besides, they were fighting different wars now. Compared to the 16.83 billion visits made to Wikipedia between March and May 2020, Britannica.com attracted 124.7 million. (Though tiny in comparison, the figure is far larger than the number of people who ever consulted its print edition.)

Towards the end of our alphabet, we confront one arresting paradox: we know more about our lack of knowledge today than at any previous time in history. Maybe that's one of the things that keeps us going, the old hunting and gathering. A famous Map of Ignorance, constructed in the early 1980s by Ann Kerwin and Marlys Witte of the Arizona University Medical School, only heightened the value we place on learning. They applied it specifically to medicine, but it is fairly applicable to all fields of research.

Known Unknowns: All the things you know you don't know
Unknown Unknowns: All the things you don't know you don't know
Errors: All the things you think you know but don't
Unknown Knowns: All the things you don't know you know
Taboos: Dangerous, polluting or forbidden knowledge
Denials: All the things too painful to know, so you don't

Dr. Kerwin, a philosopher-in-residence at the medical school, was delighted to see her chart travel the world online, calling it "a cosmic swerve . . . a silly prompt for exploration and celebration of the fertile home territory of learning." Her colleague Marlys Witte reasoned that unanswered questions are the raw material of knowledge, "and (current) knowledge is the raw material of (future) ignorance, i.e., answers and questions shift with time and the accumulation of answers."

Or as the Danish polymath Piet Hein put it:

Knowing what
thou knowest not
is in a sense
omniscience.

The Germans have a nice name for the study of the cultures of ignorance: *Nichtwissenskulturen*. One reason I like it is because it forms a triumvirate with two other words

Informationwissenschaft (the organization of knowledge) and *Wissensgeschichte* (the study of the history of knowledge).

This book has not been a history of knowledge, but it has tracked how one aspect of our knowledge has been communicated, circumscribed and passed on. When I drove down to the outskirts of Cambridge to retrieve a pristine set of encyclopedias at the beginning of this book, I was using elements of my knowledge of finance, markets, communication, cartography, risk and safety, travel and technology. Driving back with the set, I was adding knowledge to ignorance, and knowledge to knowledge, which, as Denis Diderot knew in 1751, is all one can ever hope learning to be:

> The goal of an Encyclopédie is to assemble all the knowledge scattered on the surface of the earth, to demonstrate the general system to the people with whom we live, & to transmit it to the people who will come after us, so that the work of centuries past is not useless to the centuries which follow, that our descendants, by becoming more learned, may become more virtuous & happier, & that we do not die without having merited being part of the human race.

Z

ZEITGEIST

This is what we knew then.

The great deceit of the encyclopedia is that its obsolescence will necessarily render it redundant. Every generation believes its world to be changing faster than the last, and with a greater clarity of purpose, but we make a mistake if we think it necessarily contains more valuable knowledge. A fine encyclopedia will stand you in good stead like an old wristwatch: its timing may be out, and sometimes it may not work at all, but its mechanics will always intrigue. These old volumes show us what we thought we knew, and we discard them with a rash disregard for the work of our forebears. Ancient editions carry a secret knowledge of their own, the enshrined accretion of learning. If nothing else, they are materially wonderful objects. Run your fingers down their raised spines and tell yourself you are not transported. As Albert Einstein once reported, the pursuit of truth and beauty is a sphere of activity in which we are permitted to be children all our lives.

And what of the last jagged letter? Have most compilers run out of zest? Do the strings of their hearts still go zing as the presses ready their cranks? Here are a handful of entries in the rear-view mirror, heavily truncated, loaded with distant and noble erudition. Some appear willfully naive; many check the "Who Knew?" box. I hope they show the benefit to be had from not rejecting old things just because they are not modern. When we ascend to space in a rocket we are only able to do so because of those who once paddled uncharted in canoes.

From *Encyclopédie* (1751-65)

Zimbi: Small shells that serve as everyday currency in the Kingdom of the Congo, as well as in a great number of other countries in Africa, along whose coasts they are found. We find a large quantity near an island that is opposite Luanda Saint Paolo; these are the most valued. These shells are a gold mine for the Portuguese, who hold the sole right to collect them, and that helps them purchase from Africans their most precious merchandise.

From *A New and Complete Dictionary of Arts and Sciences, Comprehending All the Branches of Human Knowledge* (1763-64)

Zythogala: Beer posset, a drink recommended by [seventeenth century physician Thomas] Sydenham as good to be taken after a vomit, for allaying the acrimonious and disagreeable taste the vomit has occasioned, as well as to prevent gripes.

From *Encyclopaedia Britannica*, First Edition (1768-71)

Zapata: A kind of feast or ceremony held in Italy, in the courts of certain princes, on St Nicholas's day; wherein people hide presents in the shoes or slippers of those they would do honour to, in such a manner as may surprise them on the morrow when they come to dress.

From *Encyclopaedia Britannica,* Second Edition (1777-84)

Zaleucus: A famous legislator of the Locrians, and the disciple of Pythagoras, flourished 500 years BC. He made a law by which he punished adulterers with the loss of both their eyes. His son offending was not absolved of this punishment, yet to show the father as well as the just law-giver, he put out his own right, and his son's left eye. This example of justice and severity made so strong an impression on the minds of his subjects, that no instance was found of the commission of that vice during the reign of that legislator.

From *Encyclopaedia Britannica,* Fifth Edition (1815)

Zest: The woody thick skin quartering the kernel of a walnut; prescribed by some physicians, when dried and taken with white wine, as a remedy against the gravel.*

From Abraham Rees's *Cyclopaedia* (1819)

Zabda: A large and pleasant town of Syria, chiefly, if not solely, inhabited by Christians, which furnishes 700 men fit for war. The town is sheltered by mountains, but the locusts are very destructive.

From *The Children's Encyclopedia* (*c.* 1930)

Zeppelin: Although his name came to be hateful to humanity, Count Ferdinand Zeppelin, born at Manzell, near Lake Constance, in 1838, must have credit for the change from the helpless balloon to the successful lighter-than-air craft.

* The gravel: kidney stones.

He saw he must depart entirely from the pear-shaped gas-bag which had been for a century in use, and that he must have a vessel which would not crumple up when driven against the wind. It must be rigid and steerable. So, after many trials and failures which ultimately brought him almost to beggary, he devised the famous and infamous Zeppelin. Nothing else counts in the history of steerable airships. They are as much ahead of all rivals as our ocean liners are ahead of sailing ships.

From *The Columbia Encyclopedia*, Single Volume (1935)

Zaharoff, Sir Basil: 1850–, International financier and munitions manufacturer. Zaharoff, often called "The Mystery Man of Europe" because of the secrecy surrounding his personal and business affairs, was born of Greek parents in Anatolia, Turkey. He is generally considered the greatest armament salesman the world has known. For his services to the Allies in the World War, Zaharoff was knighted by George V and decorated by the French government. He has, however, been subjected to harsh criticism on the grounds that he fomented warfare, and has been accused of exerting a baneful influence on politics by secret intrigue through his association with European statesmen, notably Lloyd George.

From *Children's Britannica* (1960)

Zoo, Regent's Park: In Regent's Park many of the animals, such as lions, wolves and monkeys, are kept in cages. Many people think that wild animals roam over very large spaces and will therefore feel cramped if they are shut up in cages. As long as they have enough space to move about in, most animals seem able to live quite comfortably in cages. Some creatures seem to enjoy being looked at by visitors and play all kinds of tricks, as if they are "showing off." Among these are the chimpanzees, orang-utans and gibbons, which perform acrobatics, often leaping all round the cage, or wrap themselves up in newspaper.

From *Grolier Encyclopedia International* (1967)

ZAHARIAS, MILDRED DIDRIKSON ("BABE"), 1911-56: American athlete, born in Port Arthur, Tex. She was voted the outstanding woman athlete of the first half of the 20th century in an Associated Press poll. As "Babe" Didrikson she distinguished herself in track and field by setting world records in the javelin throw and 80-meter hurdles in the 1932 Olympic Games. In 1938 she married the noted wrestler George Zaharias. An outstanding performer in basketball, baseball, and billiards, she later concentrated on golf. Her courageous but losing battle against cancer won the admiration of the sports-minded throughout the world.

From *Encyclopaedia Judaica*, First Edition, Jerusalem (1971)

ZYCHLIN: Town in Lodz province, near Kutno, central Poland. A Jewish community existed in Zychlin from the 18th century, and in 1765 there were 311 Jews paying the poll tax. About 3,500 Jews lived in Zychlin in 1939, forming approximately 50 per cent of the total population. The town fell to the German forces on Sept. 17 1939, and on the following day all the Jewish men were driven to a village 15 miles away, but after detention in a church for three days were released. In April 1940 the Polish and Jewish intellectuals, especially teachers, were arrested and deported to German concentration camps. On Purim (March 3) 1942, the [remaining] Jewish population was assembled in the market place, and 3,200 persons were loaded on carts; anyone too weak to climb up on the carts was shot on the spot. The entire Jewish population of Zychlin was thus dispatched to the Chelmno death camp and murdered.

From *Great Soviet Encyclopedia*, Third Edition, Macmillan (1975)

Zen: One of the currents of Far Eastern Buddhism. The word "Zen" itself is the Japanese pronunciation of the Chinese character transcribing the Sanskrit term *dhyana* (meditation, self-absorption); the Chinese pronunciation is *ch'an*. Zen devolved in China in the sixth and seventh centuries under the strong influence of Taoism, from which Zen borrowed the disregard for knowledge and the conviction that the truth cannot be expressed in words but can only be attained by an internal leap, freeing the consciousness not only from the beaten paths of thought but from thought in general. An idiosyncratic (vulgarized) variant of Zen flourishes among beatniks, who understand Zen as an ideology that rejects civilization.

From *Encyclopaedia of the Arctic*, Routledge (2005)

Zagoskin, Lavrentii Alekseevich: Russian explorer of Alaska in the 19th century. He discovered the mountain ridge between the Yukon Territory and the eastern coast of the Norton Bay, explored the Kotzebue Sound, studied the climate of Alaska, and published his meteorological data collected over this two year period. In 1848 Zagoskin retired from the Navy, and moved to the village of Ostrov, 20km outside of Moscow. Not content to retire from scientific endeavours, he planted a garden of apple trees and made daily meteorological observations studying the impact of climate on crop yield.

From *Encyclopaedia Britannica*, Fifteenth Edition (2007)

Zahir Shah, Mohammad: (b.1914) King of Afghanistan from 1933 to 1973, providing an era of stable government to his country. He undertook a number of economic development projects, including irrigation and highway construction, that were backed by foreign aid, largely from the United States and the Soviet Union. He was also able to maintain Afghanistan's neutral position in international politics.

In a bloodless coup on July 17, 1973, Zahir Shah—who was in Italy undergoing medical treatment—was deposed. The leader of the coup, General Mohammad Daud Khan (the king's brother-in-law), proclaimed Afghanistan a republic with himself as its president. Zahir Shah formally abdicated on Aug. 24, 1973, and remained in Italy, where he spent most of the next three decades. During that time his native home descended further and further into chaos in what came to be known as the Afghan War.

From Wikipedia (early October 2021)

Zuckerberg, Mark Elliot: (/ˈzʌkərbɜːrg/; born May 14, 1984) is an American media magnate, internet entrepreneur, and philanthropist. He is known for co-founding Facebook, Inc. and serves as its chairman, chief executive officer, and controlling shareholder.

Born in White Plains, New York, Zuckerberg attended Harvard University, where he launched the Facebook social networking service from his dormitory room on 4 February 2004, with college roommates Eduardo Saverin, Andrew McCollum, Dustin Moskovitz, and Chris Hughes. Originally launched to select college campuses, the site expanded rapidly and eventually beyond colleges, reaching one billion users by 2012. Zuckerberg took the company public in May 2012 with majority shares. In 2007, at age 23, he became the world's youngest self-made billionaire. As of October 2021, Zuckerberg's net worth is $122 billion, making him the 5th-richest person in the world. Since 2008, *Time* magazine has named Zuckerberg among the 100 most influential people in the world as a part of its Person of the Year award, which he was recognized with in 2010. In December 2016, Zuckerberg was ranked 10th on *Forbes* list of The World's Most Powerful People.*

ŻYWIEC

But human decency prevents me from giving Zuckerberg the last word. Instead, the last word—because it is the last word to appear in the last printed edition of *Encyclopaedia Britannica* in 2010, the unwitting final stop (a conclusion even) of a journey lasting hundreds of years—is Żywiec, a town on the Sola River in south central Poland in the Carpathian Mountains near the Czech and Slovak borders. The town was first chronicled in the fourteenth century, and is a popular tourist center, being

* The entry runs to around 11,000 words, with 200 references and links. In November 2008 I interviewed Mark Zuckerberg in London. He was twenty-four, and only worth about $3bn then, and Facebook only had around 100 million members (compared to the 2.85 billion active monthly users it claimed in March 2021). He already had his familiar mantra: Facebook is about sharing. "The idea was always, tell people, 'share more information,'" he told me. "And that way we could gain more understanding about what's going on with the people around you." This was long before the Cambridge Analytica scandal, and all of the other negative Facebook revelations that showed how the illicit harvesting of this shared information could be used for political ends. "People have always spent a lot of time communicating, connecting, sharing with the people who are around them and are important to them," Zuckerberg continued. "It's a very human thing." I asked him where this quest for knowledge began (the popular story was that it began as a way to meet girls). "All my friends at school, we always talked about how the world would be better if there was more information available, and if you could understand what was going on with other people more—essentially if people shared more information about themselves." Without ever calling it this, he was making the world's largest self-selecting personal digital encyclopedia. Not always an accurate one, of course, but a vibrantly active hyperlinked resource.

home to a church containing the "Dormant Virgin." It is also known for its large breweries and the estimated population in 1982 was 28,800.

Żywiec exists on Wikipedia too, where it gets more than the fourteen lines devoted to it in *Britannica*. Many thousands of useful words more. By the end of June 2019 its population had grown to 31,194. There is a history of its churches, of its role in the first partition of Poland in 1772, and about its fate in the two world wars. There is geographic and demographic information, and one learns that although between 1975 and 1998 it was located within the Bielsko-Biała Voivodeship, it has since become part of the Silesian Voivodeship. There are men's and women's football teams in the town, and the main brewery is now owned by Heineken.

Wikipedia also has several color photographs of Żywiec, and the one of the town hall ought to be in a Wes Anderson movie. Should you wish to corroborate the information or find out more there are sixteen references to sources and many hyperlinks. Notable people born or connected with Żywiec include the former IBO cruiserweight champion Tomasz Adamek, the Poland international footballer Tomasz Jodłowiec, and Tadeusz Wrona, a pilot who successfully performed a belly landing of a Boeing 767 during LOT Polish Airlines Flight 16 at the Chopin Airport in Warsaw on 1 November 2011, and so smoothly did he do it that none of the 231 passengers and crew hurt as much as a hair.

When I accessed this information on 7 October 2021, there was a blue box with white type above it:

> Please don't scroll past this.
>
> This Thursday, for the 1st time recently, we humbly ask you to defend Wikipedia's independence. 98% of our readers

don't give; they simply look the other way. If you are an exceptional reader who has already donated, we sincerely thank you. If you donate just £2, or whatever you can this Thursday, Wikipedia could keep thriving for years. Most people donate because Wikipedia is useful. If Wikipedia has given you £2 worth of knowledge this year, take a minute to donate.

Show the world that access to reliable, neutral information matters to you.

Thank you.

The pedant in me balked at the use of "1st" for "first," but I donated £12, the price of a set of *Britannica* at the end of the eighteenth century. I couldn't think of anything that provided better value.

I hope this book has encouraged you to think twice about throwing out an old set of encyclopedias, of whatever vintage, of whatever quality. I hope it may even encourage you to rescue a set from a charity shop, or AbeBooks or eBay.

But be quick, as I may beat you to it. In September 2021 I went back to eBay to look for a set of *The Children's Encyclopaedia*, the volumes I had first taken off the shelves at school fifty years before. There were a lot of copies—blue bindings, brown bindings, single volumes and complete ten-volume sets. One complete set in readable condition from the 1930s requested an opening bid of £3.50, and after a week it had attracted no interest. So I paid the minimum, and almost triple that for postage, and a large parcel arrived in a battered box after five working days. I imagined it had been thrown into the back of a lorry the way one chucks large objects into skips at dumps.

The volumes were a little lighter than I remembered, but not much. How could my ten-year-old hands have handled such things? They smelled of, yes, school. A few images were instantly familiar: the opening plate showing a dapper young Shakespeare reading to a bored Anne Hathaway; a large gathering of the world's children in national dress ("Your Little Friends in Other Lands"), a depiction so well meaning and so wholly offensive—naked "Hottentots," inscrutable Chinese—that to reprint it today would land you in scalding water.

It wasn't just a nostalgia trip for me, it was a learning trip. I can only confirm the old adage that education is wasted on the young. Did you know, for example, why we hear better on water than land? Or why some people have dimples? And does iron get heavier when it rusts? I found it diverting, hilarious, surprising.

Equally surprising was the discovery that new junior encyclopedias were still being published in heavy print. In 2020 Britannica launched a new single-volume, full-color, punchily designed edition called *Children's Encyclopaedia* (in the UK) and *Kids' Encyclopedia* (in the US). Its editor Christopher Lloyd wrote something unusual in his introduction, something few editors of encyclopedias had mentioned before: he admitted there was a lot he didn't know. The known unknowns, he suggested, might be as interesting as anything else, for they were the inspiration for future generations (and future editions). He hoped that an inquiring mind rewarded in an orderly way—and is this not the best value of an encyclopedia yet produced, even at this late hour?—would prove to be a reliable and satisfying alternative to the maelstrom online.

I learned a lot. A nebula cloud the size of Earth only weighed as much as a small sack of potatoes. I read how crystals form. I discovered that the oldest living things on earth were the

Great Basin bristlecone pines in the Rocky Mountains (around 5000 years). I questioned the statement that a human being can make more than 10,000 different faces, and wondered how one measured them. I was disappointed to find that the Bugatti La Voiture Noire hypercar would cost me $18.7 million. And I regained my faith in human ingenuity when I saw that the first artificial kidneys were adapted from washing machines. A lot of these were the sort of hey-wow factoids I had learned to distrust as an adult, substitutes for deeper learning. But they made the child in me want to know more.

The book joined the unsteady piles of encyclopedias to the left of my desk. I counted eighty-seven volumes in all, a wildfire of information. The whole spinning world continues to revolve in those pages, pungently outmoded as they are. And to handle just one of those books is to be transported to a place of dedication and expertise, and often to obscurity, and occasionally to genius. I'm saddened that the world no longer has a use for most of them, and that this remarkable corner of history is history itself.

The Christmas You've Dreamed of
is Here Now
For Christmas and a Lifetime . .
Wouldn't you like to give—or to receive—the one gift that is truly "for Christmas and a Lifetime" . . . ? Wouldn't you like to give—either to yourself and your family, or to someone else deserving the very best—the one and only Encyclopaedia Britannica . . . 24 beautifully-bound volumes containing 38 million words that will forever enrich the lives of those who have access to them?
THE OPPORTUNITY IS YOURS NOW. A special offer—in effect between now and Christmas—makes it EASY for you to obtain this finest and most authoritative of all reference libraries. Its 26,000 picture-packed pages of factual information are the work of 4,000 eminent authorities including 36 Nobel prize winners. Send the coupon TODAY for full details and for a free PREVIEW BOOKLET describing the newest edition of Britannica. No obligation whatever.
There is only ONE
ENCYCLOPÆDIA BRITANNICA
Preferred for 185 Years
1952 EDITION—Send for Free Booklet
Encyclopaedia Britannica, Inc., Dept. F-7
425 North Michigan Avenue, Chicago 11, Illinois
Please let me have, without obligation, full details of your Special Christmas Offer; also a free copy of the PREVIEW BOOKLET describing the newest edition of Britannica.
Name
Address
City Zone State
Available in Canada: Write E.B., Ltd., Terminal Bldg., Toronto, Ont.
11

Acknowledgments

I would like to thank everyone who has helped me with this book. This number includes the pair I've been grateful to for many years, and whose wisdom and enthusiasm is never taken for granted: my agent Rosemary Scoular and my editor Jenny Lord.

The team at Weidenfeld and the wider Orion empire has provided untold expertise. Thank you to Steve Marking and Arneaux for the wonderfully arresting jacket design, to Sarah Fortune, Kate Moreton, Lucy Cameron and Ellen Turner, and to my copy editor Seán Costello, who detected anomalies, repetitions, questionable assumptions and repetitions.

The staff of the London Library have rooted out many rare and important editions. Much of this book was researched during lockdown, and the library's postal system was another wonderful service from this exceptional institution.

My thanks also to Johnny Davis, Leo Robson and Catherine Kanter for providing inspiration and the occasional volume. I spoke to many people at Wikipedia who do not receive a mention in the text, and I appreciate the time they spent with me. I am indebted to Andrew Bud for conducting his usual meticulous read. Professor Daniel Pick provided similarly cogent and far-sighted comments.

There are several scholars who have devoted many years to the study of encyclopedias and their contexts, and I list some of their major publications below. The works of Frank and Serena Kafker, Jason König, Greg Woolf, Peter Burke, Jeff Loveland and Ann Blair were particularly useful, combining rigorous detail with engaging readability.

This book is dedicated to my wife, Justine, who sighed hardly at all when another set of pungent old flaky books arrived in the post, and has been my index and spine throughout.

Further Reading

The following guide to further reading contains one glaring omission: encyclopedias. I've written about so many intriguing possibilities, and it would be superfluous to list them all again here.

I have attempted to record the sources of my own knowledge in the footnotes, particularly the valuable contributions from academic journals. The following books go into greater detail about much of the history and debating points I've discussed in the previous pages. All have proved invaluable in my research.

Arnar, Anna, *Encyclopedism from Pliny to Borges* (Chicago: University of Chicago Library, 1990)

Arner, Robert D., *Dobson's Encyclopaedia: The Publisher, Text, and Publication of America's First Britannica, 1789–1803* (Philadelphia: University of Pennsylvania Press, 1991)

Barney, Stephen et al., eds., *The Etymologies of Isidore of Seville* (Cambridge: Cambridge University Press, 2010)

Blair, Ann, *Information: A Historical Companion* (Princeton: Princeton University Press, 2021)

Blair, Ann, *Too Much to Know: Managing Scholarly Information Before the Modern Age* (New Haven, Connecticut: Yale University Press, 2010)

Boyles, Denis, *Everything Explained That Is Explainable: On the Creation of* Encyclopaedia Britannica*'s Celebrated Eleventh Edition, 1910–11* (New York: Knopf, 2016)

Broughton, John, *Wikipedia: The Missing Manual* (Beijing; Cambridge: O'Reilly Media, 2008)

Burke, Peter, *A Social History of Knowledge: From Gutenberg to Diderot* (Cambridge: Polity, 2000)

Burke, Peter, *A Social History of Knowledge II: From the Encyclopédie to Wikipedia* (Cambridge: Polity, 2012)

Collison, Robert, *Encyclopaedias: Their History Throughout the Ages* (New York: Hafner, 1964)

Cooper, Helen, *The Structure of the Canterbury Tales* (London: Duckworth, 1983)

Courtney, Janet Elizabeth Hogarth, *Recollected in Tranquillity* (London: William Heinemann, 1926)

Darnton, Robert, *The Business of Enlightenment: A Publishing History of the Encyclopédie 1775–1800* (Cambridge, Massachusetts: Harvard University Press, 1979)

Einbinder, Harvey, *The Myth of the Britannica* (London: MacGibbon & Kee, 1964)

Evans, Philip, and Wurster, Thomas S., *Blown to Bits* (Boston: Harvard Business School Press, 2000)

Hankins, John Erskine, *Background of Shakespeare's Thought* (Hassocks: Harvester Press, 1978)

Jacobs, A.J., *The Know-It-All* (London: William Heinemann, 2005)

Kafker, Frank, and Loveland, Jeff, *The Early Britannica* (Oxford: Voltaire Foundation, 2009)

Kafker, Frank and Serena, *The Encyclopedists as Individuals* (Oxford: Voltaire Foundation, 1988)

Kister, Kenneth F., *Kister's Best Encyclopaedias* (Phoenix, Arizona: Oryx Press, 1994)

Kogan, Herman, *The Great EB* (Chicago: University of Chicago Press, 1958)

König, Jason, and Woolf, Greg, eds., *Encyclopaedism from*

Antiquity to the Renaissance (Cambridge: Cambridge University Press, 2013)

Lih, Andrew, *The Wikipedia Revolution* (London: Aurum Press, 2009)

Lough, John, *Essays on the Encyclopédie of Diderot and D'Alembert* (London: Oxford University Press, 1968)

Loveland, Jeff, *The European Encyclopedia: From 1650 to the Twenty-First Century* (Cambridge: Cambridge University Press, 2019)

Lynch, Jack, *You Could Look It Up: The Reference Shelf from Ancient Babylon to Wikipedia* (New York: Bloomsbury, 2016)

McHenry, Robert, *How to Know* (New Delhi: Corner Bookstore, 2005)

Murphy, James W., *Who Says You Can't Sell Ice to Eskimos?* (CreateSpace/Amazon, California, 2013)

Rosengard, Peter, *Talking to Strangers: The Adventures of a Life Insurance Salesman* (London: Coptic, 2013)

Salecl, Renata, *A Passion for Ignorance: What We Choose Not to Know and Why* (Princeton: Princeton University Press, 2020)

Smith, Reginald A., *Towards a Living Encyclopaedia: A Contribution to Mr. Wells's New Encyclopaedism* (London: Andrew Dakars, 1941)

Thomas, Gillian, *A Position to Command Respect: Women and the Eleventh Britannica* (Metuchen, New Jersey; London: Scarecrow Press, 1992)

Wells, H.G., *World Brain* (London: Methuen & Co., 1938)

Wilson, Arthur McCandless, *Diderot* (New York: Oxford University Press, 1972)

Wright, Alex, *Cataloguing the World: Paul Otlet and the Birth of the Information Age* (Oxford: Oxford University Press, 2014)

Illustrations

All other images supplied by author.

Index